D O M I N O ' S
M A N S I O N

Thomas Monaghan, Gunnar Birkerts
And The Spirit Of Frank Lloyd Wright

By Gordon P. Bugbee

With Foreword By Vincent Scully

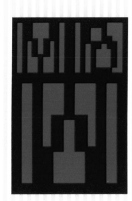

C O N T E N T S

Planning Research Organization
For A Better Environment (PROBE) Press
1599 Witherbee, Troy, Michigan 48084

© 1988 by Gordon Pritchard Bugbee
All Rights Reserved. Published 1988.
Printed in the United States of America.
10 9 8 7 6 5 4 3 2 1

Coordinating Editor: Paul Chu Lin
Graphic Design: Marino & Marino, Birmingham, Michigan
Photography: Balthazar Korab, Troy, Michigan
Printing: Pinaire Lithographing, Louisville, Kentucky

Library of Congress Catalog Card Number: 88-62139
ISBN Number: 0-9621045-0-7

P R E F A C E

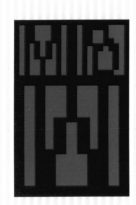

1. The books *Megatrends* by John Naisbitt; *Forecast 2000* by George Gallup, Jr. and William Proctor; *The Future 500* by Craig R. Hickman and Michael A. Silva; *America By Design* by Spiro Kostof; *Man-Made America: Chaos or Control?* by Christopher Tunnard and Boris Pushkarev; *The Reckoning* by David Halberstam; *In Search of Excellence* by Thomas J. Peters and Robert H. Waterman, Jr.; *Thriving on Chaos* by Thomas J. Peters; *Quality, Productivity, and Competitive Position* by W. Edwards Deming; and *Quality Is Free* by Philip B. Crosby all focus on these concerns, as do articles as *U.S. News'* 'American Competitive Drive—Are We Losing It?', *Time's* 'The Hapless American Consumer—Why is Service So Bad?', and *Time's* 'What Ever Happened to Ethics—Assaulted by sleaze, scandals, and hypocrisy, America searches for its moral bearings.'

Once, a person's word was as good as gold. Once, the American way of life was identified in folklore and tradition with integrity, fair play, virtue, accountability, exploration, creativity, self-determination, and self-motivation. The founders of this republic dreamed these goals would be their legacy to future generations. Once, the label 'Made in the United States' guaranteed high value and symbolized pride.

Now ethics, social organization, politics, business, technology, communications, and accountability seem to change rapidly. Now the world has seemingly become smaller. Unlike the 1950s, when the United States was the healthiest economic and industrial nation in the world, global competition has become intense. The automobile, machine tool, electronics, steel, and clothing and shoe industries,

among others, have been battered. Industry, particularly in the United States, has had to face increasingly global competition—in some cases to survive.

The covers of books and magazines reflect America's introspection, reawakening a desire to revive the basic values and traits we all assumed were ingrained in and sacred to our way of life.[1] These publications confirm the changes we all are undergoing— some pleasant, some humbling, some violent, some we would wish away, but cannot.

In such times, architecture cannot merely create self-indulgent *'objets d'art'*; rather, it must respond to all its contexts, and serve to express lasting values. In the present case—that of a corporate headquarters—architecture must not only respond to considerations of use, site and design, but must first respond to—and express—the corporation itself, from the values which affect its well-being, employer/employee relationships, reputation, and image down to its strategic plans, policies, and successes.

Domino's Pizza, Inc. has grown phenomenally; it has begun to rival McDonald's among fast-food service corporations. Clearly, Domino's Pizza has responded to the anticipated needs and desires of its customers. Its corporate public reputation is excellent—and improving. It has engendered teamwork and pride in the corporation among its staff and franchisees. It has also begun to address the issues of ethics and appropriate values in the marketplace.

The headquarters facilities not only reflect these aspects of Domino's Pizza as a company, they also respond positively to national issues and concerns—through development and creative composition of functions and activities within its buildings and the way those buildings use their site. Thus, the story of Domino's Pizza's headquarters and the interplay of personalities involved in its evolution offers more than a personal history, it offers lessons in an architecture of context and responsibility.

We believe this book conveys these lessons by attempting to answer four questions:

1. How did Domino's Pizza founder and chief executive officer Tom Monaghan's own past, hierarchy of values, drive, and vision shape the growth of the Domino's Pizza facilities?

2. What can the Domino's Pizza corporation teach us about management practices, employer/employee relationships, customer/public relations, and focus on today's world-competitive marketplace; how have these issues and responses shaped the development of the headquarters facilities; and how will they shape future developments in business and architecture?

3. What consequences follow when a major corporation—as more and more are doing—moves its headquarters out of the city to the countryside and the exurban context? What about small farms within an exurban context? And the cultural enrichment of an exurban community?

4. Can an architect meet his client's desires for a particular form and style—in this case that of a master of architecture, Frank Lloyd Wright—without falsely and cheaply copying his work, without loss of appreciative capital value?

We will demonstrate the development of this project from large-scale planning and design to micro-development of details in the executive suite, using both conceptual sketches and traditional drawings.

Domino's Pizza's facilities have finally been evolved and realized through the architectural skills of Gunnar Birkerts, who brings to the project his own set of values, views, and experience. Obviously, this early book cannot show all the 'dreams' or 'visions' realized by Tom Monaghan, Gunnar Birkerts, and others to come. A future volume will have to demonstrate the evolution and assess the fulfillment of their dreams.

For this first part of the larger story of Domino's Pizza headquarters, we wish to thank Tom Monaghan, Gunnar Birkerts, John H. Howe, Paul Raeder, Larry Brink, Anthony Gholz, Richard O. Brunvand, Vural Uygur, Toni J. Hendrix, and Sara-Ann Briggs for the sharing of experiences, information, and documentation.

As coordinating editor, I want to express my personal appreciation and gratitude for their dedication and efforts in bringing this story to print to the book team: Dagmar Buerk, artist; Gordon Bugbee, writer; Susan Brozes and Margaret Anne Bugbee, book assistants; Balthazar Korab, photographer; Jay Marino and Michael Kirk, designers; Ann Marino and Kim Mangan, typographers; John Williams, aerial photographer; and to Patricia Conway for her informative address given during the East Central Regional Conference of Association of Collegiate Schools of Architecture, Miami University, Oxford, Ohio, October 17, 1986. Finally, we give special thanks to Vincent Scully for writing the foreword to this book and for sharing his insights with us all.

—*Paul Chu Lin, Coordinating Editor*

The architect-client relationship between Frank Lloyd Wright and Tom Monaghan may be unique in history in view of the fact that one of the principals was, from the beginning, no longer living. Wright has been present only as a perhaps rather unquiet spirit whose work, as Monaghan admires it, must be translated into physical reality by a second architect— in this case, Gunnar Birkerts.

Leaving aside any assessment of the effectiveness of that three-sided relationship, one cannot help but be sorry that Wright and Monaghan were not able to work together in life. They were clearly made for each other. Monaghan loves Wright and his work with faithful passion, and is exactly the kind of client Wright himself most admired and seemed to do his best work for. Monaghan is in every way a self-made man: the American paternalistic capitalist to the life, deeply and personally involved, it would appear, with every one of his people and every aspect of his enterprise. He owns his business himself, damns the banks, refuses to go public, and regards pizza making as an art. Wright was consistently sympathetic to such clients, homegrown middle-western tycoons, educated in the school of hard knocks and, perhaps, at Michigan, say, but never, as Eaton has shown, at Harvard or Yale. Wright, too, leaving

aside his well-known gastronomic refinement, would have been delighted by the pizza image itself. The modern pizza, especially Monaghan's delivered variety, has become one of the most American of foods and is now a favorite throughout the world. True enough, it originated in southern Italy, but it was never a big thing there until it was reworked in America and brought back to local attention by American tourists. It was around in New Haven, Connecticut, in the nineteen-twenties, and was spelled 'apizza', pronounced 'ah-beets' in New Haven Italian. Nobody much but Italians ate it at that time, and, as a child, one could under certain circumstances address an Italian friend as 'Ah-beets' without fear of reprisal. It was only in the nineteen-forties that New Haven came to be regarded by all its inhabitants as the pizza capital of the world, a distinction now enjoyed, one supposes, by Ann Arbor.

In any event, Wright would surely have been delighted to build for Monaghan. The impression also persists that Monaghan, foiled by economics in his attempt to become an architect himself, more or less unconsciously set out from the beginning to become the kind of client Wright would have admired. And he has achieved that objective to an admirable degree. Since that is so it might at first seem strange that Monaghan did not assign the role of Wright's stand-in to the Taliesin Fellowship, which is after all in the business of imitating Wright's work much more literally, if perhaps no more correctly, than Birkerts can be expected to do. But Monaghan has said that he regards Birkerts as the greatest architect practicing today and therefore as the one best able to interpret Wright's work and to develop appropriate new forms out of it. Monaghan's judgment here might not be shared by everyone. Despite Birkerts' long-standing respect for Wright, the two architects are very different in kind. Birkerts' work has always seemed rather thin and hard-edged, in the International Style manner. It is bold and confident, like Wright's, but tends toward surface rather than depth and, perhaps paradoxically, reflects a kind of northern mystic idealism which Wright, for all his talk about Romance, not to mention the mystical predilections of his wife, Ogilvanna, rigorously shunned. Nor do direct suggestions from Nature seem to play much part in Birkerts' work while, in one way or another, they pervade much of Wright's.

Despite all that, one cannot help but feel that Birkerts has turned out to be a good choice and has done a creditable job on the exterior massing and detailing of Monaghan's incomparably long, Prairie-Style building. The heavy planes of the overhanging copper roofs are the major elements of the design, and they are strikingly effective in laying out the vast form on the site. Their overhang is perhaps not quite deep enough, and that, coupled with Birkerts' rather unWrightian (at least unPrairie-Style) use of large panes of clear glass beneath them, thins out the design and confines it within a boxy volume in ways Wright would have avoided. One wants the planes more detached, more floating, with deeper shadows below them, but the tension between Wrightian plasticity and International Style surface is perhaps appropriate here, since it prepares us for the interior space, which is pretty much straight 1980s office building with nothing of Wright about it. It is more fun than most office buildings, however, with the long central

corridor, a considerable road, running right through it and Monaghan's office, with its fine view along the prairie, set skimming the contours like a zeppelin's car. It is served by a marvelous bathroom, a classical construction of gleaming marble, modelling vaulted spaces like those of an especially affluent Roman bath. It is a decidedly Post-Modern design and casts some doubt upon the validity of the various anti-Post-Modern views which are attributed to Monaghan in the text of this book. Splendid facilities for gymnastic exercise are provided for the staff—Monaghan is a fitness enthusiast—but no real dining room. Any eating done in the building is of Domino's Pizza, delivered hot and instantaneously and consumed where convenient.

The building's most memorable quality is its relation to the site. Two vast express highways intersect on the rolling plain, and the building stretches itself out toward the angle they form. Here the long, hovering roof planes come into their own, celebrating and shaping, as it were, the whole continental space. In this, the building can be regarded as the ultimate triumph of the Prairie-Style house type of the period 1900-1910, which Wright had actually used to complement and to shape flat suburban lots in the suburbs of Chicago but which evoked in form and name the vaster topographical setting across which those suburbs had been laid out. Moreover, Monaghan's building is explicitly modelled upon a specific Prairie-Style design. It is Wright's project of 1908 for the Harold McCormick house at Lake Forest, on the shore of Lake Michigan north of Chicago. At the last moment, after Wright had almost entirely developed the design, the McCormicks took the commission away from him and gave it to Charles Platt, of New York, who built an actually very beautiful Italianate villa on the site, one long since torn down.

The loss of the commission had a serious effect upon Wright. Monaghan shares the view that it may well have had something to do with bringing to a boil the restlessness and dissatisfaction that led him to flee Oak Park with Mamah Cheney in 1909. Wright himself told Henry Russell Hitchcock in the 1940s that he remembered Mrs. McCormick coming down the lawn to give him the news. He said that he somehow knew from the way the plumes of her headdress were nodding that he was going to lose the job. It meant so much to him precisely because it was, or would have been, the culmination of all his Prairie-Style work up to that time. Far larger than the Robie house of 1908-09, its size would almost have rivalled that of the Imperial Hotel of the following decade. It is even possible that the Prairie Style was stretched too far in it. The low-lying planes of flat hipped roof do seem to go on and on, proliferating in ways that, for all their marvellous energy, begin to give the impression of being additive rather than integral, creating space after space in interwoven profusion and mounting up above the lake in a monumental composition of enormous, almost Mayan, scale. One wonders whether Mrs. McCormick felt something of that. Platt's building was markedly simple, volumetric, bright, and cool, as if conceived in some conscious reaction to richness, chiaroscuro, and complexity. It is, nevertheless, very sad that the McCormick project was never built, and it is especially touching that Monaghan has always been drawn to it and specifically chose it as the model, indeed the symbol, of his own headquarters building. Here, perhaps, was an old challenge Monaghan could take up *for* Wright, a doomed project, maybe one that aimed too high for its moment, which he could do his level best to bring off at last. Monaghan clearly sensed as well that the McCormick design wanted to be even bigger than it was. The farther those interminable roofs could be made to wing out across the landscape the better. It might all become simpler and stronger at vaster scale—and Wright's vision thus justified, the unfinished made whole.

Whether the project as now in building does come off entirely may still be open to question. We will have to wait to see it finished, stretched full length like a hurrying railroad train across the site,

to form a reasonable idea of what it really is. At some time it will be joined by Birkerts' contrasting tower, leaning dynamically toward it across water about midway along its length. As presently conceived, that monument has a decidedly Russian Constructivist character, recalling the urgent diagonals of projects designed in the first years after the Revolution. It seems, at least in project form, to be even more compatible with Wright's dynamic roof planes than the tower Wright himself designed at a later date, 'The Golden Beacon', which Monaghan originally intended to raise on that site. Early negotiations with the Taliesin Fellowship concerning the construction of the Beacon eventually fell through, and by 1987 Monaghan was seriously considering Birkerts' design. If it should become a reality the three-way collaboration between architects and client will have turned out even richer and more creative than seems the case at present.

But Wright remains the hero, or perhaps better, the old king whom Monaghan champions. When fully occupied by a number of going business concerns, and accompanied by its complementary farm, the long, low-rise office building between the superhighways will inevitably be read as a bold emblem of Broadacre City itself and a glorification of Wright's beloved image of urban decentralization along the automobile roads. Monaghan, too, loves automobiles, as Wright did all his life. His distinguished collection of Wright's furniture—on which he says no bank will ever loan him a nickel, although it accrues in value more rapidly than anything else—is therefore complemented by a collection of magnificent cars, of which certainly not the greatest but surely the most endearing is a Lincoln Continental painted Wright's Cherokee Red, once totalled and remodeled by Wright with no rear window. It might be said that, like Monaghan, Wright moved fast and never looked back at all. But Monaghan has in fact looked back in this critical instance, piously and with hope, to Wright's early days and the promise they bore.

—*Vincent Scully*

8

BOOK ONE

Prologue

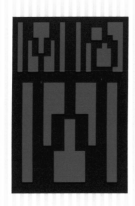

Introducing The Client:
Domino's Pizza And Tom Monaghan

1

Once upon a time of William McKinley or Calvin Coolidge, upstart American manufacturers made fortunes underselling the established world. Today, when obsolete plants litter the Rust Belt and the new upstarts are overseas, we can look back wistfully on this era. Its showmanship was almost legendary in its own time. In addition to manufacturing, the fields of finance, transportation, merchandising, and the press amassed comparable wealth.

Corporate ostentation came to focus on two building types, the company headquarters and the mansion of the mogul who built and owned the company. By the turn of the century, the downtown headquarters building became tall. It often took the form of an ornate pavilion or a classical temple mounted atop floors and floors of windows for clerks. The very important guests on their way to executive suite hospitality rarely looked in on these workaday intermediate floors.

Equally symbolic of the company was the mansion of the mogul, located in the city at first, and later in the suburbs. Outsiders only glimpsed its opulent seclusion through the wrought iron gates that received these same very important guests, now as personal friends of the mogul. Headquarters and mansion alike were the mogul's personal instruments. Manhattan led in such extravagance, but every important city had these landmarks according to its own specialties: McCormick farm machinery and Pullman

cars in Chicago, Carnegie and Frick in Pittsburgh steelmaking, the Hannas and Mathers in Cleveland ore, and Jim Hill's trains in St. Paul.

Time passed, and the moguls gave way to a line of corporate managers who could never claim the mansion on the same symbolic terms. The mansion went, and the headquarters no longer had to share the prestige. In postwar years the headquarters often became a sprawling suburban palace in a garden landscape, fit for an oriental potentate. The imperial presence was now invisible and impersonal, for it was now the spirit of the corporation, itself—the *esprit de corps* of IBM, for instance. The clerks now became significant exhibits in their coordinated open office landscape, seated with their cybernetic servants. This was true also of those corporations that elected to stay downtown in new glass-and-metal office towers.

Most recently, these urban counterparts have moved their clerks to cheaper back offices in the suburbs in order to sublet a prime vacancy for prestigious offices. The corporate headquarters remaining upstairs has become divorced from everyday business operations, and is purely a corporate symbol. The building has retained the corporate logo, and the managers have kept their sumptuous aerie. This new corporate mansion is a penthouse where the directors and very important guests are received and entertained. The image makers have prevailed, while the alienation of manager and managee is complete.

In the Midwest an entrepreneur named Thomas S. Monaghan has found a more democratic way to combine the mansion with the corporate home office. Monaghan is Founder, President, and Chairman of Domino's Pizza, Inc., which grew from modest beginnings into an international fast food empire. The business was built upon motivation, and motivation suggested sharing the rewards with those who helped to build it. In such a new exurban corporate mansion the help and the neighbors frequent the drawing room and even mingle with the very important guests.

Tom Monaghan probably never thought of his new showplace as a sort of mansion—an overgrown home, perhaps. His inspiration nonetheless was from drawings of one of the grandest mansion designs of the era of the moguls. The design Monaghan admired was never built; the McCormick family which commissioned it changed architects instead and built a different style of villa on their suburban estate north of Chicago.

Architects working in the Postmodern idiom welcome such archetypes if their symbols still arouse a modern audience. There is a trap in such eclecticism, however. A well-informed client may know precisely what he wants in terms of a specific prototype from the past; little latitude for creativity may be left to the architect. Monaghan's inspiration is a case in point, but it happens to lie outside the Postmodern catalog of sources. It is a 'Prairie house' design of the master architect Frank Lloyd Wright. The Postmodern critic praises Wright as a historical figure, but consigns his work to the general body of mainstream modern architecture of the midcentury. This was a mainstream which Wright despised, but which Postmodernism wishes to supplant to make a place for itself.

Gunnar Birkerts is the architect Monaghan entrusted with interpreting his wishes. Their narrow scope became Birkerts' dilemma. Birkerts is acknowledged as one of America's top ranked architects, but his design methodology has little empathy for eclectic image making. This book is the story of his collaboration with Tom Monaghan to produce a very special building which neither would have conceived independently.

The site for the building, farmland rechristened 'Domino's Farms', lies on the eastern edge of the city of Ann Arbor. The city is best known as the home of the University of Michigan. The university presence draws many high-tech research laboratories to town. Ann Arbor is the western anchor of 'Automation Alley',

Thomas S. Monaghan, Portrait
Credit: Domino's Pizza, Inc. Archives

Gunnar Birkerts, Portrait
Credit: Domino's Pizza, Inc. Archives

Original Domino's Pizza Shop, 1960, Ypsilanti, Michigan
Credit: Domino's Pizza, Inc. Archives

1. 'Former Rust Bowl is now Automation Alley', in *Crain's Detroit Business,* 11 May 1987, p. 9, as reprinted from 11 April 1987 issue of *The Economist.*

2. Thomas S. Monaghan and Robert Anderson, *Pizza Tiger* (New York: Random House, 1986), pp. 56-61.

a fast-growing high-tech corridor stretching eastward past Domino's Farms toward Detroit, forty miles away. Thus the site for Domino's Farms lies under intense pressure for some sort of development. Some see the industrial automation makers of Automation Alley as Detroit's ultimate salvation from the Rust Bowl curse.[1] But Domino's Farms belongs to the service economy, not to smokestacks. This is home to the management of the world's largest pizza delivery company.

The initial groundbreaking took place on August 30, 1984. The development package announced for Domino's Farms seemed nominally like many others for metropolitan areas around the country today. An office complex and perhaps a hotel were planned, close to a pair of superhighways cloverleafed to one another. The highways would feed such a commercial center, together with the myriad homesites that must someday fill up the open fields nearby.

Tom Monaghan had a more personal vision for the barns and cornfields existing at Domino's Farms. He wanted his headquarters building to share its 300-acre site with a real working farm. Such a farm would demonstrate the dependence of pizza products on agriculture. It might also keep alive among its future neighbors something of that appreciation

for farm life that Monaghan had acquired as a boy on a farm in northern Michigan. He also saw his new headquarters building as a home of cultural activities outside of business hours. The hotel he proposed would be a conference and training center, bringing Domino's Farms to life around the clock welcoming Domino's Pizza people coming from around the country. Conserving a rural setting for these buildings would be a valuable demonstration of a continuing balance between urbanity and the countryside. In this, Tom Monaghan would come as close to reviving the message of Frank Lloyd Wright as in any recognizable Wrightian features adorning the buildings.

Tom Monaghan once wanted to be an architect, himself. As a young veteran he enrolled in the architectural school at the University of Michigan and attended classes for several weeks, but money was short. Then his brother Jim took over the DomiNick's Pizza Shop in the nearby town of Ypsilanti. Tom joined him to earn college expenses, and the partners reopened the shop on December 9, 1960. The workload became more demanding than the brothers expected, and Jim Monaghan bowed out to protect his other job. Tom Monaghan put off college indefinitely, for he had business debts to pay off. He was in the pizza business for good.[2]

Imperial Hotel Entrance
Credit: © 1988 David L. Hawkins

Imperial Hotel, 1916-1922, Tokyo, Japan
Credit: Museum of Modern Art, New York

3. Lucian Swift Kirtland, *Finding the Worth While in the Orient* (New York: Robert M. McBride & Co., 1926), p. 35.

4. Thomas S. Monaghan, untitled introductory address to symposium, '*The Wright Hand*,' at University of Michigan, 13 April 1985 (reprinted in edited unpaginated proceedings).

He retained an abiding interest in Frank Lloyd Wright. As a boy of twelve he had first encountered Wright's work while scanning books in the public library at Traverse City, Michigan. He became convinced of Wright's merit from a published list of the ten greatest architectural works of the first half of the twentieth century; seven of the ten buildings cited were by Wright. Later, when Monaghan became a Marine stationed in Japan, he often went sightseeing at Wright's big Imperial Hotel, built in Tokyo during the First World War era. The hotel was big enough to be a small world arrayed in Wright's taste. As a guidebook commented, 'there existed a magic potency in the curves and angles of its marvelous design,'[3] and Tom Monaghan felt this magic. Back home in Ann Arbor once again, he sought out all the Wright homes he could find in the area.[4]

The original Ypsilanti store did its best trade delivering pizza to college dormitories. Early on, Monaghan found it wise to confine the business to delivering a limited selection of pizza and soft drinks, with no dining tables on the premises, and this has remained the operating formula. Now renamed 'Domino's Pizza', the business added successful outlets in other college towns. Other shops located in residential neighborhoods did poorly at first; for a time, their poor performance threatened the whole pizza enterprise. Then Amstar Corporation brought suit over use of the trade name 'Domino's' on behalf of their Domino sugar products. The litigation further inhibited growth of outlets during the rest of the seventies until Domino's Pizza won the contest in 1980.[5] That was a period to consolidate gains. Most of the dynamic growth of Domino's Pizza has taken place since then.

5. Monaghan and Anderson, *Pizza Tiger,* pp. 137, 143, 187, 231-32.

People are supposed to be too cynical for such a story, but the public has embraced Tom Monaghan as a return to the Horatio Alger stories. There is his boyhood; he spent six years in an orphanage (when he was four, his father had died on Christmas Eve, and his mother's long working hours as a nurse brought about his stay at a Roman Catholic orphanage). There is his upbringing; the farm life up north and then the hitch in the Marines taught self reliance and discipline, so vital to a youngster who would someday run his own pizza shop.[6]

6. Monaghan and Anderson, *Pizza Tiger,* pp. 22, 27, 32, 44.

Finally, there are the rewards, beginning with the groundbreaking ceremony at Domino's Farms and all that it meant that late summer day in 1984.

The Tigers were another reward. The wholesome, youthful-looking Tom Monaghan seemed almost anointed with the privilege of buying the precious baseball franchise in late 1983 from the respected John Fetzer. Monaghan promised to serve an apprenticeship under Fetzer's guidance to learn the ropes of being a responsible owner. The Detroit Baseball Club was rich in tradition. The Tigers had played in eight world series contests over the years. Ty Cobb, Harry Heilmann, Mickey Cochrane, Hank Greenberg, Al Kaline all had been Tigers. The team had played on the site of its ballpark longer than any other major league club. Along with Boston's Fenway Park, Tiger Stadium will be baseball's oldest when the White Sox replace their ballpark in the near future. For Tom Monaghan in his first season as owner in 1984, the Tigers were storybook stuff. That spring the team won thirty-five of their first forty games, a major league record. For the first time since the fabled 1927 Yankees, a team never surrendered first place all season long.[7] Now Tom Monaghan's picture was in all the newspapers, and not just on the business pages.

7. George Lee Anderson, *Bless You Boys* (Chicago: Contemporary Books, Inc., 1984), pp. 1, 70; Michael Betzold and Marc Okkonen, 'Tigers' Lair Has a Corner on Lore', in *Detroit Free Press,* 13 September 1987, p. 9D.

Tigers' Kirk Gibson in World Series Victory, 1984
Credit: *Detroit Free Press,* Mary Schroeder

There were perquisites of the very successful businessman as collector. Artifacts of Wright's buildings—patterned leaded art glass windows, furniture, documents—were bought piecemeal at auction to display at Domino's Farms. There were two big Duesenberg automobiles, each costing Monaghan over a million dollars, as the nucleus of a growing collection of exotic cars. The classic cars toured the country for exhibits on behalf of Domino's Pizza. There was also a very active new Indy-type racing car in red-white-and-blue Domino's Pizza markings. In 1985 Al Unser took this car to second place standing in national competition.[8] The cars weren't just toys; they sold pizza.

The pizza business has been good to Tom Monaghan. It has also been good by degree to many of those who grew along with it. Critics of the growing service economy—and of the fast food industry in particular—say that it sustains itself with low-paying dead-end jobs for teenagers. As a substitute for the decreasing number of better-paying factory jobs, the trend implies a lower standard of living ahead for America. But Domino's Pizza has grown with many up-by-the-bootstraps outlets like the original Ypsilanti shop of 1960. In keeping with the work ethic, hard workers can become store managers and franchisees by the time they are in their early twenties. They can look to a financial arm of Domino's Pizza to help establish their business if the bankers are skeptical. Successful franchisees can be promoted into the parent organization, even into its upper reaches, without the obligatory MBA degree that American business expects.[9]

One small bit of pantomime illustrates this spirit of leveling and solidarity within the whole Domino's Pizza organization. On one day each month, all Domino's Pizza employees in the headquarters building don the same uniform worn by the pizza throwers and delivery drivers of the Domino's Pizza franchise outlets. All are reaffirmed as 'Dominoids,' company lingo for a Domino's Pizza employee. This costume also erases the distinctions of hierarchy

8. Monaghan and Anderson, *Pizza Tiger,* p. 280.

9. Monaghan and Anderson, *Pizza Tiger,* pp. 19, 261.

Working at Domino's Farms is another incentive like these annual performance awards that build the pizza business.
Credit: Domino's Pizza, Inc. Archives

of a company headquarters for the moment. 'You can be sitting next to a vice-president in the cafeteria,' a Dominoid will explain, 'and it won't show.'

The new headquarters building at Domino's Farms plays a role in this motivation. Dominoids share this pleasant place to work as one of the rewards of the fastest growing food chain in the history of the restaurant business. The customary playthings of a rich man are for all to enjoy in this corporate mansion. The collection of valuable artifacts is of Wright's work, placed prominently in a nearby exhibition building. The classic cars have joined the Wrightiana in that new building north of the offices, to be more accessible to the public. The barns of this corporate country house stable the everyday farm animals of a children's petting farm. The striped tent for special festivities out on the lawn presents summer theater entertainment for the whole community on evenings and weekends. The very important guests at this corporate mansion are Dominoids from all over and the curious public as well.

The analogy to a mansion will be complete when the conference/training center is built with its tower of guest rooms and when the pond is created to flow between the buildings of Domino's Farms. The existing offices are a place of work, after all, despite the informal ambiance. To spend a day and evening in the pleasant setting of Tom Monaghan's dream, and to awaken the next morning beside a window looking down on the copper roofs, to linger over breakfast at pondside before a new day's activities is, as any tourist knows, the way to really feel at home.

Mansion And Home Office: The Heritage Of Domino's Farms

2

The story of the company headquarters building as a showplace in architecture is well known, especially when it concerns the skyscraper, America's best recognized gift to architecture. The mansion in American life is also familiar, whether on the plantations of colonial Virginia or on the opulent Edwardian estates of the moguls of American commerce. The intertwining of these two themes, however, presents a special heritage for Domino's Farms.

In colonial times, the Virginia mansion *was* the home of big business. In the eighteenth century tobacco economy, the large plantation was the prime social and economic unit. Towns like Williamsburg or Richmond existed primarily as political capitals, not as centers of transatlantic commerce. The plantation shipped its tobacco directly to London from its own James River docks. Back across these same docks it received the latest fashions from London and fabricated items for building the new mansion, such as window sash, wrought iron gates, and even bricks carried as ballast.

A colonial plantation owner like William Byrd at Westover was turning to the same sources for his mansion design as his later Edwardian American counterpart in commerce. Both emulated the way of life of the eighteenth century English country house. The American mansion builders of the two periods differed from one another in that Byrd's wealth lay in his productive land, like that of the English gentry in his time. The Edwardian showplace represented wealth accumulated entirely separately in commerce in cities and towns. In the end the Edwardian mansion proved to be superfluous.

In the northern colonies, the coming separation of big business from the home was already evident. New England still had an agricultural economy in colonial times, but it was one of small family farms in contrast to the big tobacco plantations. Families were large in order to run such farms. While elder sons stayed on to inherit the farm, younger ones came of age and slipped off to town to make their fortunes in shops and counting houses; alternatively, they became itinerant country peddlars or went seafaring in Salem windjammers trading to China. In these various ways capital accrued slowly to form the foundation for the infant American industries of the early nineteenth century.

In the early years of the New England textile mills, the earliest large-scale American industry, the company offices were not yet given any special distinction. The factories typically developed away from the large cities near a convenient river or stream to turn the water wheels that gave them power to run their looms. The mill workers came from farms in the surrounding countryside at first. Even when the mill towns arose around the huge masonry buildings, their location usually remained too isolated from big cities to justify much ostentation for the sake of prestige. The mill building was typically dignified with a cupola for a factory bell placed over a stair tower projecting from the many-windowed masonry wall of the mill. The proudest monument of the mill town might be the owner's house on the hill— if, indeed, the owner did not live in Boston. As for the home office of the mill, this was usually tucked away in an inconspicuous corner off the factory floor.[10] For another century emerging new industries had their headquarters down at the works, as in the early years of the Ford Motor Company. These industries were created or overseen by practical men who felt most at home amidst their factory's operations.

In the cities of the early nineteenth century the company showplaces housed a bank, an insurance firm, or a publishing house. These buildings often featured a classical portico or a Medici Palace facade pasted on the front as a reassuring connotation of stability and prosperity. An early example was the Girard Bank in Philadelphia. Until the elevator came, no tenant or client willingly climbed more than four flights of stairs.

The first commercial building to have a passenger elevator, the invention of Elisha Graves Otis, was the Haughwout Store of 1857 in New York City. Its five story facade was a Renaissance-style Venetian palace executed in cast iron, more evidence of technology at work.[11] In this case the height of the building did not take advantage of the elevator's promise of vistas from windows up among the church spires.

10. Martha and Murray Zimiles, *Early American Mills* (New York: Bramhall House, 1973), pp. 113, 130, 135, 149, 164, 167.

11. Marcus Whiffen and Frederick Koeper, *American Architecture* (Cambridge, MA: The MIT Press, 1983) I, p. 205.

Westover Plantation House, c. 1730, James River, Virginia
Credit: Gordon Bugbee

Typical 19th Century New England Mill
Cambridge, Massachusetts
Credit: Gordon Bugbee

Girard Bank, 1797, Philadelphia, Pennsylvania
Credit: Historical Society of Pennsylvania
Philadelphia, Pennsylvania

With elevators, height of a building became a finite measure of prestige. Now upper stories with a panoramic view of town commanded the highest rents, rather than the lowest rents as in buildings without elevators. In New York City in 1875, the *Tribune's* new home could boast of double the usual five stories, and competition in height was on its way. The Tribune Building was commissioned to satisfy the vanity of the publisher Horace Greeley, just before his unsuccessful presidential campaign of 1872 and his death soon afterwards. Even the best of architects was daunted by the problem of suitably composing the facade of a tall elevator building. Richard Morris Hunt, the building's architect, simply superimposed several conventional buildings on top of one another. A tall mansard roof with dormer windows three stories high capped the facade, together with a spindly clock tower with a pyramidal peak. After 1905 the solid masonry walls of this pile strained under a new load of another nine stories of offices treated in similar fashion, with the same sort of mansard and tower reconstituted above the whole.[12] Even without this new height, the design was an astigmatic nightmare.

12. Paul R. Baker, *Richard Morris Hunt* (Cambridge, MA: The MIT Press, 1980), pp. 219-23.

When the Tribune Building was finished, Hunt was on the threshold of creating the ostentatious city mansions and palatial summer 'cottages' of the Vanderbilts for which he is best remembered. These established the grand scale and pretentious form of the American mansion in a turn-of-the-century golden age he didn't live to see.

Before the end of the century, Chicago architects made the tall office building more practical with a steel skeleton jacketed with a lightweight masonry curtain wall. The architect Louis Sullivan conferred visual coherence to the facades of such buildings by letting the lines of the facade reveal the disposition of elements inside. A prominent entrance, big shop windows and those of walk-up mezzanine offices were grouped in the lowest visible zone. An ornamental attic cornice in front of mechanical and storage space capped the building mass. In between in the tripartite composition was an array of identical windows representing those offices reached only by elevator.[13] A textbook example was the Guaranty Building he designed in 1894 for Buffalo, New York. Sullivan enriched this new architecture with original plant-like or geometrical detail often executed in terra cotta.

13. Louis H. Sullivan 'The Tall Office Building Artistically Considered', in *Kindergarten Chats and Other Writings* (New York: George Wittenborn, Inc., 1947), pp. 203-05.

Chicago celebrated its coming of age in the early nineties with a set of monumental civic buildings and the 'White City' spectacle of its World's Fair

Haughwout Building, 1857, New York City
Credit: Museum of the City of New York

Tribune Building, 1874, New York City
Credit: Museum of the City of New York

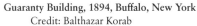

Guaranty Building, 1894, Buffalo, New York
Credit: Balthazar Korab

Woolworth Building, 1913, New York City
Credit: Museum of the City of New York

Equitable Life Building, 1915, New York City
Credit: Courtesy of *Architectural Record*

of 1893. These were classically inspired in the renewed eclectic spirit gathering force in the East. From this stimulus, typical Chicago office buildings began to acquire diluted period detail. The facade was still composed in a tripartite set of zones, but the architects now explained this approach by analogy to a classical column; it had a 'shaft' contained between the 'base' and the 'capital.' As a prophet of a new architecture, Sullivan loathed the rationale.

A historical sketch on tall buildings cannot ignore this Chicago School, but it constitutes a digression from a topic concerned with corporate headquarters buildings. Speculators promoted the Chicago School office buildings to house a multitude of tenants in small office cubicles. There were few corporate signature buildings in the lot.

After the turn of the century, the scene of innovation shifted back to New York City once again. The city was now home to giant trusts and huge corporations wanting prestigious skyscrapers to match their new exalted magnitude. Special recognition

came to whichever spectacular new skyscraper was momentarily the world's tallest office building (no building had yet exceeded the height of the Eiffel Tower in Paris). At fifty stories the Metropolitan Life Tower was an oversized paraphrase of the St. Mark's Campanile in Venice; at sixty stories the Woolworth Tower was an essay in Gothic detail applied repetitiously in pressed units of glazed terra cotta. These were true towers, rising in slender shafts from a broad base of office space below.

In a controversial way, the Equitable Life Building was the most influential building, even if it was not quite in the Metropolitan and Woolworth league. This monstrous Chicago style classical column rose all forty-two stories flush with the property line from sidewalk to cornice in its rapacity for rentable space. Its notoriety helped to bring about New York's Zoning Ordinance of 1916. This legislation prescribed setbacks for taller buildings in order to give their humblest neighbors some slight chance of capturing a fresh breeze and a sunbeam.

Meanwhile in Chicago again, Colonel Robert R. McCormick was puffing his *Chicago Tribune* as 'The World's Greatest Newspaper'. To suit this image, the Colonel sponsored an international competition in 1922 for architects to design 'the most beautiful and distinctive office building in the world'.[14] Over two hundred entries from twenty-three countries sought a share of $100,000 in prize money. The entries of American architects generally were lackluster exercises in classical or Gothic eclecticism, often with nearly interchangeable massing of superstructure. The winning design by John Mead Howells and Raymond Hood is arguably far superior to these in its finesse. The Tribune Tower in their version became a sort of inhabited 'Butter Tower' of Rouen Cathedral. Its crown was hemmed in with giant buttresses which made structural nonsense but which were crucially dramatic in silhouette. Other architects couldn't hope to emulate it. The sort of cut stone detail that would have covered the richest society church of the day was now distributed over a thirty-six-story tower.

The architects didn't try to emulate it. The prizewinners included, they considered the Second Prize design to be the definitive statement of the tall office building. It was submitted by Eliel Saarinen, whose Helsinki Railroad Station headed a respectable body of work in his native Finland. His work had been obsessed with a telescoping motif for some years. There was the polygonal pylon of receding planes he proposed over a classical parliament house design for a Finnish competition of 1908, for example. Now, drawn directly upward in subtle transitions from its rectilinear base, the motif reached the height of a Chicago office tower. It had found its mark in a type of building Saarinen had never seen. At the same time, the setbacks ordained by the New York Zoning Ordinance had found architectonic expression. 'Rising from the earth in suspiration as of the earth and as of the universal genius of man', wrote Louis Sullivan of the design, 'it ascends in beauty, lofty and serene…until its lovely crest seems at one with the sky'.[15] Sullivan was less generous to the Gothic alternative, disparaging it as 'an imaginary structure—not imaginative'.[16] There was a touch of the medieval in Saarinen's design, too. In general, however, its vision helped to free architects of obligations to substantiate their designs in historical precedent. They turned to new forms heralding the Art Deco in America.

During the twenties, stalagmite shapes of skyscrapers began to crown the Battery skyline of New York City and the downtown districts of other

14. *The International Competition for a New Administration Building for the Chicago Tribune MCMXXII* (Chicago: The Tribune Company, 1923), p.13.

15. *Tribune Competition,* text opposite plate 13.

16. Stephen Longstreet, *Chicago 1860-1919* (New York: David McKay Company, Inc., 1973), p. 458.

Chicago Tribune Building as Built, 1925
Chicago, Illinois
Credit: Balthazar Korab

Saarinen Tribune Tower Proposal, 1922
Credit: Museum of Finnish Architecture
Helsinki, Finland

cities. The supreme example of Art Deco virtuosity
was a signature building for Chrysler Corporation
in midtown Manhattan. Four short years before, this
corporation had emerged from a fragmentary
tangle of decrepit auto companies nobody else wanted.
Since then, Walter P. Chrysler had made it the
third of a Big Three of American auto companies.

Chrysler's sons didn't expect to follow
their father into the automotive world. Instead, he put
them to work promoting an office building that
would at last be taller than the Eiffel Tower in Paris.[17]
William Van Alen's design of soaring verticals
was crowned by stainless steel parabolic arches surging
upward into a slender spire; the spire had emerged
as if by magic late during construction in order to
exceed the height of a rival Wall Street tower that had
just been topped off.[18] The exterior was mono-
chromatic, but the interior blossomed in rich, colorful
veneers and in inlays of its elevator doors and cabs
and the like. With the Saarinen design before it, this is
our lingering image of the ideal skyscraper to the
extent that Postmodern architects have revived and
adapted its form.

Saarinen would see no skyscrapers of his
own built. Indeed, the city planner in him rebelled at
the urban density demanding such skyscrapers.
There is irony in the fact that his prize money from the
Tribune Competition allowed him to emigrate to
the United States in 1923. That autumn, he joined the
architectural school faculty of the University of
Michigan in Ann Arbor; for two years he taught a select
class of advanced students much like the studio
course Gunnar Birkerts has taught there for many years.
(While there, Saarinen did design a memorial
bell tower for the campus, which remained on paper;
the rather similar Burton Tower eventually built
there was designed by others.)

Two of Saarinen's students at the university,
Henry Scripps Booth and Robert Swanson,
drew him to Bloomfield Hills in suburban Detroit.
There in stages he planned the academic community of Cranbrook for Booth's father, George Gough
Booth, publisher of the *Detroit News*. In the late
twenties Saarinen built two preparatory schools for the
campus. Probably the most popularly admired of
his Cranbrook work was the Cranbrook Boys' School,
in a manner suggesting the vernacular medieval.
The Kingswood Girls' School was more advanced in
design, rather Wrightian in an informal massing,
yet moderately formal in elements and materials.

At Cranbrook Saarinen was more influential
as an educator. George Booth had always intended

17. Walter P. Chrysler and
Boyden Sparkes, *Life of an
American Workman,* 2nd ed.
(New York: Dodd, Mead
& Company, 1950), p. 198.

18. Paul Goldberger,
The Skyscraper (New York:
Alfred A. Knopf, 1981),
pp. 82-83.

Chrysler Building, New York City, 1928-1930
Credit: Museum of the
City of New York

Cranbrook Boys School, 1925, Bloomfield Hills, Michigan
Credit: Balthazar Korab

the teaching of arts and crafts to be foremost in priorities for his new community. The Cranbrook Academy of Art coalesced only by 1932, in the depths of the Depression. Eliel Saarinen became its Director, serving until 1946. Saarinen believed in 'self education under good leadership', so this postgraduate program focused on the students' own projects. Until degrees were granted, starting in the forties, the informal program needed no courses and formal critiques. The Art Academy became a humanistic response to the Bauhaus in Germany, seeking an integration of the arts under the primacy of architecture. Students of Saarinen's regime became familiar postwar leaders in architecture (Harry Weese, Ralph Rapson), planning (Edward Bacon), sculpture (Harry Bertoia), textiles (Jack Lenor Larsen), furniture, (Charles and Ray Eames), and contract interior design (Florence Knoll). The versatility of Saarinen and his wife Loja and their son and daughter, Eero and Pipsan, particularly explains the success of the Art Academy in embracing the various disciplines.[19]

Before the school arose, Cranbrook had been a country estate. Albert Kahn designed Cranbrook House for George Booth in 1907 in a cottage vernacular manner sympathetic to the English Arts and Crafts Movement. The property had originally been a farm. Eliel Saarinen's original mandate at Cranbrook was to make over the farm buildings as the proposed boys' school.

George Booth's move to Cranbrook from his city mansion was part of the turn-of-the-century shift to country house living for the wealthy; it had been stimulated by Richard Morris Hunt with his string of Vanderbilt mansions imitating Italian palaces and French chateaus. Although this trend found formal expression in French and Italian styles, the true sociological impetus was a yearning for the life of the English country gentry. In reality, the American manufacturers, bankers, and publishers were looking over the shoulders of their English counterparts in commerce as they turned the pages of *Country Life* magazine and went about raising their own Edwardian showplaces.

In an era that adulated the mogul, the corporation was an extension of his personality, and the mansion was a personal statement of his success. The mansion's period dress was a carefully chosen stage setting, whether it alluded to England, France, or the Mediterranean countries. George Booth was uncommon in choosing the less pretentious Arts and Crafts style for his view of how a wealthy man should live. Alternatively to a Tudor mansion, most

wealthy men chose something classically dignified like the giant Whitemarsh Hall in the Philadelphia suburb of Chestnut Hill. For the Morgan partner Edward Stotesbury, Horace Trumbauer designed it in the very formal eighteenth century English Palladian mode as an appropriate setting for the antiques and collection of English portrait paintings Joseph Duveen assembled for his client. The effect was supremely ostentatious. In all innocence, Henry Ford supposedly said of his stay at Whitemarsh Hall, 'It's a great experience to see how the rich live.'[20]

Whitemarsh Hall was magnificent, but among the Edwardian estates some Postmodern architects of our own day are more attracted to a Mediterranean country classical manner as practiced by the New York architect Charles A. Platt. A case study for our purposes is his largest house in this vein, Villa Turicum, built in 1911 for Harold and Edith McCormick in Lake Forest, Illinois. The house, no longer standing, interests us also as the building which supplanted the design by Frank Lloyd Wright which later came to fascinate Tom Monaghan in drawing form.

Charles A. Platt was an attorney's son who studied painting in Paris and gravitated to a painterly interest in Italian gardens. Wealthy relatives and friends asked him to design gardens for them, complemented with appropriate houses. Thus he became an influential landscape architect and an architect. A large monograph of his country houses was published in 1913, but it was really a retrospective collection.[21] After the war years he moved on to designing larger buildings and campus groupings, as for the University of Illinois and Phillips Academy at Andover, executing the latter with a Morgan partner's fortune.[22]

Harold McCormick was a younger son of Cyrus McCormick, who had protected his inventions against a swarm of imitators to create the family's big farm implement company. Edith McCormick was a daughter of John D. Rockefeller. When Villa Turicum was built, Harold McCormick was Treasurer of International Harvester Company, the trust which absorbed the family firm. He succeeded his older brother as President in 1918. The several McCormick sons built homes in Lake Forest, a North Shore suburb of Chicago, as did the *Chicago Tribune's* Colonel McCormick, whose grandfather was a brother of old Cyrus. Harold and Edith McCormick continued to keep a city residence, his father's old mansion, on Chicago's north side Gold Coast. Their marriage survived completion of Villa Turicum by only ten years.[23]

19. *Design in America: The Cranbrook Vision 1925-1950* (New York: Harry N. Abrams, Inc., 1983), pp. 42-44.

20. James T. Maher, *The Twilight of Splendor: Chronicles of the Age of American Palaces* (Boston: Little, Brown and Company, 1975), pp. 35-36, 78.

21. *Monograph of the Work of Charles A. Platt, with an Introduction by Royal Cortissoz* (New York: Architectural Book Publishing Company, 1913).

22. Norman T. Newton, *Design on the Land: The Development of Landscape Architecture* (Cambridge, MA: Harvard University Press, 1971), Chapter 25.

23. *Chicago: Its History and its Buildings* (Chicago: S. J. Clarke Publishing Company, 1912), I, pp. 741, 750, 752; Albert N. Marquis, ed., *The Book of Chicagoans* (Chicago: A. N. Marquis Company, 1911, 1917); Albert N. Marquis, ed., *Who's Who in Chicago* (Chicago: A. N. Marquis Company, 1926, 1931).

Villa Turicum, Garden Side, 1911, Lake Forest, Illinois
Credit: Courtesy of the Platt Family

Platt understood that a villa in Italy was not a house alone, but a unity of gardens and house architectonically extended into the varied Italian hillscape. His own work encouraged American architects to treat houses in a larger context. Villa Turicum illustrates Platt's customary arrangement of grounds around the four distinct facades of a freestanding house. The entrance facade on the west was dignified in its symmetry, but modest for its size, its stucco walls, shuttered windows, and tile roof. A vaulted loggia facing the lake vista across a paved fountain court made the east facade only a little more formal. The chief bit of ostentation was a baroque garden stairway beyond. It led down the steep lakefront bluff to a pool and prospect for viewing Lake Michigan over the treetops. The latticed south facade was more reserved, facing the garden planted rather informally within a grid of gravel paths. The north facade was assigned the service entrance.[24]

Apart from the lakefront side, only surface materials and discreet detailing gave the house its Mediterranean flavor. Inside, however, a sequence of chambers in Italian period dress had replicated stone mantels, door casings, coffered ceilings and the like. The most distinctive room at Villa Turicum was a glass-roofed 'Pompeiian Court', set opposite an open courtyard in the heart of the house. Platt, himself, designed all this work and selected the furnishings, tapestries, and the like. The client expected this complete product in order to cast a convincing spell for parties and entertainment. At Whitemarsh Hall, Trumbauer and Duveen, architect of the shell and purveyor of antiques to the owner, were allied with French decorators to complete this service. The client did not expect to move in with his own furniture, at least in the most prominent rooms. (Frank Lloyd Wright has been criticized for forcing a similar design control on his patrons, but the practice was more customary than we realize today. Unlike American architects who merely selected furniture usually, Wright was closer to European counterparts who designed the furniture and accessories as well.)

24. Keith N. Morgan, *Charles A. Platt, The Artist as Architect* (New York: Architectural History Foundation, 1985), pp. 113-20; *Platt Monograph,* pp. 61-65.

The upstairs plan of Villa Turicum reveals at least nine generous bedrooms, each with private bath. One was the master suite, of course. But the McCormicks' three small children wouldn't need so ample an establishment (indeed, children were often tucked away with a governess in attics of the mansions.) The extra bedrooms were for the extended visits of house guests, true to the English country house manner. In effect, Villa Turicum and Whitemarsh Hall and their counterparts were very exclusive small hotels. The kitchen belonged to a sort of short order restaurant. If an eccentric houseguest wanted lobster for breakfast, why, fresh lobster should probably be on hand, just in case. The chef contended with a multitude of doctor's-orders diets for diners who were mostly middle-aged or elderly.

Before Platt began his studies for Villa Turicum, the Wright Prairie house mansion design and the scheme of another earlier architect had been set aside. Little evidence survives to show why Harold and Edith McCormick even considered a Prairie house, but the Platt design seems preordained for them.[25]

25. Morgan, *Charles A. Platt,* p. 116.

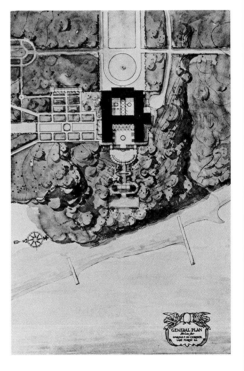

Villa Turicum, Site Plan, Lake Forest, Illinois
Credit: Courtesy of the Platt Family

Villa Turicum, Drawing Room
Lake Forest, Illinois
  Credit: Courtesy of the Platt Family

Villa Turicum, Pompeiian Court
Lake Forest, Illinois
  Credit: Courtesy of the Platt Family

Villa Turicum, Floor Plans
Lake Forest, Illinois, with unbuilt wings
  Credit: Courtesy of the Platt Family
  Columbia University, Avery Architectural and Fine Arts Library, N.Y.

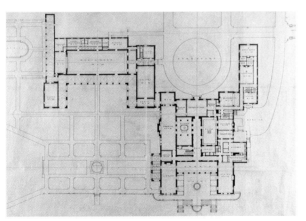

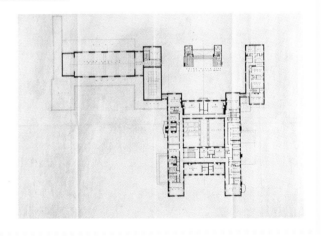

About twenty-five years ago Professor Leonard Eaton published a comparison of Wright with a contemporary mansion architect, Howard Van Doren Shaw, whose work paralleled Platt's except perhaps in preferring English fashions. The book was titled *Two Chicago Architects and Their Clients*. The author, a University of Michigan professor, will join our story more directly later on as the man who introduced Tom Monaghan to Gunnar Birkerts. Dr. Eaton found that those who chose Wright's Prairie houses were usually self-assured, self-made businessmen, perhaps practical-minded owners of small manufacturing concerns. They hardly fitted the avant garde mold one would have expected of people attracted to Wright's work. One suspects that they admired him for his practical problem solving.

Most of Shaw's clients were businessmen, too. Often they were the Ivy League college educated sons of the founders of big companies. Many hired Shaw to build homes in the same aristocratic Lake Forest community where Shaw, himself, lived. Where Wright's clients might be close to the arts, often as amateur musicians, Shaw's clients would be passive patrons of art organizations.[26] Dr. Eaton's book does not consider Harold McCormick, for his Prairie house mansion was never built, of course. But he fits the Shaw pattern closely. Harold McCormick and his brothers were Princeton men. He and Edith McCormick generously supported the symphony organization and grand opera in Chicago. Aline Saarinen

has written that Edith McCormick tried unsuccessfully to supplant Mrs. Potter Palmer as Chicago's social autocrat.[27] It seems obvious that the role Villa Turicum had to play for a captain of industry and a leader of society was too circumscribed to permit an aesthetic adventure. Indeed, one is pleasantly surprised by their discretion to eschew a Whitemarsh Hall.

Cranbrook House, Whitemarsh Hall and Villa Turicum all stood isolated from the outside world on ample grounds. In contrast, many 'country house' mansions were displayed as a collection of corporate landmarks all in a row. They might stand back on deep green lawns along a lakefront road, as in the Detroit suburb of Grosse Pointe. There, Edsel Ford's Cotswold mansion by Albert Kahn happened to be hidden from the road in a landscape setting by Jens Jensen; a mansion-sized gatehouse was its proxy for the Ford name to gawkers on Lake Shore Drive. In full view from the road was Alvan Macauley's smaller Cotswold clone by Kahn, representing the Packard presidency. A Georgian mansion John Russell Pope designed for Roy Chapin was 'Hudson cars' before Henry Ford II moved in and made it 'Ford cars.' The role pursued widows tied to a company only by dividend checks. 'Rose Terrace,' which Horace Trumbauer designed for Anna Dodge Dillman in 1934, would always be 'Dodge cars' even though Chrysler Corporation had bought the Dodge Company six years earlier from the New York bankers who had received it still earlier from the heirs of Horace and John Dodge.

26. Leonard K. Eaton, *Two Chicago Architects and their Clients: Frank Lloyd Wright and Howard Van Doren Shaw* (Cambridge, MA: The MIT Press, 1969), pp. 32, 41, 139.

27. Aline B. Saarinen, *The Proud Possessors: The Lives, Times and Tastes of Some Adventurous American Art Collectors* (New York: Random House, 1958), pp. 23, 345.

Alvan Macauley House, 1929, Grosse Pointe Shores, Michigan
Credit: Albert Kahn Associates, Architects and Engineers, Detroit, Michigan

The era of mansions is gone. Popular memory pictures it as revelry of Gatsbyesque bacchanals that gave the mansions a final flourish in the twenties. The demise of the mansions is attributed to many causes: The income tax, the stanched flow of cheap, obedient servants, the Depression, the desire for privacy and security, and the rising land values that overwhelmed the Grosse Pointe lakefront estates and the 100-acre grounds of Villa Turicum in Lake Forest. Most fundamentally, the impersonal corporate stewards who succeeded the founding moguls didn't inherit their claim on the mansion as corporate symbol with a lifestyle of country gentry.

Russell Lynes, then Managing Editor of *Harpers Magazine,* wrote in its 'After Hours' column about his visit to Grosse Pointe in 1959. He found its estates being fragmented into what were advertised as 'gentlemen's estatelets'. Lynes was in Detroit to see the new General Motors Technical Center, north of Detroit in Warren Township. Inspired by portraits of company directors he saw there, he contrasted his two experiences:

'In the days when the mansions of Grosse Pointe were built, the businessman's glorification was personal and his house was his expression of triumph. Now his glorification is corporate and it is his company's facade that matters. He doesn't build houses now; he builds whole campuses instead. Corporate ostentation affords the corporate leader the same gratification he once derived from personal ostentation and now he can call it "progress." Did the old tycoons in the Grosse Pointe mansions say: "What is good for me is good for America"? I suppose they did.'[28]

The General Motors Technical Center which Lynes came to visit heralded that new breed of suburban corporate showplaces that would rival its downtown conterpart. A corporation selling automobiles was a befitting midwife to the trend. The corporation's first criterion was for a half hour's driving time from downtown headquarters. The site chosen was also about midway in the eighteen miles separating executive enclaves in the Grosse Pointe and Bloomfield Hills suburbs. Chairman Alfred P. Sloan, Jr., whose benevolent gift to motorists was the annual model change, first contemplated a Technical Center during World War II. According to Harley Earl, longtime styling chief at General Motors, Sloan 'envisioned a place having the atmosphere of a college or university campus where GM's Central Staff group dealing with advanced creative thinking would be free to explore the future for new ideas and new concepts in automotive styling and engineering.'[29]

Axiomatic to this new type of showplace was the pleasant working environment promising a more effective staff. The new suburban office campus would contrast with the clerks in drab cubicles in a typical downtown headquarters. The fundamental workspace of the downtown skyscraper had hardly changed since Louis Sullivan's day. A corollary opportunity for the new suburban campus was to showcase its contented staff in its handsome setting for the benefit of the very important guests like Russell Lynes. That this outlook could be born in so sensitive a facility as the Technical Center is paradoxical, for one would have expected corporate reflex to demand a 'fortress' instead to protect trade secrets in gestation. That the Technical Center has since become so is merely a contradiction in its story, and it is not unusual in this.

As architects General Motors chose the Saarinens, father and son, 'for another Cranbrook', as Eero Saarinen recalled later.[30] The corporation got something visionary instead. The initial conception was Eliel Saarinen's. It established the giant scale of magnificent distances that would prevail in this motorist's campus. His design arrayed the various departmental buildings as extremely long and low masses around a large central lake. In the drawings, one prominent building seemed futuristic, with an expressionistic airfoil roof. Another recalled the rooftop monitors of Albert Kahn's Chrysler Truck Plant four miles down Mound Road. The charcoalesque renderings of Hugh Ferriss, with their usual ambiguity between daytime and night, announced the Saarinen scheme in 1945. Then the project was shelved for three years. For the moment, new factories had priority at General Motors.

When construction began at last in 1949, the buildings followed Eero Saarinen's design, although they were still distributed roughly according to his father's master plan. The visible spirit was of yet another architect, however, the German emigre Ludwig Mies van der Rohe.

The final director of the Bauhaus when Hitler closed it, Mies came to head the architectural school at Illinois Institute of Technology. In the late thirties he had begun to build its new Chicago campus. Its buildings and his postwar Chicago apartment towers prophesied an era of gridded facades in steel and glass prescribed universally for all building types. For a time Mies' idiom seemed to be the full flowering of the 'International Style', the budding creation of avant garde European architects of the prewar era. As we know in retrospect, Americans are

28. Russell Lynes, 'The Erosion of Detroit', in *Harper's Magazine,* January, 1960, p. 25.

29. Harley J. Earl, 'Styling in General Motors', in *General Motors Engineering Journal,* 3, No. 3 (1956), p. 78.

30. Allan Temko, *Eero Saarinen* (New York: George Braziller, 1962), p. 20.

General Motors Technical Center, 1951-1957, Warren, Michigan
Credit: Balthazar Korab

Connecticut General Life Insurance Company, 1957, Hartford, Connecticut
Credit: Ezra Stoller © ESTO All Rights Reserved

too restless to have accepted such a confining discipline for long. Eero Saarinen evangelized his client to accept this Miesian formula in steel and glass as having the pristine quality of automobile manufacture. Many innovations there became standard practice. Neoprene gaskets adapted from car windshield technology held window glass and panels in place. The thin insulated sandwich panels were prefabricated with finished inner and outer surfaces of porcelain enamel on steel. Luminous suspended ceilings of modular plastic panels also became part of the designer's working vocabulary.[31]

Eero Saarinen was already showing his own restlessness toward any such universal principles. The blank end walls of his metal-gridded buildings were dressed in glazed brick in brilliant colors Mies might have disavowed. On the gargantuan scale of the Technical Center, such flourishes are welcome.

A styling auditorium under a big, shiny stainless steel dome foretold the architects' growing satiety with the boxes of the International Style. Most showy was the variety of staircases in entrance foyers, often dramatically suspended or cantilevered, as trademarks of the various departments. The new buildings for the Technical Center accumulated gradually. The campus was fully landscaped and ready for public viewing at last in 1956.

As construction resumed in this postwar era the corporate office building was already the most prestigious building type, followed perhaps by airport terminals and college buildings. The center city office tower was transformed fundamentally with its metal-and-glass curtain wall and its suspended acoustical ceiling—an assembly recessing the new fluorescent lighting and concealing the new air conditioning.

31. Aline B. Saarinen, ed., *Eero Saarinen on his Work,* 2nd ed., rev. (New Haven, CT: Yale University Press, 1968), pp. 30, 32.

The name of Skidmore, Owings and Merrill ('S.O.M.') became closely associated with the pristine new office towers, beginning with the prototypical Lever house the firm had designed in 1951 in New York City. S.O.M. had battened on large scale projects (prewar world's fair planning and the wartime Oak Ridge atomic weapon community) before high quality design became its forte. A year after the Technical Center opened, S.O.M. completed its first suburban headquarters project, a lowrise office complex for the Connecticut General Life Insurance Company on a 280-acre site outside Hartford. Monographs of S.O.M. work through 1973 show twice as many urban office towers as suburban office buildings, but the suburban genre was established.[32] A typical suburban example would be one to three stories high, of long span bays framed in concrete or heavy steel members, serene in its simple classical regularity against a richly landscaped setting. Architects like S.O.M. and Eero Saarinen would give the same complete care to furnishings, partitioning, and choice accessories and artifacts that Platt would have composed for a drawing room in the golden age of the mansion. (Many of these furnishings and accessories were produced by graduates of the Art Academy at Cranbrook.)

Eero Saarinen's crowning example of the office building in the countryside was for the John Deere Company for a 600-acre site outside Moline, Illinois. This was an eight-story slab-shaped building spanning a shallow ravine. A pond was dammed in the hollow in front of the building, flanked by woods on the high ground. To eliminate window blinds that would spoil the view, Saarinen hung horizontal sunshading from the facade, framed and fabricated in steel expressed like timber joinery. This was made possible by a pioneering use of a protective rust coating on the special high tensile steel employed. Saarinen wanted gutsy steel this time, deemed appropriate for a farm machinery manufacturer.[33] A commission for an urban office tower came to Saarinen at last from Columbia Broadcasting System in New York. Closely spaced concrete piers sheathed in dark granite rose 500 feet from ground to parapet. The bold vertical lines aptly updated the ideal of the tall building, yet anchored the whole mass to the ground as few office towers on *pilotis* could do.

Eero Saarinen died prematurely of a brain tumor on September 1, 1961. His practice passed to two of his associates, relocated in Hartford, Connecticut, as the firm of Kevin Roche, John Dinkeloo and Associates.

32. Ernst Danz, ed., *Architecture of Skidmore, Owings & Merrill, 1950-1962* (New York: Frederick A. Praeger, 1963); Axel Menges, ed., *Architecture of Skidmore, Owings & Merrill, 1963-1973* (New York: Architectural Book Publishing Company, 1974).

33. Saarinen, *Eero Saarinen on his Work,* p. 82.

Lever House, 1952, New York City
Credit: Ezra Stoller © ESTO All Rights Reserved

John Deere Administration Building
1957-1963, Moline, Illinois
Credit: Balthazar Korab

AT&T Building, 1978, New York City
Credit: Johnson/Burgee Architects
Photo Credit: Richard Payne, AIA

Transco Tower, 1983, Houston, Texas
Credit: Photo by Michael Puig
Transco Energy Company

34. Paul Goldberger, 'When Suburban Sprawl Meets Upward Mobility', in *New York Times*, 26 July 1987, p. 30H.

35. Untitled address by Patricia Conway to East Central Regional Conference of Association of Collegiate Schools of Architecture, Miami University, Oxford, Ohio, 17 October 1986, one of the best statements of current trends in corporate home office design.

36. Christopher B. Leinberger and Charles Lockwood, 'How Business is Reshaping America', in *The Atlantic Monthly*, October 1986, p. 43.

37. Raechelle Garbarine, 'Farms Giving Way to Offices as Development Pushes West,' in *New York Times Real Estate Report: Commercial Property*, Section 12, 10 May 1987, pp. 54, 58.

In the eighties downtown skyscrapers have once again become favorites of Postmodern architects, with their preference for urban forms and settings. The bellwether of Postmodernism was the new Manhattan headquarters for American Telegraph and Telephone Company in New York City. This was the split-pedimented 'Chippendale highboy' designed in 1978 by the Johnson/Burgee office. The general body of urban Postmodern towers is more evocative of the tapered Art Deco buildings of the twenties. This is a renewed affirmation of Eliel Saarinen's Tribune Tower prototype. The Johnson/Burgee office designed a classic example in the 64-story Transco Tower, built beside other towers the same architects designed in the Houston area.

A sign of the times is that the Transco Tower stands in the Post Oak development of suburban Houston, not downtown. Even more significant, the architect was chosen by the developer, Gerald Hines.[34] Today the developer takes the initiative. The developer picks a site, conjures up a building-to-be and invites the big corporation to move in with a lease. The corporation gets to put its logo on the parapet. To attract a *Fortune 500* corporation, the developer may turn to Philip Johnson of the Johnson/Burgee firm to design a showplace; that is not the tenant's prerogative. The tenant corporation expresses its own personality within its own quarters through the agency of an interior architect of its choice, or perhaps the predilection of the current corporation president for antiques determines the ambiance within.

Visually, there may be a split personality between the building shell and its interior.[35]

For lesser corporations outside the *Fortune 500* list the choice is likely to be a developer's low-rise building in the suburbs. Such buildings are often gathered into 'urban villages', a term coined by Christopher Leinberger and Charles Lockwood.[36] These are office-hotel-shopping nucleii off the expressway ramps in the midst of suburban residential development. Post Oak is merely one of the largest of these urban villages.

Other such developments are set apart in their own ample acreage, but their isolation in a natural setting is not always of their own choice. A typical example is the Perrysville Corporate Center developed by Foster Wheeler Corporation for itself and other tenants in Union Township, New Jersey. The owners will develop only two-thirds of their 270 acres. The remainder will be left as a natural buffer from residential development nearby. This separation is dictated by the township authorities, who have also bargained for the owner's investing in related road improvements that will minimize disturbance to the emerging residential character of the township.[37]

The corporation invests its own capital in its headquarters building much more rarely today than in even the recent past. Today's business climate forces the corporation to show better performance by getting more out of its revenues and resources. There is little temptation for the corporation to preen itself in a home office monument that ties up

38. Jo Ellen Davis, 'Can Transco Wriggle Out of the "Take-or-Pay" Mess?', in *Business Week,* 28 September 1987, p. 67.

39. Robert A. Bennett, 'Corporate Boon: Real Estate', in *New York Times,* 20 August 1987, p. 23

40. Sam Howe Verhovek, 'Builders Got Tax Breaks, But What Did City Receive?', in *New York Times,* 24 May 1987, p. 6E.

capital idly. There is also the spectre of the corporate raider with his own personal objectives for corporate wealth so recklessly displayed. The Transco Energy Company, which ultimately acquired its Houston headquarters, is considering a partial sale and lease-back of the building to raise needed capital.[38]

Even the corporation that gave us the Chippendale high-boy has found a drastic change of heart. American Telegraph and Telephone Company will occupy half of a sixty-story developer's building as its Chicago regional headquarters. The corporation will provide no equity or financing, but in return for its presence in the building the developer will surrender a half interest in ownership to the corporation.[39]

A final sign of the times is that AT&T recently proposed to move most of its staff out of its Manhattan Postmodern monument and into cheaper back offices in New Jersey. AT&T would reserve to itself its executive offices in its namesake building back in Manhattan.[40] High rent tenants would fill the rest of the building. The remnant of an executive enclave as penthouse is of course the new form of mansion that at last the corporate officers may aspire to possess. The trend runs counter to those voices calling for management to draw closer to its employees and the consumer world, and it is not a healthy trend for American business. In their splendid isolation from reality, the managers in their penthouse mansion may become oblivious to the erosion of their corporate base.

A building does not have to promote this corporate split personality. Domino's Farms is one example of a better answer.

The Spirit Of Frank Lloyd Wright

3

41. Jonathan Lipman, *Frank Lloyd Wright and the Johnson Wax Buildings* (New York: Rizzoli International Publications, 1986), pp. 9, 15.

If Frank Lloyd Wright's wishes had prevailed with his client, the Johnson Wax Administration Building would have been the prototype of the postwar suburban corporate showplace. Wright risked losing his commission by arguing strenuously that the proper setting for a workplace was the countryside around the company's home town of Racine, Wisconsin. Company officials preferred to stay close to their factory in Racine. In depression times they were not inclined to pay for a new factory in the countryside as well.[41]

So the setting for the new office building became a nondescript neighborhood of little frame houses gathered around the old brick mill buildings of S. C. Johnson and Son. Wright responded by creating a streamlined massing of high window-less walls of Cherokee red brick. This was quite unlike the usual openness of his designs. The cloistered community within the walls couldn't see the visual discord outside. The motorist visitor passed through a portal and left his car in a pillared 'carport'. Wright led the visitor under this low ceiling to the front door; thus he magnified the spatial impression of the tall reception hall inside.

42. 'New Frank Lloyd Wright Office Building Shows Shape of Things to Come', in *Life Magazine,* 8 May 1939, p. 15.

The interior offered everything else that Chairman Sloan could have wished for the campus-like offices he would soon propose for the General Motors Technical Center. The benefits included incalculable good will in publicity. Leading its issue of May 8, 1939, for example, *Life Magazine* featured the opening of Johnson Wax in preference to the coinciding one for the New York World's Fair. The offices in Racine, the *Life* writer observed, were 'a truer glimpse of the shape of things to come' than the fair's 'freak and futuristic buildings'.

The writer could see past the streamlined shell and the dramatic skylighted hypostyle hall of the Main Workroom, 'spectacular as the showiest Hollywood set'. What seemed really significant was 'creative genius applied to the problem of designing the most efficient and comfortable, as well as beautiful, place in which Johnson Wax executives and clerks could do their work'.[42] Anticipating the trend of postwar open office planning, desks and files of two hundred clerks were placed on the main floor of the great room. Several specialized departments occupied a perimeter mezzanine. This Main Workroom allowed as efficient a flow of paperwork, along with flexibility for future needs, as any factory floor might want of its production facilities.

Johnson Wax, Exterior, 1936-1939, Racine, Wisconsin
Credit: S.C. Johnson & Son, Inc.

Johnson Wax, Interior, Racine, Wisconsin
Credit: S.C. Johnson & Son, Inc.

For so mundane a purpose, the spirit of the Main Workroom was exalting. Slender, tapered concrete uprights in serial ranks rose up to turn into the saucer shaped ceiling mass they supported. These gargantuan 'golf tee' forms were silhouetted against skylights of hollow Pyrex tubes set parallel between mastic joints. Wright developed the glazing using chemical tubing manufactured by the Corning Glass Company.[43] There were no conventional windows, and no exposed ceiling lamp fixtures, yet the writer from *Life* found no aggravating glare in the 'soft, shadowless illumination'. Quoting the architect, he found this 'designed to be as inspiring a place to work in as any cathedral ever was to worship in'.[44]

Still less prepossessing surroundings greeted the only comparable commercial office building Wright ever built. Early in his career, in 1904, he designed the headquarters of the Larkin Company. This was a self-contained mail order soap products firm in an industrial district a mile east of downtown Buffalo, New York. The new offices stood across Seneca Street from the company's monstrous multistory warehouses. Across a side lot was the Seneca Street railroad station where locomotives of departing trains sent up slowly-settling clouds of smoke and soot.[45]

Visitors weren't so important to the Larkin mail order business as they were to Louis Sullivan's Guaranty Building of a decade earlier, standing on its prominent corner of downtown Buffalo. The pair of tan terra cotta street facades of the Guaranty Building, rising to the gentle outward curve of the attic cornice, were among the most unified and most pleasing of Sullivan's work. Behind its twelve-story facades, however, this was only another example of what were now conventional tall office buildings. Its plan was U-shaped to give light and air to office windows facing away from the street. Windows in the light court recess looked out at other windows and over the alley toward backsides and flat rooftops of neighboring structures.

Such a light court, a necessary afterthought to conventional downtown office buildings, now became the central focus of Wright's five-story Larkin Building. Open galleries replaced the windows in this simple monumental space, now sheltered under a skylight high above. Perhaps Wright was influenced by old-fashioned office buildings where the galleries of such a skylit well led to partitioned office cubicles for a multitude of tenants.[46] But here, all was open space, as a single-tenant building could be. Here the staff was fully in view with easy

43. Lipman, *Johnson Wax Buildings,* p. 65.

44. *Life Magazine,* 8 May 1939, p. 15.

45. Reyner Banham, *The Architecture of the Well Tempered Environment,* 2nd ed., rev., (Chicago: University of Chicago Press, 1984), p. 86.

46. Meredith L. Clausen, 'Frank Lloyd Wright, Vertical Space, and the Chicago School's Quest for Light', in *Journal of The Society of Architectural Historians,* March 1985, pp. 66, 72-73.

Larkin Building and Building Entrance
on Seneca Street, 1904
Credit: Buffalo and Erie County Historical Society

Larkin Building Atrium Skylight
with Typical Work Messages, Fifth Floor Level
Credit: Buffalo and Erie County Historical Society

communication possible in its mail-order processing work. As in the later Johnson Wax offices, Wright designed the office furnishings, in this instance some of the earliest metal desks, chairs, and files to be manufactured.

All was not merely hierarchical overview, with clerks below and supervisors and executives upstairs. There were some staff amenities at the top of the building. On a top floor gallery near the skylight was a restaurant, with railing planters trailing ivy into the well, a Wright trademark.[47] There was also a pipe organ for music. On the roof deck above was a paved recreation area.[48]

Unlike downtown office towers maximizing real estate coverage within property lines, the Larkin Building was free-standing on its site. Its principal windows were on the long side walls. This was one of the earliest office buildings to have its windows sealed shut. This kept out railroad soot, and treated air was distributed through the building in duct shafts. The air was taken in at rooftop level where the airborne particles from railroad pollution would not linger so long.[49]

The mass of the Larkin Building was fragmented into the brick box shapes and layered planes so characteristic of Wright's early work. The entrance to the building was through glass doors of the type that was just coming into vogue when the building was demolished in 1950. Windowless brick stair towers at the four corners gave the building a robust appearance that could coexist with its huge warehouse neighbors across Seneca Street. In its customary way, in Buffalo as later in Racine, a Wright building would take its outer form both from its internal arrangements and from its surrounding environment.

Unlike his earlier Chicago colleagues, Wright would make his mark not with large commercial buildings like these, but with houses. The Larkin building arrived alongside the first of Wright's Prairie houses just after the turn of the century. Like Venus from the sea, the Prairie house seemed to come full-blown into being in the kind of complete, consistent ordering that usually takes generations of undistracted evolution in a vernacular logic.

Most people today see the Prairie house in just those forms that pleased Tom Monaghan—horizontal lines including hipped roofs over broad eaves and ribbon windows. The typical house was of balloon framing, that light wood nailable framing which Chicago gave to America seventy years before. It had a stucco weathering surface outside and plaster inside. When money allowed, Wright

would build in solid brick instead. In any case, there would be a massive masonry chimney at the center, visually anchoring the house.

Free flow of space was the chief distinction of the Prairie house from its Edwardian suburban neighbors. In the Prairie house space spread horizontally away from the central hearth, often in fingers extending at right angles to one another. Generous expanses of casement windows and glazed doors pointed this vision of space farther to walled terraces and the outdoors. Here, most often, the Prairie house design collided with the reality of a suburban lot. The Prairie house hugged the ground, without basement or useable attic. Its Edwardian neighbors stood tall on raised basements just beyond a five-foot side yard, and were topped with steep roofs cluttered with gables, dormers, and chimneys. This ultimate incongruity certainly drove Wright to insist on a spacious exurban setting for his houses once the automobile made this practical. Wright came to dislike the suburbs, just as the Larkin and Johnson Wax experiences substantiated his disdain for city living.

At least sixty Prairie houses of all sizes can be counted for the first decade of the century in Storrer's listing of Wright's work actually built.[50] Among the best of the more typical designs would be the house built in River Forest in 1908 for Isabel Roberts, Wright's office secretary. Its design answered to the qualities recited above. Its two-story living room was especially pleasing, ending in a large bay window with leaded diamond-shaped panes. The visitor today finds the house different from its appearance in old photographs. A later owner asked Wright's help in restoring the house. Impatient with freezing the life of a building as 'history', Wright persuaded his client to update the house instead. Brick veneer replaced the stucco outside, and new woodwork was installed inside.[51]

Wright designed several large Prairie houses, including the unbuilt McCormick scheme. A large, rambling brick house was built in Buffalo for Darwin Martin, President of the Larkin Company. The best known Prairie house is one of the most creative designs, the house built for Frederick Robie in 1909. While the Isabel Roberts house feels smaller than one expects from photographic impressions, the Robie house is larger. Layering of brick terrace and balcony walls seems to present a long, low house on a hillside, for a full story at grade level is disguised by the terrace walls. At the ends of the house are long cantilevers of the hipped roofs reaching out far beyond the body of the house beneath them as dramatic accents of Prairie house space.

47. Grant Carpenter Manson, *Frank Lloyd Wright to 1910: The First Golden Age* (New York: Van Nostrand Reinhold Company, 1958), p. 153.

48. Robert C. Twombley, *Frank Lloyd Wright: His Life and His Architecture* (New York: John Wiley & Sons, 1979), p. 99.

49. Banham, *Well Tempered Environment*, p. 91.

50. William Allin Storrer, *The Architecture of Frank Lloyd Wright: A Complete Catalog*, 2nd ed., rev. (Cambridge, MA: The MIT Press, 1982).

51. Thomas A. Heinz, *Frank Lloyd Wright* (New York: St. Martin's Press, 1982), p. 7.

Isabel Roberts House in Stucco, 1908, River Forest, Illinois
Credit: David R. Phillips Photographic Collection

Isabel Roberts House in Brick Veneer, 1955, River Forest, Illinois
Credit: Hedrich-Blessing

Frederick Robie House, 1909, Chicago, Illinois
Credit: Richard Nickel, Courtesy of the Richard Nickel Committee

Frank Lloyd Wright
Credit: Balthazar Korab

The Prairie house was a fundamental challenge to the Renaissance heritage in its various permutations which governed most buildings of any pretentions down to the present century. Much Edwardian eclecticism offered interchangeable sets of bas-relief facades to be grafted onto the body of the building. The array of chambers inside was manipulated to satisfy the facade design chosen. As we have seen in Platt's country houses, the chambers, themselves, could be similarly treated in a selection of period dress. The same house might contain an 'English' library with a ceiling of oaken beams, the mistress' 'French' bedroom, and the like.

Changes in thinking had been occurring as succeeding generations of architects nibbled at the Renaissance heritage of architecture for at least 150 years before the Prairie house appeared. Wright as a boy received a copy of John Ruskin's *Seven Lamps of Architecture*.[52] In his writings, Ruskin proposed to replace the neutral stucco skin of buildings with harmonious combinations of exposed materials of good quality, each having its own expressive character-

istics to bring out. As an apprentice architect, Wright studied the *Dictionnaire Raisonné* of Eugene-Emanuel Viollet-le-Duc.[53] His writings drew conclusions about rational structure from the Gothic cathedrals and recommended introducing the new materials such as iron into the vocabulary of formal building. This is only an oversimplified capsule commentary, of course, and it would be ludicrous to expect any brief account to summarize influences on Wright.

Wright came out of a farm community and small town boyhood in Wisconsin and elsewhere to apprentice himself to a Chicago architect. By the early nineties Wright was Chief Draftsman in the office of Adler and Sullivan. People look to Louis Sullivan as Wright's mentor and chief influence. Perhaps Sullivan's most useful counsel was to seek out the outer form of a building in its inner nature. But, except for elevators and extra stories, office space had not changed very fundamentally in half a century, and Sullivan had little more opportunity than to compose their facades. He could not guide Wright very far by example in Wright's quest to transform the house.

52. Manson, *First Golden Age*, p. 11.

53. Manson, *First Golden Age*, p. 21.

54. Aristotle, 'Poetics', Chapter 8, lines 33-35, tr. by Ingram Bywater, in Richard McKeon, ed., *Introduction to Aristotle* (New York: Random House, 1947), p. 635.

In architecture, as in art or literature, the creator customarily gives unity to his work with some dominant theme. Aristotle felt the same impulse, explaining, 'For that which makes no perceptible difference by its presence or absence is no real part of the whole.'[54] In the interests of such unity, the architect usually plays down the presence of other themes or requirements which must be satisfied but which would become distractions. In his Crown Hall Architectural School building at Illinois Institute of Technology, Mies van der Rohe exercises a pair of major themes separately. The bold rooftop girders and their supports express structure, the support of the roof deck, without intruding into the interior space with deep beams. The interior, in turn, is free to express a universal space bounded by six plane surfaces.

In this striving for thematic unity, the apparent simplicity of Wright's Prairie houses and other work is misleading. At its best, a Wright building may be judged fruitfully on any of a number of possible themes: Those of space, of structure, of construction and materials, of visual ordering, of manner of use, of siting, of comfort and environmental adaptation, and even of symbolism. The whole does not suffer for the complexity of its conception.

55. Vincent Scully, Jr., *Frank Lloyd Wright* (New York: George Braziller, Inc., 1960), pp. 13-14.

56. Frank Lloyd Wright, *The Natural House* (New York: Horizon Press, Inc., 1954), p. 46.

57. Frank Lloyd Wright, *The Living City* (New York: Bramhall House, 1958), p. 142.

'Organic' is the word Wright used to describe such a complete, integrated philosophy of design. This began with inducing a harmony of the whole with its parts. In terms of a building, the design process worked outward from the space it contained. Wright argued that the resulting appearance was almost inevitable as taken from a given set of conditions. The term 'organic' appeared with the description he published of his Prairie houses accompanying his *Wasmuth Portfolio* of drawings in 1910. In later years he used the term as a sort of code to explain different aspects of his work, so that a precise definition became elusive. Nonetheless, throughout Wright's career, while the context grew in scope, the inferences of 'organic' remained consistent.

In a biography of Wright, Vincent Scully best explained the sense of 'organic' design when he wrote:

'When a building built by men to serve a specifically human purpose not only celebrated that purpose in its visible forms but became an integrated structure as well, it then took on the character of an organism which existed according to its own complete and balanced laws. In this way it dignified by its wholeness and integrity the purely human intellect and hand which had created it. This is what Wright meant by "organic." Few architects have attempted so much and have been willing to ignore so little in order to achieve it.'[55]

Organic design takes its example from the harmony of plant life. Louis Sullivan was also inspired by plants in the vegetative forms of his wonderful ornament. Wright warned against a literal approach, however, one preoccupied with surface appearance. He explained that organic design does not mean imitating the outward form of the plant.[56] Finally, Wright responded to Sullivan's well known dictum, to sum up that 'we must realize form and function as one.'[57]

Crown Hall, Illinois Institute of Technology, 1952-1956, Chicago, Illinois
Credit: Balthazar Korab

Wright produced the Prairie house for a particular time and place. Organic design did not imply that Prairie house forms were universal, even in the Midwest of their origin. Wright's career lasted long enough to demonstrate this. In the mid-thirties, when other men of his age would have retired from business or professions, Wright devised what he called the 'Usonian house'. By the end of his life, Usonian houses well outnumbered the Prairie houses.

Like its predecessor, the Usonian house had horizontal lines and ribbon expanses of casement windows and doors. The Usonian house generally spread out in a single story, however. Typically, a flat roof covered it, although hipped and shed roofs appeared in some postwar examples. At one corner would be a carport. Prewar Usonian houses almost universally had masonry piers and chimneys and cypress board siding with horizontal battens, covering walls inside and out. Most Usonian houses had one large living space to maximize the sense of spaciousness; a dining area at one end replaced the formal dining room of the Prairie house. Much furniture was built in, and heat radiated from hidden sources in the concrete floor slab.[58]

A regular grid governed the design of each Usonian house. In all his buildings Wright insisted upon some geometrical ordering of design. In the Usonian plan the grid was usually in double squares, but often hexagons or diamond shapes were used instead. Some postwar houses were based on portions of circles.

One example of a diamond grid was in a house called 'Snowflake'. It was built in 1941 for the family of Carl Wall in Plymouth, Michigan, just up Highway M-14 from the future Domino's Farms. With a diamond grid, space flowed more smoothly and turned less abruptly than in the typical L-shaped Usonian house. As a Marine on leave, Tom Monaghan visited Snowflake while on a date with a girl whose family—he discovered avidly—lived in a new Wright house next door to the Wall family.[59] Almost thirty years later Monaghan bought Snowflake. The company uses it as a guest residence for visiting Domino's Pizza franchisees.[60]

Parenthetically one may interject the obvious conclusion that Tom Monaghan would have been the ideal client for Frank Lloyd Wright at Domino's Farms, had the architect lived long enough. Here at last was the opportunity to put an office building in the countryside where Wright thought it belonged. But Monaghan was interested in reviving the seventy-five-year-old design of the McCormick house

and in using Prairie house forms in general. For Wright an appropriate idea could remain alive for a relatively long time. A quarter of a century might pass between the germinating idea for a building and the opportunity to build it in a mature form. But Wright almost surely considered that the Prairie house had had its day. He designed what he called the 'last of the Prairie houses' in 1937 for Herbert Johnson, his client for the offices in Racine, just as the Usonian house took shape.[61] One suspects that Wright would have greeted Tom Monaghan warmly, but would have charmed his new client into wanting an updated form of building. In death, Wright had no such control over the perpetuation of the Prairie house.

The looks of a Usonian house were also an end product. The conditions that favored the Prairie house no longer really existed in the thirties. This was true even though the Usonian house multiplied especially throughout the same Midwestern states where its predecessor thrived. As for the Prairie house and the 'restoration' of the house of Isabel Roberts, we have seen that Wright believed that a building might evolve during its lifetime.

Organic architecture concerns a process and not a set of immutable forms and materials. The Usonian house was never so static in appearance during the last quarter century of Wright's life as the Prairie house was in its own era. Organic design was adapted to current conditions. For example, during the Depression, savings in labor costs came from prefabricating core panels which the cypress siding stabilized in place. In his study of Usonian houses, John Sergeant has shown that postwar inflation neutralized this advantage; solid masonry accordingly replaced this panel system frequently in exterior walls.[62] When government postwar priorities made other materials scarce, concrete block was used, often in decorative shapes. Conditions change, and one following organic design principles today might react to the poor quality of available wood or the high energy costs of making brick without gravitating to flimsy construction by default.

Like Wright's other buildings, the Usonian houses were also adapted to different regions and conditions of climate. At any one time, new Usonian houses were not homogeneous in form across the country in the way that air conditioning has allowed the ubiquitous development house to become today.

The Usonian house was built most often for families of modest means. Wright was trying to reduce building costs to make his houses available to as many families as possible. He was not dealing

58. John Sergeant, *Frank Lloyd Wright's Usonian Houses: Designs for Moderate Cost One-Family Homes* (New York: Watson-Guptill Publications, 1976), pp. 19, 21.

59. Monaghan, 'Wright Hand' address, n. pag.

60. Monaghan and Anderson, *Pizza Tiger,* p. 273.

61. Lipman, *Johnson Wax Buildings,* p. 175.

62. Sergeant, *Usonian Houses,* pp. 81, 86.

Carl Wall House, Exterior, 1941, Plymouth, Michigan
    Credit: The National Center for the Study of Frank Lloyd Wright at Domino's Farms

Carl Wall House, Plan, Plymouth, Michigan
    Credit: © 1986 Frank Lloyd Wright Archives

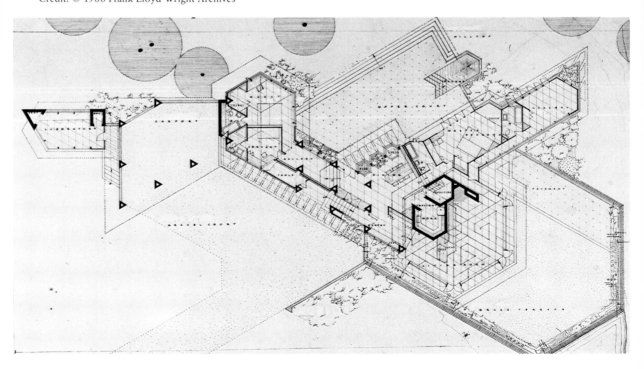

63. Kenneth Frampton,
Modern Architecture:
A Critical History, 2nd ed., rev.
(London: Thames and Hudson,
1985), p. 306.

in esoteric images for a small, appreciative avant-garde. Kenneth Frampton has observed that the sheer quantity of Usonian houses built bears that out.[63] One suspects that his clients were drawn to the same practical side of design as Prairie house owners had been—the ingenious mechanical systems, the adaptation to prevailing climate and the problem solving in general. Especially in the thirties, the quantity of Usonian houses would have been larger still, but conservative lending institutions and agencies turned down many houses. Some families could afford their Usonian house only by building it with their own efforts, even to sharing with neighbors the molds for concrete blocks which they cast themselves. The process had to be simple enough to encourage this.

The Usonian house related to the land in a way that the Prairie house rarely could do. The Prairie house usually had the same flat, trimmed lawns as its neighbors. The Usonian house on a suburban lot was positioned to maximize and shield its garden. Wright usually succeeded in having his client buy at least an acre of land as far as possible from the city and its suburbs. Wright foresaw the engulfing future of urban sprawl. The glory of the Usonian house was its adapting to topography that would have to be flattened and denuded of trees to build a conventional house. The Usonian house encouraged the natural landscape to come up to the house, even to pass beneath it.

An Agenda For Exurbia From Broadacre City

4

Organic design in Mr. Wright's hands had a a life of its own. It promised a way of living extending beyond the entities of a single Usonian house or a single place of work. These were simply part of a greater panorama he called 'Broadacre City'.

Wright was always a populist in the mold of Emerson and Thoreau. Similar inclinations in Louis Sullivan as a mentor amplified this spirit in Wright. His domestic troubles after the Prairie house years probably toughened his self-assurance. The Roaring Twenties were deaf to so old-fashioned a philosophy, as Norris Kelly Smith has observed,[64] and for

various reasons construction starts of Wright's projects dwindled while the boom surged for other architects. The Great Depression brought out soul searching in everyone for the causes of what went wrong. It was then that Wright's thinking crystallized in this concept of Broadacre City. In the confident, prosperous postwar era when at least a Levittown home seemed to await everybody in the suburbs, the nation put aside its social concerns. Wright continued to refine his Broadacre City proposal in a series of books, writings, and exhibits, culminating in *The Living City,* published a year before his death.

64. Norris Kelly Smith,
Frank Lloyd Wright: A Study
in Architectural Content
(Englewood Cliffs, NJ: Prentice-
Hall, Inc., 1966), p. 109.

The city as it existed was at the core of Wright's malaise, whether in the Prairie house years, the helpless thirties or the prosperous fifties. Wright disliked the overcrowding and traffic congestion that came from the centralizing impulse which he considered a survival from an obsolete era. The city thrived on speculation that played upon land values which this centralization drove upward. Buildings seemed to exist for the sake of real estate transactions and their use was secondary. Most troubling to Wright was the image of a citizen as a tenant, always vulnerable to forces beyond his control and living in perpetual anxiety.

In the city the benefits of machine production went to tycoons whom nobody idealized anymore in the depression years. Nor did Wright consider government very promising as a palliative. Its bureaucratic 'mobocracy' threatened the democratic instinct, what Wright saw as the 'Sovereignty of the Individual.'[65]

The goal of Broadacre City was to make every person become what it was possible for him or her to be as an individual. The automobile offered people freedom in mobility. Wright thought they would be renewed in moving to the countryside in possession of at least one acre of land to live on. So Broadacre City was not a recognizeable city. The nation would become a sort of continuous state of urbanity integrated with the countryside. This new balance would respect the natural terrain, and the indigenous character of a region would assert itself.

In Broadacre City, good roads would keep work, school, markets and cultural opportunities within easy reach. Supplementing family income, the citizen could grow food on the family property, and the family might ride out another depression. For those lacking agrarian instincts, there would still be apartments, but they would benefit from the rural setting. Tall buildings once born of the speculative urge downtown would now exist in a park as the object of beauty and pride they were meant to be.[66]

65. Wright, *Living City*, pp. 79, 110-11.

66. Wright, *Living City*, pp. 81, 110, 121-22.

Broadacre City, 1935
Credit: © 1984 Frank Lloyd Wright Archives

Midway Barns, Taliesin, 1938, Spring Green, Wisconsin
Credit: Pedro E. Guerrero

The role of the small farm was crucial to this Broadacre City. Wright foresaw futility in its trying to compete with large-scale agriculture of the West. The small farm should turn to 'intensive farming, as varied as possible' in raising specialties favored by the consumers living in their vicinity. The farm should be convenient to markets where the farmer could sell his products directly, without a middle-man.[67] Of any building type other than houses in his Broadacre City repertory, Wright was most specific about what a farm building should be. The Midway Barns he built on his property at Taliesin in Wisconsin were the best example among his built work. There was an unbuilt farm building project of 1932 for Walter Davidson that, for want of other evidence, Kenneth Frampton considers the most important build-ing type Wright defined for Broadacre City.[68]

Cultural opportunities were another prime concern of Wright's Broadacre City proposals. Existing culture in cities was, to him, imposed and artificial. True culture would have to be associated with daily activities. In a similar way, education should be partici-patory; one should learn by doing.[69]

A microcosm of Wright's Broadacre City existed on his own land, Taliesin, near Spring Green, Wisconsin. The great rambling house at Taliesin had grown in pulsations after 1911 despite the setbacks of three fires. It, too, was a mansion, but dedicated not to a rich man but to a wholesome way of life.

In 1932 Wright formed the Taliesin Fellowship. This communal entity at Taliesin trained architects while exploring related arts and crafts and inculcating all in a philosophy of life. Apprentices of the Fellowship not only helped to design buildings under Mr. Wright's direction. They built buildings as extensions of work at Taliesin and at his Arizona camp of Taliesin West. The senior apprentices made field visits to administer construction of Wright build-ings elsewhere. At the least, the apprentices were an extension of Wright's practice, just as earlier archi-tects had learned their profession under a senior architect.

67. Wright, *Living City,* pp. 158-60.

68. Frampton, *Modern Architecture,* p. 191.

69. Wright, *Living City,* p. 184.

70. Sergeant, *Usonian Houses,* pp. 99-100, 102.

At Taliesin, a complete way of life was the difference. The apprentices also raised and prepared their own food. The talents they brought to Spring Green enriched communal musical and cultural gatherings at Taliesin.[70] The drafting room where the apprentices worked had the outdoors in full view. (This would contradict any notion that the inward focus of the Larkin and Johnson Wax projects should be the norm for workplaces.) The Fellowship was partly Wright's response to the Bauhaus, which was expunged so soon afterward in Hitler's Germany. In this country its closest parallel may have been Eliel Saarinen's Art Academy at Cranbrook, but the way of life at Cranbrook was nonetheless more institutional in spite of its intentions.

When Wright died in 1959, the Broadacre City concerns seem to have gone with him as a utopian vision. But the conditions he foresaw are gathering. At the time he began to formulate his proposal in the early thirties, census data considered the United States population about equally divided between urban and rural residents. In contrast the 1870 Census taken just after Wright was born designated only a quarter of the population as urban and the rest rural.[71] The ratio is now about reversed in the 1980 Census.[72]

71. *Historical Statistics of the United States, Colonial Times to 1970* (Washington, DC: U.S. Department of Commerce/ Bureau of the Census, 1975), I, pp. 11-12.

What the Census calls 'urban' means 'suburban' to most people today. In some areas of megalopolis the suburban sprawl extends continuously past several center cities that have lost their meaning as centers; the suburbs largely ignore them. The urban tendency toward concentration and resulting pressure on land values that Wright railed against has also followed the population to the suburbs.

72. *Statistical Abstract of the United States 1986,* 106th ed., rev. (Washington, DC: U.S. Department of Commerce/ Bureau of the Census, 1985), p. 15.

Farms cannot survive anywhere near such metropolitan areas; land speculation and presumptive taxation drive the farmer to sell out to those who can afford to hold his land until development is appropriate. There seems no natural deterrent to the trend and few measures to counter it. Some states like Massachusetts have an agricultural preservation program wherein the state reserves farmland by paying the owner the difference between its agricultural value and its value to the developer.[73] The desire to reserve such land must become politically recognized and palatable, however, before the occasion is lost.

73. Anne Gerard-Flynn, 'Worthington, Mass., Preserving the Farmland,' in *New York Times,* 9 August 1987, Section 8, p. 1.

A generation growing up today has never been out of the suburbs very long and knows neither the countryside nor the downtown city. To these people food is no longer a symbol of its source, but is merely a wrapped package with a brand name. An age-old disdain for the countryside as a haven for hicks threatens to return to join a newfound abhor-

74. *Annual Housing Survey 1980, Part A: General Housing Characteristics, United States and Regions* (Washington, DC: U.S. Department of Commerce/ Bureau of the Census, 1982), pp. 59, 93, 127, 161.

75. William H. Whyte, *The Last Landscape* (Garden City, NY: Doubleday & Company, 1968), pp. 202-07, 218-19.

rence of the center city and its crime. A sublimely provincial outlook results.

The centrifugal flow of population to the suburbs has also fulfilled Wright's prediction that the city as he knew it would become obsolete. In his time, few people foresaw the abandonment of the center; urban unrest and riots began to accomplish that a decade after *The Living City* appeared. Abandonment of buildings in lieu of transfers among residents accelerated.

The metropolitan suburb that absorbed the urban energy ought to represent an ideal attainment of democracy. After all, the Central Western region, where Prairie and Usonian houses became most numerous, had seven out of ten homes deemed owner-occupied in the 1980 Census (that region led the rest of the country in degree of homeownership).[74] Many of these homes were relatively new suburban ones; they had many Usonian features, although these were diluted in a way Wright would have disavowed.

The suburbs do not live up to much civic pride in the old fashioned way, however. More than becoming lost in megalopolis, however, they have become homogenized across the country. Individual suburbs have an elusive identity. In the suburban fabric, the civic focus and the 'piety hill' of an older town are missing. The new centers emerging in the run-on suburbs are the commercial 'urban villages' we have referred to, the regional shopping malls and office-hotel clusters alongside the freeways. Suburban life centers on them. Local magazines reduce suburban existence to money-spending lifestyles amid trendy restaurants and boutiques; they have little to offer families lacking money to spend or the inclination to spend it their way. Metropolitan daily newspapers have always had a city desk; today they seem baffled and miserly in covering comparable suburban life except in lifestyle features almost interchangeable with those of other metropolitan dailies. With this imbalance and the rosy implication that there fortunately isn't much news in the suburbs, their strident city coverage seems merely anti-urban.

The suburbs are no longer that vision of wholesome countryside that suburbanites once came seeking. In the sixties, critics like William Whyte tried to arrest this loss of open space. The cluster development they proposed offered row houses in compact groupings so that a residue of land could be recaptured for parkland shared among these homes.[75] This rationale had to overcome resistance where owning a detached house standing in a yard was an attainable ideal. The trend to smaller families and households of 'dinks' (double income/no kids) promoted acceptance.

Once people have been persuaded to surrender front lawns and back yards for patio slabs and such communal open space, the developers now wish to minimize the open space. To be fair, they are only reacting to higher land values. The new cluster development is said to offer virtues of small town living and the informal ways of resort life. Suburban formlessness is supposedly rectified by urbanizing it in nostalgic exercises of Queen Anne neighborhoods or Victorian villages.[76] The original suburban impulse for getting closer to nature is now supposed to be met by keeping a second home 'up north'.

Postmodern architecture is often a handmaiden to this urban suburb. Classical forms of Postmodernism are often urban images wanting tightly-clustered buildings forming plazas and definite streetscapes. Postmodernism would like to offer civic symbols if only a civic client would come forward; on an intimate scale Michael Graves has created several pleasing civic groupings in California and New Jersey, for example. Commercial clients are more amenable. In the suburbs Postmodern forms are at home inside enclosed shopping malls that have usurped the civic imagery that the municipalities have vacated. The symbols are selective; there should be no monumental clocks to remind shoppers that time is passing. More commonly, Postmodernism shows up beyond suburban parking lots in the form of flat commercial facades punctured with thermal windows or oversized fanlights and crested with pediments-without-roofs.

The Postmodern spirit seems apropos in downtowns that have grown by accretion; its broad compendium of forms tailors building features to a context of interesting existing work. Its popularity could help to reverse the increasing suburban bias against encountering center cities. More often, however, it produces an empty urbanity in a suburban locale that projects no empathy for urban living and offers little context which the architects find worth exploiting.

There is some poetic justice that tracts of ranch houses are not considered a fruitful context. The ranch houses in their time blotted out their own context of farms that had to be platted to receive them. The Postmodern pioneers Robert Venturi and Denise Scott Brown have long argued for a 'learning from Levittown', empirically sensing patterns to build upon. They maintain reasonably that their body of built work shows that they are serious.[77] On the

Housing Development, 1951, Levittown, Pennsylvania
Credit: Wide World Photos

Development of Tract Housing, 1950
Los Angeles, California
Credit: © 1950 William A. Garnett

76. Carol Vogel, 'Clustered for Leisure: The Changing Home', in *The New York Times Magazine,* 28 June 1987, pp. 13-16.

77. Robert Venturi, Denise Scott Brown and Steven Izenour, *Learning from Las Vegas: The Forgotten Symbolism of Architectural Form,* 2nd ed., rev. (Cambridge, MA: The MIT Press, pp. 152-55.

Shingle House, 1980-1983, East Hampton, New York
Credit: Robert A.M. Stern Architects, Photo Credit: Langdon Clay

78. Robert A. M. Stern,
Pride of Place: Building the American Dream (Boston, MA: Houghton-Mifflin Company, 1986), pp. 151, 154.

79. Vogel,
'Clustered for Leisure', p. 16.

other hand, Robert A. M. Stern, whose television lectures have made him a popular Postmodern spokesman, simply dismisses suburbia as 'nightmarish'. He gratuitously attributes its essence in part to the 'dream' of Broadacre City,[78] and asks the question, who wants to take care of five acres today?[79] It appears that some of his clients for expensive homes do.

Venturi and Stern, among others, come closest to redeeming the suburban ideal with homes derived from the shingled New England seacoast cottages of the late nineteenth century that Vincent Scully revived thirty years ago and labeled 'the Shingle Style' in his book of that name. Significantly, Wright's earliest work was in that vein, so rich in forms and the flow of interior space. California architects following the lead of Charles Moore have produced other suburban alternatives for Postmodernism; appropriately, all of these have strong regional character.

There are usually no clients for architects in most residential suburban work except in planned developments. Faced with the monotony of suburbia, the architectural vanguard changes the program. This is not new; except for Wright, the vanguard has closed its eyes to the essence of suburbia for half a century.

Perhaps it is no fault of Postmodernism that the suburbs lack a civic and cultural focus or that the shopping malls possess the empty symbols of these by default. A narcissistic culture now glorifies the citizen in the role of enthusiastic consumer; the compulsive yuppie had to be invented. Our culture is largely in the hands of commercial media that tailor it to the most marketable citizen-consumer segment. The new citizen does not feel inclined to

80. Wright, *Living City*, p. 110.

81. John Herbers,
The New American Heartland (New York: Times Books, 1986).

use or pay for civic or communal cultural facilities; the sedating culture of cable television costs the family enough.

The neighborhood school retains most of what little civic focus survives in suburbia. The privacy its mission requires is largely incompatible with the role of social center that planners and sociologists have long advocated for it. The churches today seem to be incidental fragments in the suburban fabric; communities are loath to permit such tax-free property to lie in any prominent location. Even the new county buildings that replace the pompous nineteenth century monuments are usually workaday structures.

Wright proposed that the county should become the principal center of political leadership. Instead, the suburbs have collected the power but have remained too fragmented to want to cooperate with one another. They seem united only by their antipathy to the center city from which most of their residents came. There are a few exceptions where a dominant county government has been attained in metropolitan areas. Miami is an unfortunate example, overwhelmed by unique problems, but it may shine yet. Indianapolis is the outstanding example, but its success is little known and little emulated.

'Nevertheless, the free city we are considering is…already here all around us in the haphazard making', Wright wrote in *The Living City*.[80] A recent book by John Herbers shows that this is true today in what Herbers calls 'the new American heartland'.[81] The Interstate freeway system was just getting under construction when Wright died. Herbers points out that corridors of scattered development followed it amid existing rural villages and townships and into territory independent of incorporated areas.

Herbers writes that a people more affluent than the native population has taken over old farmhouses and moved into new subdivisions and mobile home parks scattered through farmland. The newcomers are in the image of Wright's self-reliant citizen finding security in his land: 'A factory worker with five acres of soybeans and a vegetable garden growing behind his house.'[82] Their jobs are in small factories scattered throughout the same rural territory. Herbers shows that this is a nationwide phenomenon and cites examples. Tenth in population among the states while lacking significant industrial cities, North Carolina employs a greater proportion of residents in manufacturing than does any other state.

Who would underwrite the task of fleshing out this pale ghost of Broadacre City? Wright would

82. John Herbers, 'America's Profile Shifts', in *New York Times Magazine,* p. 74.

expect his citizens to cooperate on a county-wide basis. He did not look to the captains of industry he blamed for a share in the shortcomings of the traditional city. The Great Depression still troubled him twenty years afterward when *The Living City* became his final statement on the Broadacre spectrum.

Perhaps he was looking still further back to the 1880s, the time when he first arrived in Chicago looking for a draftsman's position. On four thousand acres south of the city, beside Lake Calumet, George Pullman was then building a model town named for himself. Beside his new factory making Pullman railroad cars, an attractive village grew up from the designs of Solon S. Beman. There were mansarded brick row houses for his employees on a grid of streets beyond a great park. Intermingled in the fabric were a shopping arcade and theater, a market hall

Pullman, Illinois, c. 1880-1930
Credit: Paul Petraitis, Pullman Research Group

First Christian Church, 1939-1942
Columbus, Indiana
Credit: Balthazar Korab

and square, the Green Stone Church, the Florence Hotel, a school, and a library, commodious buildings all. The town sewage fertilized an outlying farm that grew food for the tables of Pullman. Many other ingenious features rounded out this benevolent picture seen by a nation that instinctively distrusted company towns.

The Chicago World's Fair of 1893 drew appreciative sightseers to this idyllic exhibit. The same year brought a crippling financial depression. As employer, George Pullman trimmed his workers' paychecks as a magnanimous alternative to closing down the factory. As landlord, George Pullman felt no compunction to reduce the rents of his tenants, who would lose their valuable jobs at the Pullman Works if they moved outside the village. Within a year, the squeeze helped to bring on the violent Pullman Strike, and the most enlightened of company towns stood disgraced.[83]

83. Almont Lindsey, *The Pullman Strike* (Chicago: University of Chicago Press, 1964), pp. 40-41, 43-46, 92-93.

Nobody looks to company housing today, but the cultural ingredient of exurbia is hard to fulfill. Mr. Wright's expectations to the contrary, tax dollars are not a likely source. Escaping high property taxes has motivated much of the move to the countryside. There is some problem to persuading anybody that culture is lacking or indispensible. People simply push their television antennas up higher, but this is hardly the indigenous participatory medium Wright would have considered healthy.

There remain the employers who make their fortunes in the region. Their pride in enhancing the cultural activity of their locale might prime the pump for enlisting further support from other sources. The effort might help the region to learn to take pride in itself.

84. Paul Goldberger, 'Prairie Showplace', in *The New York Times Magazine,* 4 April 1976, pp. 47, 49-50.

The Midwest has a long tradition of such munificence. Outstate cities and towns in Western Michigan offer an example. There is Kellogg money (cereals) in Battle Creek, the Upjohns (pharmaceuticals) and Gilmores (department store) further along Interstate 94 at Kalamazoo, and the Plym family (Kawneer store-fronts) more modestly in smaller Niles. Their liberality seeds programs that are fulfilled with broader sources of contributions.

In such a way over the course of a century a cultural center of buildings gathered by accretion in Kalamazoo in a manner too expensive to achieve all at once. The Bronson Park there is ringed with such civic foundations along with churches and governmental buildings. The Ladies Library Association building of 1878 stands just around the corner, behind an Art Deco civic theater designed by the once fashion-

able New York architect Aymar Embury II (its postwar auxiliary facility by Norman Carver stands a block away). Across Park Street from these is a sleek Miesian art center. Skidmore, Owings and Merrill was given its commission along with the one for the magnificent exurban corporate headquarters building that the Upjohn Company built south of town in 1961.

The town of Columbus, Indiana holds a special place of honor in such corporate philanthropy. In 1940 Eliel and Eero Saarinen were asked to design the present First Christian Church, one of the earliest important modern churches in the country. In later years Eero Saarinen designed the spire-like North Christian Church there, together with a bank and a residence for J. Irwin Miller. Miller was a Yale classmate of his who became President of the Cummins Engine Company in town. Miller was the first layman President of the National Council of Churches.

In 1954 the Cummins Foundation of Miller's company broadened the spectrum of modern architecture in town by offering to pay architects' fees for schools and public buildings. The School Board and public agencies would be expected to hire architects of national reputation and to cultivate promising younger architects. The town profited handsomely from the program. The architects engaged made special efforts in what has become a showcase of modern architecture.

Outside of the Foundation funding, church building committees, merchants and others followed this lead with their own resources. Visitors come from all over to study this wealth of modern architecture so conveniently gathered in Columbus.[84] No building by Wright is there, but in his lifetime the program had barely commenced with a single elementary school. The major works to be seen date from succeeding decades. The Cummins Company also benefits in the resulting quality of life in town, for it can attract new staff people to what otherwise would have been a commonplace small town isolated almost halfway between Indianapolis and Louisville.

It has been many years since Tom Monaghan read *The Living City*. Other than for the appropriate place of an office tower in a rural setting, he has not stressed the Broadacre City aspect in his ideas for Domino's Farms. There is nonetheless an uncanny resemblance, if a haphazard one, to the cultural and agricultural goals of the Broadacre City concept and the extended program of demonstration farms and cultural activities he is promoting at Domino's Farms that go beyond the function of a dignified corporate home office facility.

Introducing The Architect:
Gunnar Birkerts

5

Gunnar Birkerts was chosen to design the sixth of the schools the Cummins Foundation subsidized in its program for Columbus, Indiana. Other architects already selected were truly national, with offices located between Boston and San Francisco. They were already among the 'first rank American architects' of the Cummins Foundation mandate: Harry Weese, John Carl Warnecke, The Architects Collaborative and Edward Larrabee Barnes.[85]

Birkerts, on the other hand, was probably one of the 'promising younger architects' that the Foundation wished to encourage. He had spent five years with the Saarinen organization, and had been in practice with a partner or independently for six years. The Lincoln Elementary School which he designed for Columbus was the first of the Foundation program to win national awards of the American Institute of Architects on its own right.[86] The building was also a turning point in Birkerts' own development, establishing some themes that continue in his work today. In recent years, now as one of the truly 'first rank American architects', he has returned to Columbus to design the St. Peter's Lutheran Church being built across from the Lincoln School.

Gunnar Birkerts came to this country from his native Latvia by way of Germany in 1949. His goal was to work for Eliel Saarinen. As a student in the Technische Hochschule in Stuttgart, he had seen the Hugh Ferriss drawings that announced Eliel Saarinen's

early design for the General Motors Technical Center. Saarinen was from Finland, which shared a Northern Baltic architectural heritage with Birkerts' Latvia. There being no openings at the Saarinen office at the moment, Birkerts went on to the Chicago firm of Perkins and Will for experience in a large architectural office.[87]

Gunnar Birkerts never met Eliel Saarinen, who died in 1950. The next year, Birkerts was invited to work for Eero Saarinen to assist in developing the design of buildings for the General Motors Technical Center project. The Saarinen office was in Bloomfield Hills, two miles from the Cranbrook campus. With Eliel Saarinen's passing, there was now only the most casual connection between the office and the Art Academy. Instead, the working atmosphere of Eero Saarinen's office was as intellectually stimulating as any university design studio could hope to be.[88]

Saarinen alumni became familiar names among the leaders of American architecture in succeeding decades. Kevin Roche and John Dinkeloo directly succeeded to the practice, of course. Others besides Birkerts included Charles Bassett, Anthony Lumsden, Cesar Pelli, Warren Platner and Robert Venturi.[89] Critics gathered the later work of several of these under the 'Minimalist' label of extreme simplicity in a manner often showing special care taken with the continuously glazed skin following the geometries of the building.

85. Columbus, Indiana: A Look at Architecture (Columbus, IN: Columbus Area Chamber of Commerce, Inc., 1974), p. 95, 97, 99.

86. Columbus, Indiana, p. 100.

87. Gunnar Birkerts, 'Autobiographical Notes', in GA Architect 2: Gunnar Birkerts and Associates, ed. Yukio Futagawa and William Marlin (Tokyo: A.D.A. EDITA Co., Ltd., 1982), pp. 214-15.

88. Birkerts, in GA Architect 2, p. 216.

89. Birkerts, in GA Architect 2, pp. 217-18.

90. A. Saarinen,
Eero Saarinen on his Work,
p. 6.

91. Eliel Saarinen, 'My Point
of View of our Contemporary
Architecture', 1931 address
to American Institute
of Architects, in *The Saarinen
Door: Eliel Saarinen, Architect
and Designer at Cranbrook*
(Bloomfield Hills, MI:
Cranbrook Academy of Art,
1963), p. 59.

92. Author's interview with
Gunnar Birkerts, 26 May 1987.

That anything resembling a 'school' might come out of Saarinen's people is surprising, considering the extreme diversity of Saarinen's work in the productive fifties. There is hardly any family resemblance among his buildings identifying a common source. Examples include the simple spherical 'triangle' shell of the Kresge Auditorium at Massachusetts Institute of Technology; the romantically irregular footprint of stone walls in his Yale dormitories; the monumental regularity of the American Embassy in Portland stone frames in London; and the expressionistic catenary roof of the Dulles Airport terminal outside of Washington, D.C. These in turn differ markedly from the buildings we have already discussed, the John Deere and CBS office buildings and the General Motors Technical Center.

Such variety contradicted the advice of the Modernist historian Sigfried Giedion to his Harvard classes during these years: The student could choose only between the International Style path and that of Wright, with no crossing over between the two. Saarinen was disturbed by the increasing rigidity he saw congealing architectural design in keeping with such advice. His own variety was not a goal in itself, but a result of fundamental design method. 'I feel, therefore, a certain responsibility to examine problems with the specific enthusiasm of bringing out of the particular problem the particular solution', he wrote.[90]

The great influence of Louis Kahn as teacher and mentor to younger architects has tended to overshadow the important role that Eero Saarinen played in opening American architecture to other alternatives. For Gunnar Birkerts, this exploratory design method is probably Saarinen's most positive bequest.

There is a legacy transmitted in some way from Eliel Saarinen as well in what Gunnar Birkerts calls his own 'non-dogmatic approach' to architecture. Writing as an educator, the elder Saarinen emphasized, '*Do not kill the intuition with theories. Art based on theories is a dead art.*'[91] As Eliel Saarinen was in his time, Birkerts is uncomfortable about the current intellectual approach to architecture and the *a priori* role given to theory in the design process. Theory comes into the design process 'always in retrospect', Birkerts says.[92]

Dulles Airport, 1958-1962, Washington, DC
Credit: Balthazar Korab

Design commences with a gathering and synthesizing of the contributing information. At this stage there should be no preconceptions about the ultimate form of the building. Theory is an intrusion at this state. Its role, rather, is to clarify the nature of form that is the end product. In this, one may recognize an affinity with what Wright expects of organic architecture as part of a process.

Where Eliel Saarinen's possible influence draws Birkerts away from Wright, perhaps, is in recognizing the essential role of intuition for an experienced designer. 'Style can *not* be artifically made', wrote Saarinen. 'It comes or it does not come. But if it does come, it comes only through intuition.'[93] Birkerts echoes this: 'Intuition is based on genuine knowledge. …The creative process is subconscious, on a higher level. You need time and certain stimulation, exposure to experience, music, images. … You are able to make intuitive leaps, and then go back and fill the gaps.'[94]

Birkerts stresses the difference between the synthesizing process and the intuitive role. The synthesizing process is 'to consciously search for and analyze the intrinsic structure of any design problem'; the intuitive role is 'to subconsciously sense the intrinsic structure of the problem. One approach deals more or less with external factors, the other with internal feelings, but both are part of the struggle to respond to human needs as they appear out of the nature of the problem.'[95]

Gunnar Birkerts left the Saarinen office in 1956. There was a short term in the office of Minoru Yamasaki in the nearby suburb of Birmingham, Michigan. Yamasaki was on the threshold of producing the elegant McGregor Conference Center at Wayne State University in Detroit, his masterpiece in the traditional sense of becoming a master. Yamasaki's intuitive ease in making design decisions impressed Birkerts.[96] This seemed in contrast with the thorough and methodical analysis of alternatives that led to such decisions in Eero Saarinen's office. The two approaches were not necessarily antithetical, however, and Birkerts came to draw from both in his own approach to design.

Birkerts left Yamasaki's office with Frank Straub in 1959 to form a partnership practice. The time of apprenticeship was over, and Birkerts could now speak for himself as an architect. Two years later he joined the faculty of the University of Michigan. The partnership was dissolved in 1962, and the office of Gunnar Birkerts and Associates was opened in Birmingham.[97]

Even more significant for Birkerts than these personal milestones was a trip to Finland in 1962. There he encountered the work of the architect Alvar Aalto at first hand. The experience of one building was especially moving. 'Vuoksenniska Church for me is the greatest manifestation of Aalto's form language', Birkerts wrote later. 'There, Cartesian geometry merges with the natural free forms, generated by the interior functional or aesthetic requirements.'[98] Birkerts stresses that 'Aalto is much more non-dogmatic than Wright',[99] and one remembers that Wright probably would not have tolerated a design departing from continuity of a geometrical ordering.

93. Eliel Saarinen, in *Saarinen Door,* p. 59.

94. Author's interview with Gunnar Birkerts, 26 May 1987.

95. Gunnar Birkerts, 'On Methodology', in *Gunnar Birkerts: Buildings, Projects and Thoughts, 1960-1985* (Ann Arbor, MI: College of Architecture and Urban Planning, University of Michigan, 1985), p. 24.

96. Birkerts, in *GA Architect 2,* pp. 219-20.

97. Birkerts, in *GA Architect 2,* p. 220.

98. Birkerts, 'On Aalto', essay from *Architecture + Urbanism,* May 1983, in *Gunnar Birkerts: Buildings, Projects and Thoughts,* p. 26.

99. Author's interview with Gunnar Birkerts, 26 May 1987.

Vuoksenniska Church, 1956-1958, Imatra, Finland
Credit: Courtesy of Gunnar Birkerts

Lincoln Elementary School, Exterior, 1965, Columbus, Indiana
Credit: Orlando R. Cabanban

100. Birkerts, 'On Aalto',
in *Gunnar Birkerts: Buildings,
Projects and Thoughts,* p. 28.

101. Birkerts, 'On Aalto',
text from *Progressive Architecture,* April 1977, in
*Gunnar Birkerts: Buildings,
Projects and Thoughts,* p. 26.

Birkerts sums up Aalto's posthumous influence, 'His architecture provides the more likeable definition of the Modern Movement; more likeable, perhaps, than Bauhaus or International Style. The many-faceted Modern Movement is carrying on at present with its latent thrust continuing to draw from the strong humanistic force of Alvar Aalto'.[100] Of Aalto's influence on his design, Birkerts cautions, 'I am not a disciple of his'.[101] One senses, however, that Birkerts would like to be judged as part of the same humanistic tempering of the Modern Movement someday.

Twenty years after the event, there is not much need to second-guess the Cummins Foundation and the School Board in Columbus in foretelling Birkerts' qualifications for their project. The early work of his practice sometimes appears to be derivative, but one expects this of a young architect's manner. There is a crisp design for a savings bank in Royal Oak that uses window openings (and accordingly the backlighting of artificial illumination at night) in positions where one expects to find the solidity of a post-and-lintel structure. This is perhaps a refinement of similar lighting effects found in the house Eero Saarinen designed for J. Irwin Miller in Columbus. In the year of the Lincoln School commission, Birkerts designed a Grand Rapids home that seems to be an enrichment of the design for the Goldenberg House of Louis Kahn. Perhaps the prospective clients saw studies in gestation for a college campus in Mississippi, however. The buildings were still in the future, but the design was promising and would one day influence Tom Monaghan in choosing an architect.

The Lincoln School in Columbus was a mature statement. In plan it is a chamfered square of brick walls set within a circle of a concrete retaining wall bermed on its outer side, two complete, basic geometrical shapes. The brick walls of the building proper seem to recognize its relationship to the brick mass of the Saarinens' First Christian Church a block away. House-scaled buildings surround the school, however (except for the later St. Peter's Church, of course). In deference to these, the school's apparent bulk is reduced by dropping it half a story into the depressed circular precinct, leaving segments where the smaller children play, close to the building. The foliage of trees standing on the berm around the circle contributes to this concealment, seeming to recognize that this building exists for small children, after all. One senses that the breadth of the entrance steps is less a reversion to monumental scale than an anticipation of a horde of children waiting for doors to open in the morning or pouring out after the day's last bell rings.

On the inside of the Lincoln School is a multi-purpose room surrounded by a two-story galleried corridor illuminated by clerestory windows. Even before he saw the similar effects in Aalto's work in Finland, Birkerts was already preoccupied with the effects of diffusing daylight within a building through a system of baffles, both for visual effect and for softening the distressing glare of direct sunlight. In the Lincoln School the multipurpose room receives its daylight from the corridor clerestory by means of borrowed light windows. Habitual practice for gymnasiums and multipurpose rooms then was to block up windows to keep disconcerting sunbeams from disrupting children's games; here, the room can still benefit from daylight. It is a small point, but typically Birkerts' approach is more humanistic than complete reliance on fluorescent lighting by design rote would be.

There are other notable projects of the decade following the Lincoln School commission. These had a role of guiding Tom Monaghan's attention to Birkerts, and we may defer considering them until later, in that context. It would be useful to examine two other more recent projects of Birkerts, however. These show something of his methodology at work, anticipating the direction his design work is taking independently of Tom Monaghan's preferences for Domino's Farms.

The first of these is the Glass Museum addition for the Corning Glass Company in the upstate town of Corning, New York. Birkerts did earlier municipal work for the town, including two unexecuted design proposals for a public library in 1969, and a fire station completed near the museum site in 1974.

The museum lies within view of the Chemung River, and the addition backs up to a confusing array of existing museum and manufacturing buildings that the approaching visitors previously found too ambiguous to guide them. The new museum addition accordingly establishes the public identity of the Corning buildings. The museum proper is raised off the ground one story to protect fixed museum exhibits from possible river flooding, and museum offices occupy the recessed ground floor. (One remembers that Schinkel reached the same solution for the same reason by comparable design methodology in his pioneering Altes Museum in Berlin a century and-a-half before.)

Corning Glass Museum, 1976, Corning, New York
Credit: Balthazar Korab

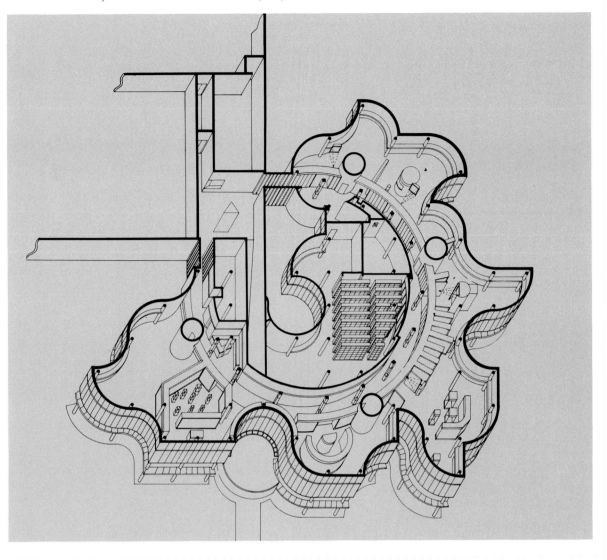

On the museum level an exhibit promenade circles around the museum library placed at the core of the building. Reaching outward from this promenade is space for specialized exhibits varying in extent according to need. The result is an irregular perimeter wall which in plan is really a set of flat walls and faceted quarter-circle arcs contained in a square grid. Birkerts arrived at this parti when he was in residence at the American Academy in Rome in 1976. He believes that the curvilinear Baroque architecture of Rome may have subconsciously influenced his design.[102]

The glass of the museum walls is a special product developed for the building, coating the inner surface with a film of stainless steel. As the facade planes change direction in their faceted arc, the appearance varies between 'glass' and 'metal' according to the incident angle of viewing it.[103] Exploiting the special properties of modern materials is another parallel between the work of Birkerts and of Eero Saarinen—

and of Wright, for that matter. (One remembers the role the Corning Company played in working with Wright on the glass technology of the Racine offices for Johnson Wax.)

The seemingly amorphous shape of the Glass Museum offers a metaphor of glass, both in its molten state of processing it and as frozen in its crystalline state. Appropriately to his design approach, Birkerts explains that this symbolism occurred to him after the form of the building was determined, rather than as a preconception.[104]

At the windows under the main body of the building, a sloping spandrel reflects daylight directly into the museum space to help illuminate exhibits. Once again Birkerts' work manipulates the effects of sunlight. (He used the same principles of daylighting along with other energy saving features in his 1974 design for the IBM regional office in the Southfield suburb of Detroit.)

102. Author's interview with Gunnar Birkerts, 23 June 1987.

103. Birkerts, in *GA Architect 2*, p. 202.

104. Author's interview with Gunnar Birkerts, 23 June 1987.

St. Peter's Lutheran Church, Columbus, Indiana
Credit: Balthazar Korab

St. Peter's Lutheran Church, Building Section
Columbus, Indiana
Credit: Courtesy of Gunnar Birkerts and
Associates, Inc., Architects

105. Author's interview with Gunnar Birkerts, 23 June 1987.

106. Kevin Roche, untitled essay, in *Gunnar Birkerts, First Recipient of the Plym Distinguished Professorship in Architecture* (Urbana-Champaign, IL: School of Architecture, University of Illinois at Urbana-Champaign, 1983), n. pag.

The conceptual approach Birkerts explains for the St. Peter's Church in Columbus may be even more characteristic of his current work. A circle represents the congregation as it sees itself gathered like a family in one body (balcony seats are excluded as being divisive). An axis cutting the circle, off-center, represents on the one hand the direction of worship towards an altar, and on the other the direction from which choral music is sung to the congregation. Opposite conditions lie to each side of this axis. One side completes the curves of the enveloping circles and half circles of apse, congregation and choir. To the other side are parallel wall planes layered in orthogonal relationships. The opposites occur in the absence of a real symmetry. On one side direct daylight enters harmlessly from the north. On the other side sunlight is deflected by baffles once again as indirect lighting. Birkerts relates this study of opposites metaphorically to the opposites in life.[105]

The opposing conditions modify the balance of the massing so that the inner and outer aspects of the church do not coincide. As a corrective, the spire is accordingly placed off-center to its external relationship so that it may be centered on the congregation circle within.

An appreciative statement by Kevin Roche effectively sums up Gunnar Birkerts' place in American architecture today:

'It was clear that his education and dedication had prepared him well for a life in architecture.

It would be difficult, however, to place his design direction in relation to others. It certainly appeared to be more toward Eliel than Eero, and one sensed that he prized Eliel's lifestyle as a model over Eero's. Eliel represented the individual architect working alone in his studio, a traditional image, while Eero was the driving, brilliant pragmatist, herding a group of ambitious young architects through the intricacies of his own exceedingly complex approach to design.

'Gunnar was an individualist then, and over the years he has not changed. He works in the relative isolation of a location which is no longer, as it was in the fifties, a central element in the American consciousness. What Detroit did in the fifties, and the energy with which it was accomplished, was quintessentially American. People went there because it was one of the major centers of industrial and business activity. Unfortunately, the spotlight has long since moved to other cities.

'Gunnar utilizes this isolation, however, to buffer him from the influence of the hyperactive architectural community of the east coast (a circumstance which is most felicitous), from the sober intellectual life of Chicago, and from the more bizarre environs of Los Angeles, so he can achieve the objective which should be desired by all architects— that of making a significant contribution to society and to the history of architecture. He does so without the frenetic publicity or the tortured prose which seem to be endemic to the careers of his contemporaries.'[106]

BOOK TWO

Domino's Farms

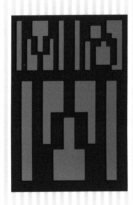

A Skyscraper And A Farm

1

Domino's Pizza moved into its new World Head-quarters at Domino's Farms on December 9, 1985. The company treats all such occasions with its own form of pageantry in the cause of motivation and fun. There was a parade of the Duesenbergs and other exotic vehicles from the old office quarters to the new place. The date for moving was especially auspicious, for this was the twenty-fifth anniversary of the founding of Domino's Pizza in the little Ypsilanti shop. The new home of Domino's Pizza was only a first phase awaiting many future additions; ground had already been broken a month before for an addition to double its length.

There would have been some sort of big office facility to house the company at this time, whether or not its Chairman invented an opportunity to honor Frank Lloyd Wright in its design. One must consider that for eight years or so Domino's Pizza, Inc., had finished each year with half again as many pizza outlets as on the New Year's preceding. On this twenty-fifth birthday there were over twenty-five hundred stores and counting.

When this period of rapid growth began, the home offices of Domino's Pizza were 'a collection of lean-to buildings and quonset huts…in the worst part of town'.[1] Domino's Farms became the fourth move of company offices in those eight years. This tally doesn't include Ann Arbor's old Hoover mansion which was to have been a classy office. Its space was outgrown even before protracted purchase arrangements could be completed.[2] Such corporate growth resulted from the goals Tom Monaghan set consciously for the company and for himself. The burgeoning need for executive space to oversee this growth was not so readily foreseen.

Tom Monaghan's first realistic opportunity to speculate on how Frank Lloyd Wright's spirit might influence the looks of his headquarters building came at the quarters just vacated. These were on Green Road in easternmost Ann Arbor, a short way beyond U.S. Highway 23 from the site of Domino's Farms. The company acquired an office building of 84,000-square-foot size there in 1982.[3] Of course it quickly became too small.

To advise him on future plans for the Green Road premises, Tom Monaghan turned to an Ann Arbor architect named Lawrence Brink. He was one of that fraternity of one-time apprentices of Frank Lloyd Wright. Larry Brink had spent two years in the Taliesin Fellowship in the last years of Wright's life. Brink went on to a more usual professional curriculum at the University of Michigan. After a brief absence, he was back in Ann Arbor to practice architecture. Commercial and industrial work came his way to design, along with a quantity of houses.

Tom Monaghan met him through a developer friend and set him to work making over his Barton Hills home in a more Wrightian flavor. The proposed alterations included a near replica of the living room at Taliesin. They were only partly fulfilled. The property wasn't equal to such ambition without crowding the neighbors. An appropriate Monaghan residence would have to be built somewhere else someday.[4]

1. Monaghan and Anderson, *Pizza Tiger,* pp. 206-07.

2. Monaghan and Anderson, *Pizza Tiger,* pp. 289-90.

3. Monaghan and Anderson, *Pizza Tiger,* p. 292.

4. Author's interview with Lawrence Brink, 24 June 1987.

Former Domino's Pizza Headquarters, 1980-1985, Green Road, Ann Arbor, Michigan
Credit: Domino's Pizza, Inc. Archives

'The Golden Beacon', Chicago, Illinois,
(1956 Design), Seen on Banner on Burton Tower
University of Michigan, April, 1986
Credit: Balthazar Korab

For the Green Road property, Larry Brink and Tom Monaghan agreed upon a complex of low buildings. It would be treated in the Prairie house idiom that Monaghan admires most in Wright's work. Horizontal lines would prevail on buildings having hipped copper roofs, sheltering eaves, and quiet courtyards. As the company's appetite for space grew, the complex could sprout more limbs and pods in true organic fashion. Throughout this campus, trees and landscaping would be interwoven with the buildings.[5]

The usual pace of growth for the Domino's Pizza organization loomed over these plans. Building and parking space would soon run out on a site of only twenty-two acres. Rather than begin filling up the courtyards, the only way to go would be up. This would call for a tower. 'Well, Tom,' said Larry Brink, 'I guess you're going to have to build the Golden Beacon.'[6]

Of Wright's unbuilt projects, the Golden Beacon was one of the most beguiling. Tom Monaghan didn't particularly care for towers; he liked Prairie horizontals. But he quickly fell under its spell.

When Larry Brink first arrived at Taliesin in 1956, Wright was preparing drawings for the Golden Beacon for a Chicago developer named Charles Glore, owner of one of his Usonian houses. At more than fifty stories, the Golden Beacon would have been the tallest of Wright's tree-like towers, save only his Mile-High skyscraper proposal of the same years.[7] The seed of the design was another apartment tower project, this being for the church parish of St. Mark's in the Bowery in New York City. This project was stillborn in the Depression year of 1929.[8]

Both tower proposals resemble trees in their trunk-like hollow concrete cores containing elevators, stairs and utilities. Their concrete floor slabs would cantilever out from the core like branches of a tree. Their lightweight outer walls of glass and copper would hang like leaves. For the St. Mark's Tower, at least, the whole mass would be faceted according to an interlocking plan grid of diamond shapes. Finally, both towers were designed to hover over the ground plane on their concrete core stem above heavy concrete foundations that resembled tap roots.

5. Author's interview with Lawrence Brink, 24 June 1987.

6. Monaghan and Anderson, *Pizza Tiger,* p. 293.

7. Monaghan and Anderson, *Pizza Tiger,* p. 294

8. Henry-Russell Hitchcock, *In the Nature of Materials: The Buildings of Frank Lloyd Wright 1887-1941* (New York: Duell, Sloan and Pearce, 1942), p. 81.

A research tower added to the Johnson Wax complex at Racine in 1950 belongs to this same family of towers. Its outer skin is more regular, however. Behind the pyrex-tubing windows, the branch-like floors show up best when the tower is lit from within at night. The only direct descendent of St. Mark's to be realized, however, was the Price Tower of 1953, built in town at Bartlesville, Oklahoma. As Thomas Heinz has explained, the Price Tower is once again tree-like in having facades that are different from one another.[9] More to the point, the profile of the building is so complex that it is hard to separate out 'facades'.

At three times the height of the Price Tower, the Golden Beacon project would be to it as the mature plant is to the sapling. In the published drawing of the Golden Beacon, there is a crown of circular cutouts of purplish hue and a green fringe of real trees topping off the vertical parallels of its skin.[10]

Translated into a centerpiece for Domino's Pizza, the Golden Beacon would be a symbol visible from the nearby highways. The rich form of the tower would be more suitably placed amid the simpler Prairie fashion growth of the Domino's Pizza headquarters on Green Road than in the urban chaos of Chicago's Gold Coast for which it was designed. The Chairman could have his office at the summit, with a view eastward toward the distant Tiger Stadium home of his newly-acquired baseball team in Detroit.

Would Wright have appreciated the tribute of a tardy apparition of his Golden Beacon? All his life he denounced architects who copied his forms instead of emulating him.[11] But a replica of his own design might have been different, a sort of archae-ology of unbuilt fantasy.

Rockefeller money restored a lost capitol building in colonial Williamsburg with only a founda-tion footprint and a picture from a library at Oxford to work with. But the chamber inside where Patrick Henry denounced the British had to be restored as guesswork that the patriot would not have recognized. The commendable goal at Williams-burg was to impress and educate the tourist more vivid-ly than any book illustrations could do.

Producing the Golden Beacon as a tribute to Wright would be a similar impulse, but reconstructing its detailing might be easier. In the eighties the suc-cessors to Wright's practice still design buildings in the drafting room at Taliesin. They now constitute the firm of Taliesin Associated Architects. People that Wright guided in the detailing he wanted to see are still at work there. Presumably, they still can refine thirty-year-old presentation drawings into reasonably valid form.

9. Heinz, *Frank Lloyd Wright*, p. 16.

10. *Frank Lloyd Wright: Drawings for a Living Architec-ture* (New York: Horizon Press, 1959), p. 172.

11. Frank Lloyd Wright, *The Future of Architecture* (New York: New American Library of World Literature, 1963), p. 38; Frank Lloyd Wright, 'In the Cause of Archi-tecture', from *Architectural Record*, May 1914, in *Frank Lloyd Wright on Architecture: Selected Writings 1894-1940*, ed. Frederick Gutheim (New York: Duell, Sloan and Pearce, 1941), p. 46.

Price Tower, 1955, Bartlesville, Oklahoma
Credit: Balthazar Korab

Their leader is William Wesley Peters. He came to Taliesin over half a century ago as one of the original apprentices of the Fellowship. Peters was a close associate of Mr. Wright, and became his son-in-law as well. In early years even as an apprentice he looked after much of the construction work. It was Peters who engineered the 'golf tee' columns in the Main Workroom at Racine. In later years under Wright he coordinated the flow of office work and the presentation drawings.[12]

Tailoring the Golden Beacon to the needs of Domino's Pizza risked diluting the majesty of the concept. The company wanted a thirty-story tower instead of the original fifty-plus. (The number 'thirty' has canonical meaning to Domino's Pizza; company policy insists that a pizza be delivered no longer than thirty minutes after the order is taken over the phone.) Would a shorter tower be noticeably superior to the Price Tower of more than half this number of stories? Modern office stories are half again as high as typical apartment stories, measured floor to floor. This would help (the Golden Beacon was designed for apartments, after all). The original proportions and scale might still be compromised, however. Offices in such a tower weren't logical either, although the Price Tower combined offices with apartments. An office building needs many more elevator shafts than an apartment building in order to maintain frequent service and carry rush hour loads. Would the increase bloat the core and squeeze out usable office space? These were serious questions, for the result might not really be a 'Golden Beacon'.

Wright's known antipathies aside, would resurrecting an adapted Golden Beacon be any more open to criticism than the quotations from past periods found today in Postmodern architecture? More to the point, only a decade ago some current Postmodern leaders like Michael Graves were refining a 'twenties revivalism' of the stark white geometrical forms of le Corbusier and the International Style. Their work carried these forms to an ingenious complexity. It was as if le Corbusier might have progressed to such refinements after the war himself, instead of turning to a concrete 'New Brutalism' as he did. Then there is the current 'twenties revivalism' of tapered Postmodern office towers in the Art Deco idiom; they, too, are carried to a richer degree in color and spatial conception as if to pretend that the Great Depression had never squelched the momentum of the wonderful ballyhoo years.

There is also the mainstream of Postmodernism which tends to a simple classicism of composed facades and distinct chambers in its search for effective symbols. Would a resurrected, adapted Golden Beacon be simply a more literal form of Postmodernism? (The nagging voice of Frank Lloyd Wright won't go away. In his Prairie house years he contended with five centuries of what he considered a misguided Renaissance and Postrenaissance classicism as lacking the integrity of his organic architecture. This was before he turned on le Corbusier and the International Style as his new adversaries.)

Tom Monaghan subscribes to Wright's philosophy of organic architecture. But at the moment we are not dealing with theory or the resonance of current architectural philosophy. The Golden Beacon, and the Prairie houses before it, went to Tom Monaghan's heart. The man who has traveled the road to Damascus needs no further justification for his passion. Nor was he alone in his feelings.

'I made a model of this Golden Beacon on the hardboard model in my office,' he said of the Green Road project, 'and I stuck it in the middle. One day after it had been there about four or five days, my secretary said, "Holy cow! Have you created a lot of excitement about that tower on the model in your office! People are going by with the door open and everybody is excited about it." Then I realized how excited everybody was about us building a tower. In fact, I call it the "Power of the Tower." '[13]

Beyond the doors of Domino's Pizza there was a broader constituency that would have to embrace the Golden Beacon idea, the officialdom and public opinion of Ann Arbor. The company needed a consultant to advise about rezoning that a tower would require on Green Road. The company retained Paul Raeder, a planner and landscape architect of the Ann Arbor firm of Beckett and Raeder Inc.

Local officials welcomed the prestige of having the Golden Beacon of Frank Lloyd Wright take root in Ann Arbor. Some sentiment preferred it as a downtown ornament, however, and this would be inconvenient to the company.[14] A downtown location would also violate all the principles of Wright's Broadacre City; a skyscraper wanted a rural setting. In all his life, Wright could never persuade his clients to build his towers outside of town. Tom Monaghan prided himself on being more enlightened.

Tom Monaghan's new planning consultant was becoming another goad. Paul Raeder argued that the twenty-two-acre Green Road site was much too small even for the remedy of a Golden Beacon. The complex would only work with some multistory parking garages, and then only for a short time

12. Twombly, *Frank Lloyd Wright*, pp. 214-15, 219-20, 344.

13. Monaghan, 'Wright Hand' address, n. pag.

14. Author's interview with Paul Raeder, 19 June 1987; author's interview with Lawrence Brink, 24 June 1987.

before the staff of Domino's Pizza grew too big for their quarters again.

Besides, the Wrightian architecture Tom Monaghan and Larry Brink proposed would want to keep a close relationship to nature. Raeder described to his client the 600-acre wooded site in which Eero Saarinen had placed the John Deere Company offices, and he let him visualize the possibilities.[15] In this advice there was that echo of Wright's usual directive to his own clients to go out and buy as much land as they could possibly afford.

Paul Raeder's recommendation aroused another of Tom Monaghan's dreams. This was the notion of having an office kept in converted farm buildings. Once he had even tried to buy a picturesque farm grouping near Chelsea, west of Ann Arbor.

He planned to put executive offices in the house and to convert the barn and outbuildings to house other company departments. The owners declined his bid, and before long the farm-office idea went the way of the Hoover mansion as another fantasy hopelessly outgrown.[16]

Now Monaghan was scouting property once again, with Paul Raeder and Larry Brink behind the windshield with him. The 300-acre parcel just across U.S. Highway 23 in Ann Arbor Township came to light. This was well more than ten times the size of the Green Road property. Moreover, there was a cluster of farm buildings on it. Now there was certainly enough space for a world headquarters *and* a working farm to coexist on the same land. The company took options on the property as the site of Domino's Farms.[17]

15. Author's interview with Paul Raeder, 19 June 1987.

16. Monaghan and Anderson, *Pizza Tiger,* pp. 290-91.

17. Monaghan and Anderson, *Pizza Tiger,* p. 294.

Tom Monaghan And John Howe

2

It was not merely a sentimental gesture to occupy Domino's Farms as a twenty-fifth anniversary celebration. Now that yet another transfer of offices was imminent, there was real urgency to get settled in permanent quarters. Afterwards, these could be enlarged without much disruption to the operations of Domino's Pizza, Inc. The company also committed itself to vacating the Green Road office building so that the original owner could move back in as a tenant. The appointed moving day was a serious deadline to meet.

It would take real wizardry to create the sort of building Tom Monaghan dreamed about for the money available. Few companies were using their own capital to build their home offices anymore.

Domino's Pizza could hardly be an exception. With the voracious growth projected for its network of new shops and distribution facilities, company earnings had to be turned back into the business even more urgently than for a normal business pace.

Bankers and lenders would have to furnish the money to build at Domino's Farms. They would dictate the limits of what they considered reasonable feasibility. Tom Monaghan would still insist on high design quality, but he was busy running a pizza empire. Another company officer would have to be chosen to find the money for buildings and to expedite the tight schedule for design and construction on a day-to-day basis.

This monitor was John E. McDevitt. He had come to Domino's Pizza as a financial consultant in the days of the quonset hut offices in 1977. His financial planning laid the foundations for the tremendous growth that followed, and it disciplined Domino's Pizza operations to achieve the Chairman's ambitious goals. When the time came to plan for Domino's Farms, John McDevitt had become President of TSM Inc., which was a holding company bearing Tom Monaghan's initials. TSM Inc. was created to provide various financial services to Domino's Pizza, Inc. and its franchisees. One of these functions was to own real estate and buildings for the regional commissaries built around the country to supply pizza products to the shops. Accordingly, TSM Inc. was designated to be the owner of Domino's Farms and to administer its construction.[18]

John McDevitt insisted on engaging a large local architectural engineering firm to compile the program requirements and to prepare the construction drawings the contractors would follow. Such a firm would have to be experienced with projects of this magnitude to assure meeting an ambitious construction timetable within a limited budget. The architect who would create Tom Monaghan's dream building would have to serve as a design architect consultant to such a firm.

Three large Detroit-area firms were interviewed. The choice was Giffels Associates, with offices in suburban Southfield. Decades earlier as Giffels and Vallet, this firm had once been the largest architectural practice in the country, with a staff of over one thousand people. The flood of postwar automobile plants and other industrial construction had raised the firm to this size. In the eighties it was still Detroit's largest architectural practice, with a staff numbering over half its original size. Its scope had broadened to encompass various large civic, commercial, and institutional building types.[19]

The Barton-Malow Company was another team member added along the way to take responsibility for the construction itself. Barton-Malow was originally simply a general contracting firm. Its reputation in construction management was made in the early seventies in administering other separate contractors as the owner's agent for the new Pontiac Silverdome, home of the Detroit Lions football team and still boasting the world's largest air-supported roof. At Domino's Farms Barton-Malow would similarly manage the phased construction of the various portions of the work. Once construction began in earnest in the fall of 1984, it hardly seemed

to cease even as the various segments of the headquarters building were completed in their turn.

The first construction would be for a lowrise office building. The Golden Beacon was intended here, too, but it would be given a later construction priority. Tom Monaghan knew the architect he wanted as design architect of the lowrise office building.

Some years before, during a vacation trip visiting homes designed by Wright, Monaghan had called upon a Minneapolis architect named John H. Howe. Monaghan wrote later, 'I remember spending a glorious day (one of the greatest days of my life) talking about Frank Lloyd Wright with Jack Howe—Frank Lloyd Wright's Chief Draftsman.'[20]

It took a man of rare quality and capability to retain the trust of Mr. Wright as his Chief Draftsman for a duration of over twenty-five years. As a young man of nineteen, John Howe came to Taliesin in August, 1932, in the earliest days of the Taliesin Fellowship. He was promoted to senior responsibility as commissions began to return to Mr. Wright in the waning years of the Depression. John Howe served as 'pencil' to Mr. Wright. He laid out drawings for which Wright had established the concept. At intervals he surrendered the stool again to Mr. Wright, who blocked in some portions in more detail. In turn, as Chief Draftsman, Howe farmed out additional detail work to the various apprentices.[21] After the death of Mr. Wright, Howe became a partner in the succeeding firm of Taliesin Associated Architects for a period of about five years.

Since 1967 John Howe has maintained his own office in Minneapolis. He usually works with one assistant while his wife tends the business books. As one might expect of a small practice, he designs mostly houses, distributed between Connecticut and the West Coast, but usually in the Twin Cities area. But on occasion he acts as design architect for larger projects in a similar working arrangement to that proposed for Domino's Farms. A hotel to be built on the north shore of Lake Superior is a recent example of such projects.

The working arrangement with Giffels Associates was satisfactory to John Howe. Giffels provided him with a room in their Southfield office, half an hour's drive from the project site. But Howe felt most comfortable doing his principal drawings at his office in Minneapolis.[22]

Tom Monaghan asked Taliesin Associated Architects to adapt the Golden Beacon for Domino's Farms, and he acquired rights to use the design. The firm had misgivings about the divided responsibilities with Giffels for the design and construction

18. Monaghan and Anderson, *Pizza Tiger,* p. 252, 288.

19. Author's interview with Vural Uygur, 30 June 1987.

20. Monaghan, 'Wright Hand' address, n. pag.

21. Lipman, *Johnson Wax Buildings,* p. 5, 25; Twombly, *Frank Lloyd Wright,* p. 214.

22. Author's telephone interview with John H. Howe, 5 August 1987.

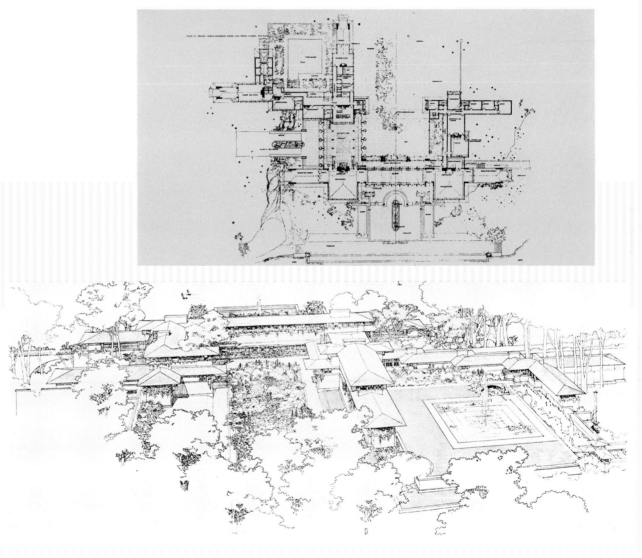

John H. Howe, Portrait
Credit: Courtesy of John H. Howe

McCormick House Plan and Rendering, 1907
Credit: © 1963 Frank Lloyd Wright Archives

drawings, for its staff was large enough to do all its own work for such a building. The difficulties were smoothed over, however. Larry Brink offered to serve as a useful intermediary for bridging the distance between the various team members in eastern Michigan, western Wisconsin, and Minnesota.[23]

To suggest a design direction for the low headquarters building, Tom Monaghan offered two of his favorite Prairie house designs, the Robie house in Chicago and the unexecuted McCormick house project for Lake Forest. Howe protested that

these were much too small to compare to the structure of 500,000 square feet envisioned then. He said he would do his best.

On a site study he sketched out a lake to run lengthwise on the property. On the western shore he placed his headquarters building, with its opposite side clearly visible from U.S. 23. The Golden Beacon was shown in position across the lake. With this grouping established, Taliesin Associated Architects began their studies of adapting the Golden Beacon design to the company's needs.

23. Author's interview with Lawrence Brink, 24 June 1987.

24. Author's telephone interview with John H. Howe, 5 August 1987.

25. Author's interview with Thomas Monaghan, 22 June 1987.

For John Howe there were many plane trips back and forth from Minnesota. Tom Monaghan wanted the pleasure and opportunity of working closely with the design architect, so they shared many breakfast work sessions in Ann Arbor. Howe enjoyed a cordial relationship with Vural Uygur, Project Manager on behalf of Giffels Associates. Howe delegated design of some of the outlying buildings to Bruce Johnson, a former Taliesin apprentice now at Giffels Associates.

At length, John Howe presented a perspective rendering of his proposed building. It was a picturesque structure of three or four stories with ribbon windows and low-pitched hipped roofs interlocking to leave courtyards as a quotation of the McCormick house planning. The mass of the building clung to the water's edge, 'with buildings poking out into the lake', as Howe described it later. These projecting wings had triangular bays to 'lighten up' hipped-roof ends that had grown broad to accommodate the amount of office space programmed.[24]

These triangular pointed ends were a special irritant to Tom Monaghan, who also said that he felt a want of unity in the informal composition. The pointed ends were missing in a second submission, but Tom Monaghan was still disenchanted with the prospect. There was a gap between the architecture of John Howe and the taste of Tom Monaghan, just as there was between even the largest of Prairie houses and the magnitude of the proposed headquarters building.[25]

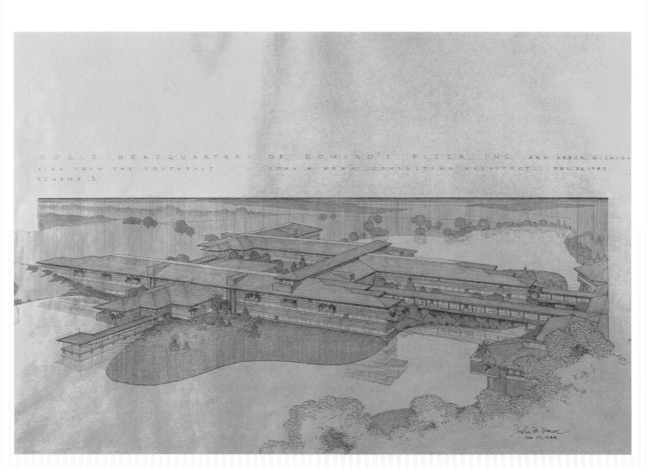

John H. Howe's Proposal for Domino's Pizza Headquarters, 1984
Credit: The National Center for the Study of Frank Lloyd Wright at Domino's Farms

Taliesin Associated Architects' Version of Golden Beacon and Headquarters for Domino's Pizza, 1984
Credit: Taliesin Associated Architects; William Wesley Peters, Designing Architect, 1984.
Tower: Based on an original design by Frank Lloyd Wright for Golden Beacon, 1956.
© Taliesin Associated Architects, 1984

26. Correspondence dated
11 January 1984 from John E.
McDevitt to Vural Uygur.

27. Author's interview with
Lawrence Brink, 24 June 1987.

Time was running out. In only two short years, a building of character would have to be designed, built, and occupied at Domino's Farms. John Howe and Tom Monaghan parted company as architect and client in December, 1983.[26] Taliesin Associated Architects continued to study the problems of adapting the Golden Beacon until the following spring, and then they put their drawings aside in turn.[27]

Today crowds of weekend visitors are escorted through the headquarters building, where they come upon colored renderings of buildings on the walls of the stairwell. One rendering is, of course, of the Golden Beacon, Wright's design. There is also a rendering of the adaptation prepared by Taliesin Associated Architects; it accommodates the changes surprisingly successfully, considering the handicaps to be overcome. John Howe's headquarters building appears on another wall, as seen from the rooftops. The Domino's Pizza project renderings could never be works of the master architect, but as dream projects with a real story they have taken on a life of their own.

3

Professor Leonard Eaton had no idea that he was setting up an architect and client relationship when he introduced Gunnar Birkerts to Tom Monaghan at lunch one day. Dr. Eaton was simply cultivating the support of a successful would-be alumnus for the wellbeing of the architectural school at the University of Michigan. This was much easier to accomplish when an unusual interest in Frank Lloyd Wright existed to cement this relationship.

For many years Dr. Eaton has been the senior lecturer on architectural history at the school. More important, he is an established scholar in Wright's story. Twenty years earlier he had published the comparison of Wright's clients with those of Howard Van Doren Shaw to which we have already referred.[28] The friendship of Dr. Eaton with Tom Monaghan has indeed benefited the school. Domino's Pizza now sponsors the annual Frank Lloyd Wright Symposium and Festival in cooperation with the school of architecture.

It should be evident by now that whatever constitutes 'the best' will interest Tom Monaghan. When Dr. Eaton said that the school ranked among the country's top five architectural schools, Monaghan characteristically inquired what it would take to make it number one. So it was to demonstrate the caliber of faculty there that Dr. Eaton arranged separate luncheon introductions to the engineer Robert Darvas and then to Gunnar Birkerts. For twenty-five years Birkerts had made the long drive from Birmingham to the school, where he conducts a design studio for up to ten of the school's most promising students.

A day or so after the luncheon with Birkerts, Tom Monaghan phoned Dr. Eaton to ask where Birkerts ranked among the country's top architects. The professor responded, 'In the first half dozen'.[29]

Not long afterwards Gunnar Birkerts accompanied Tom Monaghan through a retrospective exhibit of his own work. The exhibit was held in Eliel Saarinen's Kingswood School on the Cranbrook campus. 'You'd love Cranbrook', Birkerts assured his guest as they entered. Perhaps he was thinking of Kingswood's courtyards and its acres of low-pitched green copper roofs.[30]

28. Refer to page 26 above.

29. Author's telephone interview with Dr. Leonard Eaton, 13 May 1987.

30. Author's interview with Thomas Monaghan, 22 June 1987.

Kingswood School, 1928-1931
Bloomfield Hills, Michigan
Credit: Balthazar Korab

Of all the projects displayed, Tom Monaghan took special interest in a model of a college campus master plan. This was a study for Tougaloo College, a century-old college of predominantly black students in the state of Mississippi.

The plan proposed a multi-layered community at Tougaloo. Student dormitories occupied the upper strata, and academic and communal facilities were fitted in beneath them. The dormitories extended in parallel bar shapes across a valley, lifted up on concrete stilts. Traveling beneath the dormitories like a long gondola on an airship were concourse paths; from these the students filtered down into the public facilities arrayed laterally below on the valley floor. The waterlogged ground at Tougaloo might be unfriendly and unsupporting to the kind of earth-hugging buildings Wright might have built in another place. The 'tinkertoy' posts rising from caissons responded to these compelling local conditions.

Of this 1965 master plan, only a library and two dormitory-bridges were built, but these were enough to suggest the power of the concept. The master plan was undertaken in the year of the Lincoln School commission in Columbus. Together they belong to the early mature work of Gunnar Birkerts.

Two buildings in Minnesota also drew Tom Monaghan's attention in the Kingswood exhibit. One was the Duluth Public Library, built in 1976. It stands terraced against the steep hill panorama on which the city of Duluth faces its harbor and Lake Superior. The long, narrow city block site determined the simple bar shape, which hovers over the ground to borrow from sidewalk space for its upper story. Against the hill it stretches clearly visible from the ore carriers entering Duluth harbor, and the long form resembles these freighters that Duluth harbor was built to serve. The rounded end recalls the most modern pilot house of such freighters. Or perhaps to Tom Monaghan the metaphor was 'space ship?'

The horizontal ribbon windows of the library slope down inwardly and, with a central clerestory with the usual baffles, shed a diffused daylight that is welcome to readers inside. Under the clerestory the long central floor well and its stair seem like an updated version of the 'flower well' grand salons of the old Lake Superior liners.

Duluth Public Library, Exterior, 1969-1979, Duluth, Minnesota
Credit: Balthazar Korab

Duluth Public Library, Interior Well and Stair, Duluth, Minnesota
Credit: Balthazar Korab

Federal Reserve Bank, 1968-1973, Minneapolis, Minnesota
Credit: Balthazar Korab

31. Charles Jencks,
Architecture Today (New York:
Harry N. Abrams, Inc., 1982),
p. 60.

The other Minnesota building was the Federal Reserve Bank of 1968 in Minneapolis. At first glance it is a simple slab office building facing a public plaza. But there are solid piers forming the whole end walls; these piers lift up the slab building and a roof truss and two catenary suspension members carry its floors.

Birkerts rarely uses structure as expressively as he does here, but one discovers that it is in the service of space. The plaza passes through beneath the raised slab, visually uninhibited by columns. With a change in glazing between portions above and below the cate-nary member, the facade becomes a dramatic work of relief sculpture which some have compared to a gateway. The catenary recalls the expressionism of the Dulles Airport terminal roof in Eero Saarinen's most successful monumental building. Recent critics like Charles Jencks have ridiculed the exuberant gesture in Minneapolis, however,[31] and perhaps Birkerts sensed a grandiloquent overreaching at the time. Little of his work in nearly two decades since this design has looked to the expression of structure as the dominant basis of appropriate form.

32. Monaghan, 'Wright Hand' address (recorded transcription); author's interview with Thomas Monaghan, 22 June 1987.

33. Author's interview with Thomas Monaghan, 22 June 1987.

34. Gunnar Birkerts, typewritten memorandum dated 12 January 1987, p. 1.

35. Author's interview with Gunnar Birkerts, 26 May 1987.

36. Author's interview with Gunnar Birkerts, 26 May 1987.

'It wasn't Frank Lloyd Wright; it wasn't quite my style', Tom Monaghan observed of the Kingswood exhibit. 'It was a little too much Buck Rogers for me'. But the dramatic form of the Tougaloo model impressed him most deeply. The buildings had no brick and no roof slopes, and they 'flew' through the air. But it was a dramatic composition that hung together. 'This man can do it', he told himself. Above all, the architect was local, so that convenient dialogue was possible.[32]

The diversity of Birkerts' work might have encouraged a decision. Each building was born of the seeds of its own particular given needs, rather than answering a predetermined standard practice or the signature of family resemblance. Perhaps such flexibility might make Birkerts amenable to the special problem of Domino's Farms. Birkerts could be 'sympathetic with my organic materials', Monaghan felt, but there must be 'no space age look', only something 'more romantic'.[33]

Birkerts had mixed feelings about being named architect at Domino's Farms. Birkerts wrote of his client later, 'He liked my non-dogmatic approach to architecture and the holistic synthesis and my thrust in architecture to improve and innovate. Even as I agreed with his evaluation, some of the points he raised were going counter. Quality was not disputed, but innovation and departure did not meet his preselected and lifelong interest in the form world of Frank Lloyd Wright'.[34]

In the end, the client's most specific preferences simply became part of the given data to be analyzed. 'Since I create by synthesis, his wishes become a very strong factor, and I recognize them up to a point and say, "Now look, let's paraphrase it, let's put it into the twenty-first century,"' Birkerts explains.[35] Never in his career had a client imposed such a strong design direction.

The closest affinity Birkerts had previously found to another architect in his own work was in a 1975 design for a United States Embassy for Helsinki, Finland. It was, he says, 'homage to Aalto, to Finland, and the Northern syndrome'.[36]

In the Helsinki project drawings, the craggy walls seem to rise out of the ground slope. Window mullions and radiating batten seams of the roof seem

U.S. Embassy Project, 1975, Helsinki, Finland
Credit: Courtesy of Gunnar Birkerts and Associates, Inc., Architects

like topographical extensions of the hill site on the Baltic shore. The design is really a tribute to the high standards of Finnish architecture that Alvar Aalto helped to initiate, rather than an exercise in Aalto's vocabulary. Had Tom Monaghan noticed this project or the Lincoln School in Columbus, he might have felt more reassured about getting his 'organic materials'.

The Helsinki project remains unbuilt. It is probably deferred by the voracious appetite for funds to correct the troubled construction of the United States Embassy in Moscow.

The philosophy of organic architecture is the most suitable bridge of understanding between Birkerts and Wright. Birkerts has written:

'One can argue that organic architecture is not at the center of the Modern Movement. It provides, however, the continuity, and it is not on the fringe either, because the fringe is occupied by the International Style, personal idiosyncrasies, and highly dogmatic directions. Since these fringe factors have discredited themselves or have been abandoned, the organic core is perpetuated by Aalto, Saarinen, Erskine, Pietila, Scharoun, Rogers, Foster, Maki, Mendelsohn, Michelucci, and, of course, Frank Lloyd Wright, and many others.

'Many architectural minds have attempted to define organic architecture and in the course of the essay I will try to present my own interpretation. It has been said that architecture is either organic or it is arranged. It has also been said that the organic is *architecture* and the arranged is *building*. The description that I consider the most appropriate was given by Vasari, who said, "*Non murato ma veramente nato*." Translated, it means, "BORN, BUT NOT BUILT." So, organic architecture is not built, arranged, structured, but it is created through the process of organic generation. The great poet Wolfgang von Goethe observed the continuous growth and transformation in nature and coined the word "metamorphosis." Goethe was the strong influence of Rudolph Steiner who designed and built the "Goetheanum" in Dornach, Switzerland.

'Before I go into my description of organic architecture as I understand it, it has to be said what organic architecture *is not*. It is not imitation, it does not copy nature. Organic architecture is *not* covered by ornaments suggesting plant life. It is also absolutely wrong to take a building that is perceived as "weird" and identify it with organic architecture. And again, quoting Frank Lloyd Wright: "The ideal of an organic architecture for America is no mere license for doing the thing that you please to do as you please to do it in order to hold up the strange thing when done with the 'see what I have made' of childish pride." He also stated another interesting observation—a truism: "Eclecticism may take place overnight…(because we are working with borrowed form—G.B.)…Organic must come from the ground up into the light by gradual growth." It is inevitable that organic architecture has to grow from the inside space out. It is the synthesis of the building requirements, its site, its geographic location, the available technology, and it is concerned with conveying a meaning through metaphor or symbolism, if appropriate. It is context oriented in the physical and emotional sense, and it has to be remembered that the Zeitgeist is part of the methodology. And the result of this methodology is organic architecture.

'To paraphrase:

'Organic architecture does not mean that there are building forms that can be likened to organic growth, plant or animal. They don't look like snails or mushrooms. Organic architecture is growing out of the inner functioning, the inner meaning, the inner necessity, and if that becomes expressed in the building form, that is organic architecture. It expresses its purpose. To me, appropriate architecture is expressionistic. It expresses the purpose, the inner workings, and that particular characteristic—the "soul" of the building. The building skin is the face that carries the indication of what is really happening on the inside. I would like to call it *appropriate* expression. If the personal, idiosyncratic form giving becomes overbearing, it can create frivolous, even shocking results and they should never be sheltered by calling them organic.'[37]

When at last there was a building to dedicate at Domino's Farms, Gunnar Birkerts looked back on the beginnings:

'Tom Monaghan and I had a relationship like Michelangelo had with the Medicis or the Fuggers with their architect. To a certain extent, it was easier for Michelangelo because Michelangelo preceded Frank Lloyd Wright. The formidable genius of Frank Lloyd Wright so vividly in the mind of Tom had to be reconsidered and used as vocabulary from alphabet to syntax and a new story had to be told. Like a composer is given eight notes to compose endless music, we in architecture are given three basic forms: Circle, square, and triangle. After that we create with the use of imagination. There was this immense strength of the two minds: Tom Monaghan—there live and expressive—and Frank Lloyd Wright—posthumous and intrinsic. The result is a building.'[38]

37. Gunnar Birkerts, 'Organic Architecture, The Steady Core of the Modern Movement', draft dated 18 March 1987 as prepared for *Dimension* (Ann Arbor, MI: University of Michigan College of Architecture and Urban Planning, abridged, 1987), pp. 3-4.

38. Gunnar Birkerts, draft of dedicatory address dated 5 December 1985.

4

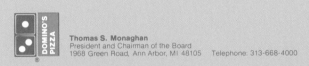

December 22, 1983

Mr. Gunnar Birkerts
Gunnar Birkerts & Associates
292 Harmon
Birmingham, Michigan 48009

Dear Mr. Birkerts:

Enclosed are materials which should help acclimate you to what we are trying to do and what the possibilities are.

Hopefully, the project will be a life long, never ending labor of love, and that you and I play a major role in it.

Sincerely,

DOMINO'S PIZZA, INC.

Thomas S. Monaghan
President

TSM/bl

Enclosures

DEC 2 3 1983

GUNNAR BIRKERTS
AND
ASSOCIATES

Correspondence from Thomas S. Monaghan to Gunnar Birkerts, December 22, 1983
Credit: Gunnar Birkerts and Associates, Inc., Architects

39. Correspondence
dated 22 December 1983 from
Thomas S. Monaghan
to Gunnar Birkerts.

This letter addressed to Birkerts formalized
the dialogue in harmony; it was dated December 22,
1983.[39] It was not long before harmony turned
to discord. When the architect delivered his initial proposal for a master plan, the owner was upset with
what he saw.

The essence of the plan was an orthogonal
matrix of low buildings with pitched roofs (the same
courtyard essence of the McCormick house that
Jack Howe had wrestled with). This was gathered into
one side of a giant circle conferring unity to all
and to the irregular edges of buildings bordering on its
perimeter. 'A circular village farm,' Birkerts called it.

The circle was bisected north-and-south by
the existing Earhart Road which then split the
Domino's Farms site. (The road would be shifted eastward to skirt the complex and its parking.)
A pond entered this circle from the south, its eastern
edge resembling the hands of a clock set at ten-
thirty. The low buildings responded to the pond with
end pavilions turned forty-five degrees—the pesky
pointed ends again?

West of the pond on the circular perimeter
stood the Golden Beacon on its small peninsula.
Girdling the circle on three sides were parking rows
arrayed in radial bands. To the west lay U.S. 23

where drivers passing at high speed would glimpse the
slender needle of the Golden Beacon at close range.

'Circle, square, and triangle,' Birkerts
would count off the basic tools of architecture. The all-
encompassing circle governed many Birkerts
designs: A recently completed law school in Iowa City,
the St. Peter's Church in Columbus, a library
addition in his own town of Birmingham. The closest
parallel was one of the unbuilt proposals of 1969
for the public library in Corning, New York, where he
later built the Glass Museum. A circular plan was
bisected by a passageway wall inside and a wall of forest
grove beyond. In the clearing, the circle remained
pure. Within the forest side, the reading room spaces
leaked out beyond the perimeter in jagged edges
merging with the growth of trees.

At Domino's Farms, once there was a tower
to look down from, the virtue of the circle's unity would
be apparent in more than a merely hypothetical
direction of view. The virtue became a flaw in the essential completeness of the circle. The ordering would
not be apparent until completion of a project destined
to be erected in stages. Once the project was 'complete,'
however, any further growth would violate
the purity of the circle. This was incompatible with
so dynamic an organization as Domino's Pizza.

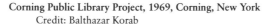

Corning Public Library Project, 1969, Corning, New York
Credit: Balthazar Korab

These objections were not the source of Tom Monaghan's displeasure, however. 'He followed my criteria to the letter in the first design he put together,' the Chairman reflected later, 'but it ended up as something I just didn't like. It was too complying, high tech or something. It didn't flow over the site, nor did it have the horizontality or drama I was looking for, and after four days I turned it down. We were both very upset by this. I wrote about five or six pages of notes about what my feelings were. They were pretty incoherent.'[40]

Time pressure was certainly part of the fit of nerves, as it certainly had figured in the decision to put aside Jack Howe's work. Moving day from Green Road could not be put back. The zoning process had commenced in December, 1983, when Domino's Pizza was between architects. With an unacceptable master plan on hand, Domino's Pizza would have to exhibit its intentions to the public with only the Golden Beacon to show.

Any rezoning effort anywhere could be daunting. Rural skyscrapers made it worse. The American public didn't share Wright's fervor for taking the towers out to the countryside. In this instance the township had already proclaimed standards for a Tech Park farther south along U.S. 23, and there was talk of keeping building height below half a dozen stories or so. There was probably no zoning ordinance in print anywhere that contemplated a skyscraper on a farm. But Tom Monaghan was adamant about getting his Golden Beacon. Domino's Pizza had put off completing the purchase of the site until the tower was confirmed as a part of it.

About two hundred people attended the town meeting to consider the Domino's Farms proposal for rezoning in February, 1984. They were reassured that the rural look of the site would be maintained. The alternative was the many homesite parcels for which the site was already zoned. 'We didn't get one person who openly objected to this tower at the zoning meetings,' Monaghan recalled later of the Golden Beacon's reception. 'As a matter of fact, many times we even got applause. That gives you some idea of the acceptance of Frank Lloyd Wright.'[41]

From the architect's office now came two separate sets of proposals for the master plan. One of these suggested something of the McCormick character still. The matrix of buildings and courtyards was now stretched out alongside the pond. Long parallel wings arrayed informally were linked by narrower transverse passageways. The parking and arrival zone followed a shallow crescent shape.

This scheme 'I loved,' recalled Monaghan, 'and it is exactly what I asked for.' As for the alternative proposal beside it, Monaghan was a bit provoked. 'Why did you do that? I didn't tell you to do that. I told you to do this McCormick house type of thing.'[42]

This alternative proposal was intriguing. It was a thing that hadn't existed before. Perhaps it would be the world's longest building. Certainly it would have the world's longest copper roof. The scheme answered Monaghan's most basic preferences of external architecture as being 'roofscapes and landscapes.'[43]

Perhaps there was a precedent for it, after all. That would be Wright's large Banff National Park Pavilion, built in 1911 in the Canadian province of Alberta and since demolished. The scale of this little-known summer hotel would be more easily compared to the scope of the present project than the Prairie houses.[44]

40. Monaghan, 'Wright Hand' address (recorded transcription).

41. Monaghan, 'Wright Hand' address (recorded transcription).

42. Monaghan, 'Wright Hand' address (recorded transcription).

43. Author's interview with Thomas Monaghan, 22 June 1987.

44. Author's interview with Gunnar Birkerts, 7 July 1987; Storrer, *Architecture of Wright,* item 170 (n. pag.).

Banff Park Pavilion, 1911-1913, Alberta, Canada
Credit: © 1984 Frank Lloyd Wright Archives

'I kept looking at it', the Chairman continued. 'It kept intriguing me. It was like changing religions. I had to do something different from what I always dreamed of doing. I went home and called him back and said, "This other building of yours is just driving me crazy. But I don't know if I want to build it or not."'[45]

A conceptual working model captured the essence of the plan. A long board contained eight equidistant parallel ridges forming seven 'tracks'. The architect would liken them to railroad tracks. Metaphor is at its best in architecture when it explains an underlying meaning or sense of order—like the 'trees' of Wright's towers.

Into each track of the model, long parallel blocks of wood were dropped at intervals. There were taller blocks near the center, and the others descended in height towards the outer tracks. The tops of the blocks were trimmed to slope away towards the side. Some blocks were chamfered on top at the end to represent nominal hips to these pitched roofs.

In each track, two or more equal-height blocks were left with intervening gaps representing courtyards separated by projecting pavilions. More blocks could be added to represent any length an ultimate building might require. Blocks of different lengths could be substituted and pushed or pulled along the tracks to manipulate the massing.

Gunnar Birkerts described how he arrived at this conceptual model:

'It was very clear that we would be facing magnitudes and growth patterns and time demands of the twenty-first century. The tranquil qualities of the Prairie architecture would have to be projected into the next century in forms that could grow, metabolize, change, and speak for themselves. Finding a systematic way to accomplish all that became the challenge. There had to be a methodology to accomplish the master planning for the rapidly and even erratically growing need.

'We decided that the expansion would take place linearly. After the analysis of the program and after establishing some growth pattern scenarios, we established a linear module of seven units, each twenty-eight feet wide, which we call "tracks." On this track module we could, not unlike the railroad switchyard, arrange program spaces in width from one to seven units and in height from a single floor up to four floors. Even if we worked with a seven-track module, the system allowed for addition of four additional tracks as required. When the building program requirements were laid out on the seven-track scenario, we realized that the building

45. Monaghan, 'Wright Hand' address (recorded transcription).

46. Gunnar Birkerts, typewritten memorandum dated 12 January 1987, pp. 2-3.

may extend up to half a mile in length.

'Now I realize that Tom Monaghan liked the Tougaloo College for its linearity, intuitively sensing the direction the master plan could take for his Domino's Farms. He began to make references to Frank Lloyd Wright's work, in particular citing the Canadian Pavilion at Banff. To me, the Domino's Farms master plan was a triumph in dealing with the magnitude of one million square feet in a low-rise corporate structure. The linear concept was functionally accommodating and visually exciting. The next challenge was to bring the nature and man-made linearity into compatible relationship. I prescribed that at the given expansion points the nature penetrates the linear structure from side to side and thus becomes woven into the linear pattern.

'The three hundred acre piece of farmland was intended to accommodate the Headquarters, its parking, and have as much farmland remaining as possible. Tom Monaghan has envisioned a working nineteenth century farm with farm animals freely moving on the landscape, practically grazing at the boundaries of the building. As the work progressed, it became harder and harder to accomplish, but it still remains as an objective, as a concept, and as a name—"Domino's Farms."'[46]

A study model in larger scale refined the conceptual track device to become the essence of a building mass on a specific landscape. The building would extend north-south just east of the to-be-abandoned Earhart Road axis. Uppermost in the building mass was a long ridge roof representing the dominant horizontal line of the building. This ridge remained continuous across the whole mass, except in dropping down one story level for a long run at either end. At these ends the building would be reduced to the breadth of this topmost roof riding on top of swelling berms engulfing the building mass to terminate the composition.

The off-center placement of the highest roof gave an extra story of height and an extra track to the west face of the building. The 'courtyard' breaches of the lower massing between projecting pavilions, as Birkerts explained, allowed nature, space, and vision to penetrate and pass through the building at these points.

To the east of the building lay the entrance zone and its parking. The parking lanes fanned out from the building to minimize monotony and were contained to the east by the relocated Earhart Road. As executed, it is unfortunate that additional parking had to encroach upon the southwestern part of

Hervanta Centre, 1979, Tampere, Finland
Credit: Courtesy of Dr. Malcolm Quantrill
Author of *Reima Pietila; Architecture, Context, and Modernism*

the site, for this was conceived as a more private zone. Once again the pond was to become the central landscape feature on the west side, and beyond it was the tower, the Golden Beacon.

Tom Monaghan gave his consent to proceed with this second concept in March, 1984. Gunnar Birkerts noticed an auspicious change in his client, who reacted in metaphorical terms for the first time in their working relationship. The first scheme, the McCormick inspiration, had been like 'mother', but the more up-to-date 'track' scheme was like 'wife'.[47]

The Chairman began daydreaming beyond the magnitude of his architect's vision. 'We were looking at the plans,' he wrote later, 'and we bought a lot of property south of us. We realized that if we wanted to, we could make that building about two thousand feet longer, and we could have a building a mile long. Someone said, "That will be the Mile High, sideways,"'[48] a reference to Wright's most ambitious tower of all.

The Mile High embodied the most palpable metaphor of Wright's 'tree' towers, but Wright saw the spirit of trees in diverse symbolic ways at Racine and Bartlesville. Critics and architects influenced by Wright continue to expand on these possible metaphorical manifestations. In his Hervanta Centre at Tampere, the Finnish architect Reima Pietila has shaped the window openings as ghost images of coniferous boughs of the trees that had to yield their place to his building, now returning as seedlings beside it.[49]

The canonical 'trees' find an appropriate context in the headquarters building at Domino's Farms, now completed to half of its ultimate length. The long mass resembles a sort of country windbreak row that a farmer might have planted long ago to keep his topsoil at home. The vision is at its best at midday when the eaves shade the red brick walls dark gray while the cascade of roofs still gleams in the sunlight. Close to the ground appear the evergreen 'boughs' where the frontal pavilions advance with their hipped roofs.

Others see it as a landform, a long ridge on the horizon. The initial name chosen for the Domino's Pizza World Headquarters building was the Welsh 'Bryn Hur', translated as 'long hill'. Wright's own buildings often bore names, as the Golden Beacon testified. 'Bryn Hur' did not stand long; perhaps it was too close a copycat of Wright's 'Shining Brow' of Taliesin, another Welsh derivative, or perhaps there were unwelcome connotations of a pun on an epic movie title on late night television.

The building was hardly occupied before Tom Monaghan changed its name. He told a gathering of the first Wright Symposium at the University, 'Ford Motor Company calls their headquarters "Glass House," the United Auto Workers call their headquarters "Solidarity House," Frank Lloyd Wright called the Seagram Building "Whiskey House." So I'm going to call this building "Prairie House."'[50]

47. Monaghan, 'Wright Hand' address (recorded transcription).

48. Monaghan, 'Wright Hand' address (recorded transcription).

49. Malcolm Quantrill, *Reima Pietila: Architecture, Context and Modernism* (New York: Rizzoli International Publications, 1985), pp. 129-30.

50. Monaghan, 'Wright Hand' address (recorded transcription).

Seen from U.S. 23, Prairie House is indeed a vision of the twenty-first century. The massing is tailored to a sense of order the motorist can comprehend in passing at a mile-a-minute clip. The most intricate modeling with the lower advancing pavilions and the intermediate penetrations occurs gathered toward what will be the central focus of the ultimate building. In the future, of course, the tower will accentuate this general focus. Falling away to the ends, the forms assume simple, strong, unbroken horizontal lines before dying into the terminating berms. Tom Monaghan likes the way the foreground foliage and knolls intervene in the highway view, so that the building passes into and out of view sequentially.

To make a six-tenths-of-a-mile-long mass of building satisfying in this way invokes some of the lessons of Baroque architecture at a huge scale. The Baroque is another architecture for a moving observer, but for a sedate pace. Maderno and the archi-tects of Rome designed church facades clustering rich detail around the entrance; detail faded away grad-ually toward the sides to become residual shapes of pilasters and entablatures, now reduced to projecting vertical and horizontal ribbons without capitals or moldings. This blurring of an architectural peripheral vision made the gaze of an approaching pedes-trian gravitate naturally to the welcoming entrance. Widening the effect from the limits of an urban piazza to the breadth of a formal garden, a Baroque palace like the Upper Belvedere in Vienna follows the same principle; there is the same reduced detail away from the central projecting pavilion, especially as the facade height drops away by one story. The archi-tect von Hildebrandt terminates his composition with polygonal pavilions topped with ornamental roofs. At the gigantic scale of Domino's Farms the effect is rendered in massing, with the end berms replacing the polygonal pavilions of the palace, now six-tenths-of-a-mile apart.

Garden Facade of Upper Belvedere, 1721-1724, Vienna, Austria
Credit: Saskia/Art Resource, New York

An Organic Shell

5

51. C. Northcote Parkinson, *Parkinson's Law and Other Studies in Administration* (Cambridge, MA: The Riverside Press, 1957), pp. 60-61.

About thirty years ago, a book called *Parkinson's Law* made a small stir in management circles. C. Northcote Parkinson's book is best remembered for the axiom that work expands to fill up the available time. Buried in the book was a chapter that should have decimated the postwar crop of pristine corporate showplaces.

The perfect headquarters, Parkinson cautioned, is designed for a static organization whose needs are fixed. In the dynamic organization, 'during a period of exciting discovery or progress, there is no time to plan the perfect headquarters. The time for that comes later, when all the important work has been done'. The author documents this phenomenon with a string of clever examples from Versailles to the British Foreign Office in war and peace. To Parkinson, the perfectly-housed organization is on the threshold of collapse, not of fulfillment.[51]

Part of the fault lies in the innate rigidity of the classical styles that for so long were the only dignified mode for a home office, commercial or governmental, pilastered or Miesian. We owe this understanding to Alberti, whose writings in the earliest Renaissance manipulated half a millenium of design practice.

Rucellai Palace Facade by Alberti
1446-1451, Florence, Italy
Credit: Alinari/Art Resource
New York

Alberti wrote of the perfect building, 'Every body consists of certain peculiar parts, of which if you take away any one,...or enlarge it,...that which before gave the beauty and grace to this body will be lamed and spoiled.'[52] In short, additions destroy the harmony of a perfect building, just as a man with three arms would look ludicrous. Alberti was not setting limits to fashion, he was stating an inherent reality of the formal classical building.

Introducing the urban skyscraper headquarters building offered little improvement. This was a finite shape encased in granite or white terra cotta. A bank of elevators preempted some of the floor space, and usually there could not be windows in all of the perimeter walls. To expand upward wasn't usually feasible; the Tribune Tower in Manhattan was an early exception. If more space was needed, another tower was built next door, again in a single building campaign, or office space was rented down the street.

This inflexibility explains Frank Lloyd Wright's antipathy to classical buildings and urban skyscrapers alike, from his earliest Prairie house years. Such spirit of static perfection was the antithesis of his organic architecture, which would nurture growth and change. Domino's Farms has evaded the curse of Parkinson's prediction because it meets the needs of a corporation whose own growth has been compounded annually.

Since the initial groundbreaking of 1984, there has been only a brief lapse between building campaigns at the Prairie House. Even before the first phase structure was occupied as the twenty-fifth anniversary celebration, ground was broken for a second unit on November 14, 1985. The new work was to be a warehouse with related offices connected by an all-weather grade-level corridor to the main office building. Since the spring of 1987 an expanded office structure has risen to link the warehouse wing with the main office superstructure on all levels. Together, these construction campaigns constitute half the length of the ultimate building. Meanwhile, on July 15, 1987, ground was broken for an exhibition building which will ultimately be the north end of Prairie House. With a wide intervening gap encumbered by farm buildings, the exhibition building needed laser technology to align it with the existing Prairie House mass. In the spirit of such perpetual growth, the architect maintains a branch office of his practice in the Prairie House.

Nestled between the two portions of Prairie House is the incongruous apparition of an idyllic rural cluster of the barns and farmhouse of the old Zeeb farm. The Zeeb barn and its sheds were the first buildings on the site to be occupied by Domino's Pizza, soon after the initial ground-breaking for the Prairie House in 1984. This became a 'petting farm' for school children to visit, making 'Domino's Farms' something more than a fancy name in developer talk. But it is also a working farm, as the occasional tractor crawling through the distant fields testifies.

The octogenarian Mrs. Louise Zeeb still lives in the farmhouse, and she seems to enjoy the activity around the place. Back in 1924 she had a year-old infant underfoot while she cooked meals for the men who raised the big gambrel-roofed barn in a two-week effort.[53] Before long, the big red barn, with its silo and shed-roofed additions, may be moved to a new location at Domino's Farms. But Mrs. Zeeb wishes to remain in her little white cottage in the grove of trees for the rest of her days.

52. Leone Battista Alberti, *Ten Books on Architecture,* trans. James Leoni, ed. Joseph Rykwert (London: Alex Tiranti Ltd., 1955), p. 195.

53. Undated 'Tour Guide Outline' provided by Domino's Pizza, Inc. for Petting Farm, item 2.

Zeeb Barn, Domino's Farms, Ann Arbor, Michigan
Credit: Domino's Pizza, Inc. Archives

The visitor's car rounds the bend in the new Earhart Road, and the length of the Prairie House unfolds beyond the windshield. The diversity among visitors shows the unique quality of Domino's Farms among corporate home offices. A housewife will be station-wagoning a herd of children to the petting farm. A tourist may come to see the decorative art and artifacts of Wright in the museum. Other visitors are friendly franchisees and timid trainees gravitating to the Domino's Pizza mecca from around the country, from around the world. Throngs come visiting on weekends for the conducted tours which feature the Chairman's Suite. All of these people complement the usual businessmen and very important guests we expect to see at company headquarters. None of these people bear the customary visitor's badge that is so intimidating for a purposeful call at home offices of other companies. Here, all enjoy the corporate mansion, including the housewife with children whom one may encounter in the office stairwell after their visit to the petting farm.

A file of tall poles bearing flags of countries hosting international operations of Domino's Pizza lines the driveway approaching the main entrance. A redwood-and-steel trellis with ridge-and-furrow skylights, casting rhythmic shadows, fronts upon a broad entrance porch. Inside on upper floors are the executive offices of Domino's Pizza, Inc., the parent organization of the pizza empire. Moveable sculpture often graces the porch, an antique Packard or the Cherokee red Lincoln Continental that was Frank Lloyd Wright's personal car, with coachwork he designed. North of the porch is the pad for the giant red-white-and-blue Domino's Pizza helicopter. From here, this craft whisks executives to conferences or the Chairman's party to Tigers games

in distant Detroit, where it is much more familiar at the ballpark pageantry than the Goodyear blimp.

When the Prairie House is finished, the additional intermediate courtyard penetrations between pavilions will offer opportunities for various departments and entities to have their own front door, their own identity in the building mass. In an office tower, such departments have all the individuality of a panel button in an elevator cab. Here, signage directs the visitor to the appropriate parking area, with the entrance of the department to be visited directly in view. The linear mass makes this possible; penetrating a sequence of courtyards in a McCormick type plan would have been more ambiguous.

Only one of these intermediate courtyards exists now, and it serves mostly lease tenants on the lower floors. As will be typical, its porch penetrates the whole building on the arrival side from the east, becoming a raised lookout platform to view the westward landscape and future pond (steps down to this garden side were omitted for the present for budgetary reasons). Sometimes a speaker will commandeer this court to exhort a faithful audience of visiting Dominoids about pizza technique or whatever, another vignette of life at the Prairie House.

One such entranceway is fully enclosed in the new office link, serving the Finance Department and Domino's Pizza Distribution Corp. upstairs. The latter maintains the largest presence among the corporate principalities at Domino's Farms. It runs the regional commissaries providing food products and equipment for the franchise outlets. Inside this entrance will be a large meeting room and small shops catering to Prairie House people who haven't time for a noonday run to downtown Ann Arbor.

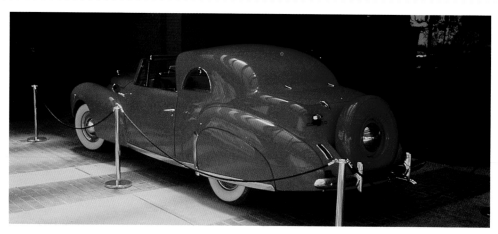

Frank Lloyd Wright's 1940 Lincoln on Porch at Domino's Farms
Credit: Gordon Bugbee

South of this new entrance stretches the long wing of the Michigan regional commissary and its related offices. These warehouses are brought under the copper roof of the Prairie House instead of being housed in a separate 'industrial' building. 'It is not a factory', reads the design directive, 'the employees are part of the family'.[54] From the bend in Earhart Road, the truck trailers parked in a paved hollow before the warehouse docks become one of the visitor's first impressions of Domino's Farms, of the pizza business at work. One of the trailers usually bears the legend, 'New Stores Division: Another Domino's Pizza Store on its Way to *You*'.

A hike awaits those who must travel between departments. An all-weather corridor spine runs the full length of the Prairie House. There is little pity for whiners with sore feet; off this passageway is a physical fitness suite with exercise equipment and a running track open to all Prairie House people. The company code favors using stairways over the slow elevators, too. The main elevator bears a dedicatory plaque with interchangeable nameplates to pillory whichever Domino's Pizza region currently records the slowest average pizza delivery time.

The tourist's first question always concerns what the building has to do with Frank Lloyd Wright. The answer lies fundamentally in Tom Monaghan's original criteria of forms and materials: The hipped copper roofs with overhangs, the berms, the ribbon windows, and horizontality in general. Raking out the horizontal mortar joints as a shadow line while leaving the verticals flush quotes Robie house practice. The red brick masonry rises from grade up to the sill line of the uppermost ribbon of windows under the eaves (any lower windows become punched openings in the wall). This is the way Wright treated his walls under the ribbon of bedroom windows in his Prairie houses. Above the topmost windows hovers the low-pitched roof with its broad eaves.

Some Wright biographers like Grant Manson consider the floating roof effect to be an early influence of Japanese timber building practices on Wright.[55] Because the bright red brickwork of Domino's Farms is unusual in Japanese examples, the world traveler here might be reminded of China instead. The gates of the Forbidden City at Peking are sentinels to the imperial pavilions beyond, some of the world's most exotic architecture. The gates, themselves, are more severe, with majestic hipped tile roofs in tiers spreading their eaves above a timber colonnade standing on massive red brick walls. There is an uncanny, if coincidental, correspondence at the Prairie

54. Memorandum No. 1 dated 2 February 1984, Gunnar Birkerts & Associates, item 1.

55. Manson, *First Golden Age*, pp. 38-39.

Forbidden City, 15th Century, Peking, China
Credit: Balthazar Korab

Robie House, Layering of Masonry Walls, Chicago, Illinois
Credit: Richard Nickel, Courtesy of the Richard Nickel Committee

Stave Church of Gol, 1150, From Borgund, Norway
Credit: William M. Worden

University Reformed Church
1963-1964, Ann Arbor, Michigan
Credit: Balthazar Korab

University Reformed Church
Ann Arbor, Michigan
Credit: Balthazar Korab

House, where the continuous ribbon of darkly tinted glass replaces the timber colonnade as a shadow line under the highest roof, which seems to float over the red walls.

Wright's Robie house is the source of many features at Domino's Farms; the wooden scale model of the house in the museum attests to its special place. The successive planes of horizontal brick bands in terrace and balcony walls in front of the house suggest something of the layered brick planes on the exposed longitudinal face of each track at Domino's Farms (here the planes are distinct; the exposed lateral facades are finished in copper and glass).

Birkerts used such layered planes in his own work. His early University Reformed Church in Ann Arbor makes these ascending planes of concrete. Inside the church, they combine with Birkerts' usual high baffles to diffuse sunlight from high windows.

The perpetual building campaigns at Domino's Farms reveal the skeletal form of the Prairie House anew from time to time. To Birkerts the skeletal shape recalls the network of huge timbers in the eight-century-old Norwegian stave churches, the oldest Western counterparts of the ancient Japanese timber buildings. The exposed construction also reveals that the massive brick walls are only a weather barrier curtain hung from the steel framing.

In his mature years Frank Lloyd Wright preferred reinforced concrete work to steel framing for large buildings. Concrete is versatile as structure and surfacing alike. What ornament the psyche desires can be cast integrally into the concrete, using repetitive patterns for economy. Such ornament cannot be added later, superficially, just as the Gothic stonecarver did not add material to the cathedral fabric for his ornamental capitals. Wright was using the material the way it 'wants' to be used, and he found its properties of integral construction satisfying to his organic way of building.

Steel is different. In a multistory building, under its crude, shapeless coating of fireproofing mastic, steelwork wants to be concealed and protected under other surfacings. Considering the magnitude of building at Domino's Farms, steelwork cannot be lightly dismissed as a framing choice. Indeed, concrete was never realistically considered. In addition to its construction economies, steel framework goes up quickly to satisfy the demanding scheduling of the appetite for space at Domino's Farms.

As for Wright's practice in steel framing, we turn again to the Prairie years. Hidden from sight in the Robie house is steel framing carrying the dramatic roof cantilevers and (apropos of our subject) the long band of balcony brickwork. We think of the Larkin Building in terms of Wright's masonry masses, but of course a hidden steel skeleton carried the window spandrels and gallery railings of brick in horizontal bands, just like any other midrise building of the day. (Of course, Wright quickly turned to concrete when it became available.)

The typical Prairie house, itself, was built of balloon framing in wood studs buried under a stucco membrane outside and plaster on the interior. Wright characteristically used the stucco as a simple surfacing membrane and not as a Pygmalion product pretending to be cut stonework in the turn-of-the-century fashions.

Robie House with steel structure reinforcement
Credit: University of Chicago, Joseph Regenstein Library

Larkin Building steelwork in demolition, Buffalo, New York
Credit: Buffalo and Erie County Historical Society

The Latent Organic Core

6

In one of the seminal writings of Postmodernism, Robert Venturi compared two basic types of buildings that he called a 'decorated shed' and a 'duck'. The former would first be conceived by arranging and shaping its innards according to a program of its needs, whereupon the shell that resulted could be dressed up with suitable ornament to be presentable. Outwardly this decorated shed conceded more caprice to the architect than Wright would admit on behalf of his organic philosophy, but the beginning premises of both might not have been very far apart.

The duck was named for what was then an obscure duck-shaped fast food hut on Long Island. To Venturi, any duck was a building of a preconceived external form chosen for symbolic reasons, with its innards being crammed to fit into the shell ordained.[56] Wright could have used the term along with the unflattering epithets he chose for banks shaped like pagan temples or the perforated stucco boxes of the International Style.

It is fair to ask the question whether the headquarters building at Domino's Farms is only a decorated shed roof.

Beyond the entrance, the discriminating visitor will easily judge so. The roofscapes of the Prairie house hardly prepare one for the familiar world of painted gypsum drywall and suspended acoustical ceilings within. Decked out with Eskimo art prints, whatever their quality may be, the bland ambiance belongs to a suburban speculative office facility. Only in the executive suite and the Chairman's own office does the presence of the form giver reappear.

Restating the question, is the Prairie House

56. Venturi, Scott Brown and Izenour, *Learning from Las Vegas*, p. 87.

57. Wright, *Living City*, p. 91.

only a duck masquerading as organic architecture, a Postmodernism that happens to choose Wrightian symbols in preference to their contemporary sources in classicism or Art Deco?

One hears Wright repeating his most fundamental dictum: 'Organic architecture cultivates "the space within" as a reality instead of the roof and walls; it is building from inside out, instead of from outside in'.[57]

The architect's 'seven track scenario' of master planning would deny that the initial conception was so trivial or capricious. It has successfully guided the dynamic growth of the building to three times its original size with more to come, the best of Wrightian objectives. Nor are the workspaces fundamentally flawed, although what they want to become is only a latent image invisible to the visitor. This is not to say that the cause of organic design will be fulfilled with some judicious redecoration.

The fundamental failing is that the building does not readily explain itself, within. The array of the various departments that make up the corporate family, the identity of each and how it may be reached is obscure. The linkages between entrances and workspaces must be visually clarified, particularly in vertical sequences of space. To accomplish this is not easy when departments are constantly expanding or relocating, but this is only part of the challenge. It is not met by gerrymandering space by expediency as in a loft space having stairs and toilets at appropriate intervals, assigned much as one would dole out rentable area to tenants. The remedies may require major surgery on floor slabs and fabric.

'Long Island Duckling', 1931, Riverhead, New York
Credit: Peter Blake, *God's Own Junkyard,* courtesy of Robert Venturi

Trailer Bank with Classical Facade, 1969, Madison, Wisconsin
Credit: *Wisconsin State Journal*

'Long Island Duckling' Sketch
Credit: Courtesy of Robert Venturi

This should not diminish the major accomplishment in creating the Prairie House. To build effectively at all to house the nerve center of the world's fastest growing food service enterprise was a strain on resources. Mortgage financing set limitations for volume sheltered under what was indeed becoming the world's longest copper roof. After reserving generous porches and courtyards, a habitable shell of a building with maximum possible floor space was the first priority. Internal skimping paid for the fine envelope. The construction went on almost endlessly on the same terms, so that the opportunity to upgrade quarters already occupied has never arrived.

The story of the eighteenth century English country house may be a parable for the strategy of bringing integrity to the Prairie House. The English mansion usually began as a Georgian or Palladian shell that was as handsome and as sturdy as the owner's purse could bear. A generation or more might pass before the family resources recuperated from the strenuous initial building campaign, but the shell was ostensibly complete for all time. When funds permitted, the interior 'rooms' were finished off, if only a small number at a time. Robert Adam gave his surname to an entire period of British architecture; his reputation, however, comes largely from embellishing the chambers of buildings designed earlier by somebody else. The innate classicism shared by the differing Georgian, Palladian and Adam modes helped to give a measure of compatibility to the whole.

Something between the spirit of Wright and the preferences of Birkerts will presumably provide the continuity someday in reworking the Prairie house, compensating for necessarily niggardly beginnings. The process cannot wait for corporate generations to pass or it will not happen; the status quo will seem acceptable. On the other hand, Tom Monaghan is not likely to be so patient.

Is this strategy possible? Where are the great interior workspaces of a Larkin Building or a Main Workroom at Racine? One must remember that this is a rural office building, a completely different problem to solve. Views of a green landscape are available, even distantly, when parking begins to encroach on the foreground. (From upper windows, a sloping expanse of seamed copper roofing tends to soften the intrusion of parking.) The Larkin and Racine buildings turned inward with lofty workspaces to compensate for surroundings so visually distressing.

In any case, the magnitude of the task at Domino's Farms rules out lofty workspaces. At full extent someday, the Prairie House alone will

Kenwood House, Library by Adam
1765, Hampstead Heath, England
Credit: Woodmansterne and the Iveagh Bequest, Kenwood, England

The Collaboration In The Chairman's Suite

7

The dormant architect in Tom Monaghan came to life to seize the chance of a lifetime. The Chairman was much too busy with selling pizza to monitor John McDevitt's staff in the day-to-day planning of the Prairie House except for the most major decisions. His own office suite was another matter.

'By golly, I'm going to work on my office, myself,' he decided. 'On top of that, I'm not going to work with Birkerts' *staff*, I'm going to work with Birkerts, himself.' Here was an opportunity for 'getting into his head and seeing how this genius worked.' Thus began a series of evening conferences between client and architect over a table at the Monaghan home.[60]

Gunnar Birkerts was amenable to such an overture. In protecting the integrity of an evolving design, 'the more public the building, the more assertive I am', he would explain.[61] Something more private, like a house or the Chairman's office, became as much an extension of its owner's personality as clothing; in its planning, the architect should welcome the owner's concerns more openly. The resulting collaboration began a close friendship between Monaghan and Birkerts.

The suite represents the most thorough development of any internal feature of the headquarters building, perhaps the only part that seems ready for the visitor's close scrutiny. The remainder of the executive suite with its skylit core is appropriate for a large corporation, but few parts of the interior of the Prairie House seem to show what Gunnar Birkerts would do by himself with appropriate resources.

The space allocated for the Chairman's suite was on the two uppermost levels across the present north end of the building. A broad floor well linking the two levels makes the upper floor a mezzanine. Stairs and a long landing cling to three sides of the well, and Birkerts suggested making them serve a wall of bookshelves. The Chairman's desk on the mezzanine would be out of sight of conferees or guests gathered on the lower level. An outdoor balcony proposed along the north end had to be deferred for cost savings.

The normative Usonian interior was Tom Monaghan's starting point. He wanted a rustic effect, rather like a lodge. He knew the kind of materials this called for, the natural materials Wright would have favored. To begin with, the walls wanted the characteristic horizontal board and batten siding, and the battens should not be merely skinny strips of wood.

Birkerts talked him into substituting polished brass splines for the battens; the materials began to be a little more sophisticated and something more slick than a lodge began to emerge. These bold splines continued as muntins into the glass doors and sidelights at entrances on each level, and the shelves on the stairs were aligned with the splines. The ceiling became a textured silk fabric; as in the other offices, Birkerts felt that a board ceiling continuing the eave surfacing inside would darken the room too much. The carpeting was thick enough 'to look like it came right off the sheep's back.' A special touch was the leather floor tile in other areas, Birkerts' idea, echoing the leather-surfaced furnishings elsewhere.[62]

60. Author's interview with Thomas Monaghan, 22 June 1987.

61. Author's interview with Gunnar Birkerts, 5 May 1987.

62. Author's interview with Thomas Monaghan, 22 June 1987.

On the lower level the south wall became brick in shaped planes, with a fireplace positioned asymmetrically—the symmetry in the first design study of it was too 'Art Deco' for Monaghan's taste. The brick continued onto the floor surface at a depressed conversation area of leather upholstered seating gathered around a low glass-topped leather table containing a model of Tiger Stadium. Nearby was a chair in the shape of a baseball mitt bearing Joe Dimaggio's autograph.

Designing and fabricating accessories for the suite became an ongoing process in Birkerts' office. The underlying design philosophy called for a thematic unity in materials and patterns at all levels of scale, compatible with the features of the building, itself. Of course, Wright's organic approach called for such a harmony between parts and the whole. Inspiration came from the same fundamental square, circle, and triangle that Birkerts considered his starting point. Thematic continuity carried over into items of daily use; placemats for the executive suite were embossed and debossed in a pattern of modified concentric circles found in the top grilles of the cylindrical lighting standards.

In some instances, the fixtures and accessories recalled the overall form of the building, itself. A long candelabrum for the fireplace mantel featured parallel bronze bars of various lengths spaced apart in equal increments, rather like the tracks of the building plan. Another track paraphrase, this time of the building cross section, was in the hovering rectangular chandelier of the executive board room, with stepped planes recalling the roof edges outside.

Such empathy in microcosm had antecedents elsewhere. Only rarely did Wright's work make such direct correlations beyond a general harmony. The circular office chairs under the saucer-shaped column capitals at Racine would be an example. But the theater curtain at Taliesin translated the pattern of Taliesin, itself, into myriad colored fabric rectangles, as David Hanks has shown.[63] Loja Saarinen wove a tapestry similarly inspired, abstracting the plan of the Cranbrook Academy of Art.[64] The impulse goes back to the medieval reliquaries overlaid in Gothic tracery forms under gabled roof-like tops imitating features of the cathedrals possessing them.

In the skylit central reception hall of the executive offices leading down to the door of the Chairman's mezzanine office, panels of patterned leaded glass in dark wooden frames are hung on the walls. These are, of course, casement sash panels of Wright's art glass. They come from 'Glenlloyd,'

63. David A. Hanks, *The Decorative Designs of Frank Lloyd Wright* (New York: E. P. Dutton, 1979), p. 144.

64. *The Saarinen Door: Eliel Saarinen, Architect and Designer at Cranbrook* (Bloomfield Hills, MI: Cranbrook Academy of Art, 1963), p. 52.

Hillside Theatre Curtain, Taliesin East, 1933
Spring Green, Wisconsin

Cologne Cathedral, Reliquary, 1200
Cologne, Germany
Credit: Marburg/Art Resource, New York

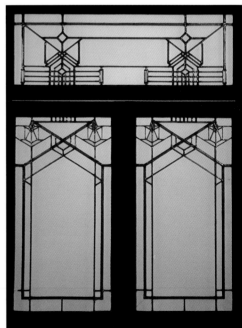

Art Glass from Bradley Residence, 1900
Kankakee, Illinois
Credit: The National Center for the Study
of Frank Lloyd Wright at Domino's Farms

the B. Harley Bradley residence of 1900 in Kankakee, Illinois, one of the most immediate predecessors of the Prairie houses. Although they are out of context of the ribbon of windows in the house as office decorations here, they are effective despite their isolation. David Hanks has explained that this compositional unity is one reason why Wright insisted on casement windows in place of the double hung sash popular at the time.[65] The sash panels here are fugitives from Monaghan's growing collection of Wrightian furnishings and artifacts in the museum.

65. Hanks, *Decorative Designs of Wright,* pp. 58-59.

The Sunday tourists generally miss the most perplexing chamber, the washroom of the Chairman's suite, but most people have been told about it. The Sybaritic set of rooms is delightful, but seems far removed from the context of the Prairie House, indeed, alien to it. It becomes a capsule of Mediterranean classicism that has somehow found its way in. Neither collaborator quite owns up to originating the washroom, but it is easy to see how the idea evolved. The ceiling is of four groin units surfaced in gold leaf. The walls of the toilet and shower areas below are of dark greenish Italian marble. Monaghan wanted thick marble slabs that would have boldly projected several inches, but Birkerts cautioned him that this was too expensive. Splined walls of wood or mirror

66. Author's interview with Thomas Monaghan, 22 June 1987.

glass carry the board-and-batten theme into the outer chamber from the walls of the suite beyond, but the pristine marble and gold dominate the overall impression. In an opposite sense of textures, the washroom contrasts with the suite beyond in the way that the gnarled, bark-covered *tokonoma* post contrasts with the smooth, precisely-jointed timbers of the traditional Japanese house. These are discordant elements to be admired for their own sake, and they reveal by contrast something of the nature of their context.

It all grew too extravagant for Tom Monaghan's comfort. 'I never asked him what things cost', he reflected afterward. 'It wasn't until later that I realized'. Late in the process he began hearing of two million dollars for the Chairman's suite, and then two-and-a-half; he never did know the final figure. 'If I had known it would cost that much, I wouldn't have done it', he concluded.[66]

The suite would simply have to become something more than one man's private office. On Sundays a brunch is served to visitors in the suite and in the executive dining room beyond. On perhaps three evenings a week, the room is made available for civic functions and organizations; an aide clears off Mr. Monaghan's desk when he leaves for the day.

Culture And Agriculture At Domino's Farms

8

Prospects for a new home for Domino's Pizza were still nebulous when Tom Monaghan bought his Tigers baseball franchise. Briefly he toyed with the idea of putting a Golden Beacon for Domino's Pizza in downtown Detroit. Maybe this impulse was intended to please new friends of his team in a city stricken by recession. The idea was dropped, and Domino's Farms materialized instead. The benevolent record of the new owner's regime at Tiger Stadium helped to put

67. 'Everybody Wins with Ilitch Plan,' in *Crain's Detroit Business,* 13 July 1987.

the matter to rest quietly, but for some the loss still rankled. Four years afterward, *Crain's Detroit Business* was still huffing editorially that Tom Monaghan was a 'loser' for 'putting up inappropriate structures in the countryside' instead of bringing his office team in from Ann Arbor.[67]

The modern corporation makes these bold chessboard moves easily, with its staff as pawns to move or discard. Among others, Mobil and J. C. Penney

68. Anthony DePalma, 'Why Penney is Moving to the Prairies: Shift to Texas Puts It in Center of the Nation', in *New York Times,* 23 August 1987, Sect. 8, p. 1; Calvin Sims, 'Mobil Sets Tower Sale to Japanese', in *New York Times,* 28 August 1987.

69. Maynard Newton, 'Correspondence', in *Crain's Detroit Business,* 27 July 1987, p. 10.

70. Author's interview with Thomas Monaghan, 22 June 1987.

are leaving their Manhattan home office towers for suburban spreads in Virginia and Texas, respectively.[68] Rumors circulating in Detroit question whether General Motors is shifting its Saturn Division headquarters to its Tennessee factory, and whether all the top executives at Unisys are buying fancy new homes in the Philadelphia suburbs for such a move.

Domino's Pizza is not among the many corporations that have now forsaken their big city offices downtown for suburban pastures. As the crow flies, Domino's Farms lies just six miles from the Ypsilanti shop where the company was born. As for the move to Detroit, one reader reminded *Crain's,* 'The howls from his employees ended that'.[69] In staying close to its origins, Domino's Pizza saved its employees long rush hour driving or a change of homes or jobs.

Tom Monaghan wants to please his employees, and he wants the beauty of Domino's Farms to 'make people happy'. That is as Wrightian a premise as any. Patriarchal this attitude may be, just as historians have read it into the Larkin and Johnson Wax establishments. The idea of employees as 'family' is even more apt for offices that look like a big house. To some this outlook is distastefully patronizing. American business increasingly comes under indictment, however, for an opposite attitude that regards all employees as inherently replaceable for a minimal bottom line advantage.

The life of Domino's Farms is more broadly synchronized with Wright's ideas than a matter of placing offices and a tower in a meadow. In agricultural matters, the 'Farms' in the name may ultimately mean much to an exurban and suburban society, by way of example. There is much to say about Domino's Farms in cultural matters as well.

The frenetic pace of 'extracurricular' activities is unorthodox for a corporate center, and the variety of functions defies even the most well-meaning drafting of zoning codes. Want of coordination shows in this enthusiasm, 'in the haphazard making', to repeat Wright's words. It is hard to fault harried managers of these activities who may be marginally aware that their efforts are significant. If Domino's Farms demonstrates the need and viability of some aspects of the Broadacre City agenda for today's society, this alone will be an effective tribute to Frank Lloyd Wright.

The farm idea came early, of course, but it is still taking shape. Tom Monaghan is uncertain whether he wants a progressive farm demonstration, perhaps an updating of Wright's own proposals, or a traditional farm preserving a way of life. At Domino's Farms, the traditional side is represented by the petting farm and a horse farm called the 'Shire Center'. The progressive side in program, if not in buildings, is known as the 'Booker T. Whatley Farm'. As a byproduct, the Chairman wants the farms to explain to visitors where ingredients of Domino's Pizza come from: Green peppers in a greenhouse, a mushroom operation, making pepperoni, a dairy herd that starts the process 'from cow to commissary'.[70]

Ironically, the original vision of the cow beyond the office window is fading. The proposed conference center will want a golf course preempting the perimeter fringe of the property. There will not be room for a golf course and a farm to coexist on the original three hundred acre parcel and still leave the offices and conference center in a reasonable expanse of prairie grass. Domino's has acquired four times as much property in the vicinity, and the farms will move just north of Highway M-14 from the headquarters site. Regrettably, the highway earthwork will conceal the barns and fields from views out the office windows.

The Whatley Farm explores the future of small family farms located near urban populations. Wright's ideal Broadacres community intermingled such farms with homes and businesses at a low density that left the continuity of the natural environment. Wright grew up in a generation when farm population greatly outnumbered townspeople in the Midwest. His esteem for the family farm institution, like that of Tom Monaghan, came from boyhood farm life stressing personal qualities like discipline, manual dexterity, and self reliance.

Of course, not all farming activities would be welcome in residential areas. Obvious nuisances would be a hog farm specialty or a farm with manured fields. Municipalities have come to outlaw farm animals routinely within their limits as a public health measure. Forces of land speculation similar to those which disturbed Wright about cities drive up land values and taxes for the small farm near a town. Finally, it seems universally believed today that the full-time farmer cannot survive economically on a small farm in any case. If this last point is true, concern about speculation in farmland becomes academic, and opinions that small farms enhance the quality of life in the presence of residences become mere sentiment.

The Whatley Farm was set up to challenge this fatalism. In the heady days of early October, 1984, when the foundations were laid for the Prairie House and the Tigers grappled successfully for their

71. Address by Booker
T. Whatley at Whatley Farm
Dedication, 23 June 1987.

championship, Tom Monaghan was distracted by
an article he saw in the *Wall Street Journal*.[71] The article
described the ideas of a retired college professor
about saving the small farm. Dr. Booker T. Whatley
had taught horticulture at Tuskegee Institute;
in retirement in Montgomery, Alabama, he edited a
technical newsletter for owners of small farms
on behalf of his Whatley Foundation and Whatley Inc.

Frank Lloyd Wright had counseled the
small farm owner that his survival lay in circumventing
the middleman, taking his produce directly to
consumers in a farmer's market. Dr. Whatley suggested
a 'U-Pick' operation instead, selling memberships
to families who picked their own produce from the
farmer's fields. For this to work, Dr. Whatley
recommended that such farms be within twenty-five
miles of towns of at least 50,000 inhabitants.
This was consistent with the relationship of farmer and
homeowner that Wright advocated. Both Wright and
Dr. Whatley said that the small farm owner shouldn't
behave like the large scale farming enterprises,
but should intensify his crops. The Whatley-type farm
might be between ten and two hundred acres in
extent. It would offer a variety of high-value crops,
alternating with the seasons and promising to give
a full-time farmer an annual income grossing at least
$3,000 per acre.[72]

Booker T. Whatley, Portrait
Credit: Courtesy of *The New Farm*

72. Richard O. Brunvand,
'Whatley Farm Dedication
at Domino's Farms', press
release of Domino's Pizza, Inc.
dated 16 June 1987.

Small farms are increasingly popular as
part-time endeavors of families with other sources of
income to subsidize a wholesome avocation.
Judy Rose has pointed out that the number of small
farms in the country increased seventeen percent
in a recent four year period, and that the last Census
showed greater percentage of population gains
in rural areas than in metropolitan ones. She describes
the frustrations of one Ann Arbor professor and
his wife who grew gourmet produce for local restaurants; a small quantity of tomatillos intricately
cultivated to order for Mexican cuisine brought a total
of $3.60, delivered. The two began exploring a
U-Pick system.[73]

Horse Drawn Wagon at Whatley Farm
Credit: Domino's Pizza, Inc. Archives

73. Judy Rose, 'Back to the
Land', in *Detroit Free Press*,
4 July 1987, page 2C.

After reading the *Wall Street Journal* article,
Tom Monaghan telephoned Dr. Whatley in Alabama,
and they met the following January at a meeting
at Michigan State University. They agreed to set up a
model farm in Ann Arbor testing and demonstrating
Dr. Whatley's principles and techniques. At the
dedication of the Booker T. Whatley Farm at Domino's
Farms in June, 1987, Dr. Whatley observed:

'Here we are today,…attempting to destroy the
myth that "Bigger is Better," or "Get Bigger or Get Out,"
which the USDA, Land Grant College System,

the Cooperative Extension Services, and the public in general labor under. ...The "Booker T. Whatley Farm" and all "Whatley-type farms" across this country are technologically advanced operations designed to produce "contamination-free" fruits, fish, feeder lambs, fallow deer, game birds, honey, herbs, mushrooms, rabbits, and vegetables. ...This farm will consist of eight Divisions: 1) Mushrooms, including Shiitake; 2) Pheasants, Grouse, Quail, and Rabbit; 3) Honeybee Apiary; 4) Christmas Trees, Fruits, Herbs, and Vegetables; 5) Feeder Lambs and Fallow Deer; 6) Fish Production, Irrigation, and Meteorology Station; 7) Slaughtering, Packaging, and Tanning; and 8) Sales and Accounting.[74]

74. Address by Booker T. Whatley at Whatley Farm Dedication, 23 June 1987.

The rural character of lands around Domino's Farms today may be deceptive. Only one private farm remains in the township as the full-time occupation of its owner.[75] Ann Arbor Township faces the usual painful tension between those who want to profit from rising land values and those who want to preserve the rural aspect, to be left alone in peace. The neighbors of Domino's Pizza are nervous about the company's reasons for its new land acquisitions, given a succession of rumors and occasional pronouncements of Tom Monaghan's latest ideas. After all, preserving a rural aspect was what won zoning acceptance of the Domino's Farms complex in the beginning. The Whatley Farm promises to explore the feasibility of the small farming business near a town, but that is as far as it can go. Its support by a landowner like Domino's Pizza becomes artificial in the long run unless legal instruments exist to provide incentives for preserving such fragments of farmland in the midst of development. On the one hand, a farmer who binds himself to raising crops instead of selling his property needs to know that his farming can succeed; but the farmer may fear becoming trapped if conditions change unfavorably. On the other hand,

75. Tina Lam, 'Not all Neighbors Relish Idea of Empire', in *Ann Arbor News,* 1 March 1987, page A5.

76. Philip D. Stong, *Horses and Americans* (Garden City, N.Y.: Garden City Publishing Co., 1946), p. 303.

towns and state legislatures that grant any compensated alternatives to development need assurance that the land will not be developed later, anyway. Motives are not necessarily obvious, even to oneself, and certainly not for a corporation, the leadership of which might change. It is not an easy puzzle to solve fairly. Until some coexistence of small farms and generous homesites is seen as desirable enough for appropriate legislation, this fundamental cornerstone of the Broadacre City philosophy will remain unrealistic.

The petting farm and the horse farm have their social usefulness, too. Compared to the objectives of the Whatley Farm, however, they are open air museums. For the moment, the petting farm remains in the old Zeeb barn and its out-buildings, but its activity may be moved beyond Highway M-14, possibly to be consolidated with the Whatley Farm. The petting farm captures the essence of a working farm to which children have somehow been admitted as city cousins without chores to do. The usual farm animals are also joined by peacocks, pheasants, and rabbits. Crops are harvested on the farm to help feed the livestock, along with vegetables and fruit to sell to Domino's Pizza people and the public. Special festive events include hayrides and bonfires and a rodeo.

The horse farm is for shire horses, bred in the English Midland shires as sturdy farm and draft horses. Like other work horses, they multiplied in the late nineteenth century on farms and in town alike before internal combustion engines made 'horse-power' merely a technical term of measure. Percherons and Belgian horses were much more common in this country, and fifty years ago less than two hundred shire horses could be counted here.[76] The Shire Center at Domino's Farms perpetuates a breed from the past and perhaps helps to find it some useful role in modern life.

Proposed Shire Horse Barns at Domino's Farms, 1987
Credit: Courtesy of Giffels Associates, Inc., Bruce Johnson, Designer

Codex Villa, Aerial and Ground Views
1983-1986, Canton, Massachusetts
Credit: Koetter, Kim & Assoc.
Photo Credits: Timothy Hursley,
Alex MacLean, respectively.

77. Fred Koetter,
'The Corporate Villa', *Design Quarterly* no. 135.

The notion of a horse farm arouses strong aristocratic connotations, but these suggest saddle horses instead of workhorses. Just such a horse farm and office facility come together as a new 'corporate villa' outside of Boston. The Codex World Headquarters building, designed by Koetter, Kim and Associates, looks out upon a horse track toward its Maresfield Farm.[77]

The contrast between the Boston and Ann Arbor office 'farms' reflects that of their divergent ancestors in American rural architecture of nearly a century-and-a-half ago: The gleaming white Greek temple farmhouse and the picturesque 'Gothick' cottage in pastel shades. The Boston villa represents the long tradition of human order imposed on nature, although blurring into it on its fringes. In this it is a successor to Platt's Villa Turicum in Lake Forest. The Ann Arbor counterpart approaches an opposing principle of blending buildings and nature.

The Postmodern Codex corporate villa draws its inspiration from imperial Roman villas and from those which Palladio designed to lend urbanity to the isolated country life of citified Venetian investors engaged in remote large-scale land reclamation. To imagine a Mediterranean context in a Boston suburb asks a suspending of judgment, but that reflex may come as easily today as it did seventy years

ago on Chicago's North Shore. Significantly, the Codex villa overcomes a Postmodern preference for urban images in taking the suburb or exurb as a starting point instead of wishing away the suburban condition.

The Codex headquarters building uses its classical villa allusions and the adjoining horse farm as symbols identifying a data communications organization with an aristocracy of the service economy. In such a setting it would be hard to imagine the range of extracurricular activities that take place in and around the oversized house at Domino's Farms.

The cultural activities that Domino's Pizza sponsors on its headquarters property are a rough model for other corporations that might culturally enrich their own communities. It is hardly a coordinated model, for managers struggle to implement a stream of spontaneous ideas from the Chairman's rich imagination. The critical see this activity and the Domino's Farms setting as Tom Monaghan's indulgent ego trip, and prefer corporations to give money to organizations to implement their own ideas. Nor is Ann Arbor, as a culturally rich university town, necessarily the most needy locale for this demonstration. Nevertheless, the test is in the end product and its value to the community, particularly for an offering that might not be feasible in any other way.

In summertime, the most obvious manifestation of this program is the big striped canvas circus tent beside the parking lot, undaunted by the dignity of the nearby corporate front door. The tent shelters a summer theater staging repertory musicals like 'Oklahoma', melodrama, and children's entertainment. This fare favors families and the elderly, segments of the population which commercial culture neglects as being outside its targeted market. Domino's Farms enlisted a professional company that produces cabaret and summer theater in outstate towns of Michigan.

Outside of the summer theater season, Domino's Farms hosts other events each weekend for families of Domino's Farms staff and tenants and the neighboring community. Some activities are oriented to the petting farm; there are harvest festivals, pumpkin carving contests, children's toy tractor pull events, and many others. More general activities include fun runs, a children's art fair, a fall color tour through Domino's Pizza property, a visiting circus, and tailgate parties to be bussed over to university football games.

Several of these events 'belong' to specific members of the Monaghan family as patrons. Tom Monaghan's event is the annual Frank Lloyd Wright Symposium and Festival. Marjorie Monaghan's special occasion is a Christmas Festival. There are visits of community choral groups and holiday players and a live nativity tableau in the barn. At this season the big Prairie House and its grounds are not too dignified to be decked out with a spectacular lighting display of 100,000 bulbs. The throngs of visitors testify to a surviving joy in holiday pageantry that characterized small town America in its turn-of-the-century past. Over Labor Day weekend, Tom's brother Jim sponsors an annual antique engine show drawing ancient equipment from all over the Midwest. Old self-propelled steam engines lumber around the meadow or puff smoke as they power belts for log-sawing demonstrations.

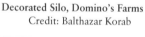

Decorated Silo, Domino's Farms
Credit: Balthazar Korab

Fall Pumpkin Harvest at Domino's Farms
Credit: Balthazar Korab

Christmas Festivities, Domino's Farms, Ann Arbor, Michigan
Credit: Balthazar Korab

Marcel Marceau, Portrait
Credit: Courtesy of Marcel Marceau

Marcel Marceau Center Proposal, 1987
Credit: Courtesy of Giffels Associates, Inc., Bruce Johnson, Designer

Domino's Farms has made overtures to the neighboring community to set up an advisory council to broaden the sponsorship and scope of some events and to be a 'think tank' for future possibilities. As proposed, the advisory council would meet twice a year, and it would include members from government, media, education, business, youth groups, and the Domino's Pizza family. The council has been dormant since an initial meeting in 1986, but reviving it would allow the community to suggest its own ideas and priorities and to help make these self-sustaining, within the limits that zoning restrictions on Domino's property will allow. Such a program would become a vehicle for volunteerism, further extending its reach. The corporation gains in the enlightened cultural climate of the community where its employees live.

Another direction for the corporation is to cultivate those cultural institutions of special excellence that can be the pride of a community while serving a broad base of tourism. Three such institutions at Domino's Farms include the Mime Center and the museum collections of automobiles and of decorative art of Wright.

The Marcel Marceau World Center for the Mime maintains its offices in the ground floor of the Prairie House. Unlike the museum collections which are owned outright by Domino's Pizza interests, this is an outside organization that is given shelter at Domino's Farms. The focus of the center is Marcel Marceau, the French pantomimist generally acknowledged as the world's greatest such performer. The center was organized through auspices of the University Musical Society, growing out of Marceau's many performances in Ann Arbor. Eugene Power, a board member of Domino's Pizza and donor of the University's fine performing arts auditorium by Kevin Roche, John Dinkeloo and Associates, brought the organizers and Tom Monaghan together.

The center seeks to conserve the heritage of pantomime for the era after Marceau's retirement as a touring performer. Lacking its own facilities but offices, the center has already promoted a summer workshop for mime in borrowed high school quarters. In the future this prototype program will grow into a year-around activity. The center proposes to build its own school building and theaters seating audiences of 500 and 2,000 spectators, respectively. Domino's Farms will furnish the land and other support, but the ambitious undertaking has drawn other funding from the Ford Motor Company Fund and the Michigan Council for the Arts. With its own home, the center will also host touring productions in mime and such related arts as Kabuki and Chinese opera.[78]

78. John Guinn, 'Miming Marceau: World Centre for Mime is a Dream Come True', in *Detroit Free Press*, 12 July 1987, p. 1E, 4E.

The museum collections at Domino's Farms opened their new temporary home early in 1988 in what will eventually be the north end of Prairie House. Domino's Classic Cars occupies a spacious ground floor, and The National Center for the Study of Frank Lloyd Wright is on the mezzanine.

To focus the visitor's attention, the automobiles appear in select groupings under downlights within the black walls and ceiling of an 'unfinished' shell of exposed construction. Curator and partner of Monaghan in the auto collection is George Crocker, a real estate investor and fellow collector with his own museum in Nag's Head, North Carolina. His own cars join Monaghan's in an array numbering over two hundred. The collection highlights postwar cars familiar to many visitors as the barely attainable dream cars of their own youth (and Monaghan's); these include a first generation Cadillac Eldorado, several early Thunderbirds, and a Tucker Torpedo. Rounding out the assortment are Jeeps and station wagons, together with elegant classic cars of the prewar period.[79]

The pearls of the collection are among the classic cars. That they are among the 'best' and 'largest' tells much about the taste of the man who commissioned Domino's Farms. The two Duesenbergs were acquired in 1985: A 1929 model 'J' roadster and a supercharged 1934 model 'SJ' dual cowl phaeton, both with Murphy bodies. When the cars were new, the conservative buyers of luxury cars didn't quite warm up to having elegant coachwork placed on America's biggest sports car chassis, and the big Duesenbergs were associated with movie stars instead. Just this combination of the best in design, craftsmanship, and machinery characteristically appealed to Monaghan.[80]

The biggest of all classic cars was the French Bugatti Royale. Only six were built. The rest of the 13-liter engines produced for unbuilt cars were put to work running passenger railcars around France. Thirty years ago, one of the Royales found a home at the Henry Ford Museum in Dearborn, thirty miles from Domino's Farms; it was given by Charles Chayne, a General Motors vice-president, who rescued it from a junkyard. Tom Monaghan acquired his own Royale in 1986 for what was then the highest price ever paid for an automobile. But again, it belonged to the best. The last-built Royale, this *Berline de Voyage* had been the personal car of Ettore Bugatti, and bore *le Patron's* monogram.[81]

79. Richard A. Wright, 'Cars, Color and Culture: Domino's Museum will Take New Approach to Auto as Art', in *Detroit News,* 15 July 1987, p. 1F.

80. Griffith Borgeson and Eugene Jaderquist, *Sports and Classic Cars* (Englewood Cliffs, NJ: Prentice-Hall, Inc., 1955), pp. 210-11.

81. Ronald Barker, *Bugatti* (New York: Ballantine Books, 1971), p. 95, 102-03, 139; Raymond Serafin, 'Tom Monaghan's Royale Obsession', in *Auto Gallery,* June 1987, pp. 22-23.

George Crocker, Portrait
Credit: Courtesy of George Crocker

Monaghan's 1932 Bugatti Royale
Credit: Domino's Pizza, Inc. Archives

Monaghan's collecting of Wright's furniture and artifacts placed Wright's own work at the top of the prevailing market for twentieth century furniture. American antiques are coming to be more valuable than corresponding European ones. Monaghan set auction records for individual pieces by bidding $198,000 for a chair and then $264,000 for a nine-drawer chest. The chair was from the Ward Willitts house of 1901, commonly acknowledged as the first complete Prairie house. The chest was a rare freestanding storage piece from the Francis Little house of 1902 in Peoria, Illinois; Wright almost universally preferred built-in storage casework, perhaps because homeowners couldn't rearrange it.[82]

Ward Willits House Dining Chair, 1902
Credit: The National Center for the Study of Frank Lloyd Wright at Domino's Farms

The market prices are dismaying to Wrightians, just the people Monaghan would like to please with his activities on behalf of Wright. The escalating prices handicap restoration budgets for Wright houses in reclaiming objects that may have left the premises long ago. Monaghan showed his strategy for this dilemma in late 1987 in a New York auction featuring items from the Susan Lawrence Dana house of 1902 in Springfield, Illinois. One of Monaghan's prize possessions among earlier acquisitions was a copper urn from this house. Governor Thompson of Illinois arrived at the auction with $600,000 in privately-raised funds to bid on five lots of items for the house. Since the successful bid would restore these to the context of a house that already preserves one of the most complete Wright settings, Monaghan declined to bid on the Governor's choices; half of the Dana house spending money was saved. Monaghan emerged from the auction with Wright material from other sources, including a house for a pet cat, designed at Taliesin in 1954 for the six-year-old daughter of a client.[83]

The Dana auction is an incident in Monaghan's emerging policy on acquisitions and preservation. To discourage the stripping of intact houses, he refrains from buying items directly from homeowners, although this can't prevent their making an end run to the auctioneers. More positively, items from his collection can be made available for reproduction in restoration projects or sent on long term loan to Wright house museums.[84] Domino's Pizza has just created an annual preservation matching grant of funds for restoration projects in Wright buildings that are open to the public (the 1987 recipient of $20,000 was the Unity Temple in Oak Park, Illinois).[85]

In time to occupy its new home, the Wright museum and archives at Domino's Farms have been

Copper Urn from Dana House, 1902
Credit: The National Center for the Study of Frank Lloyd Wright at Domino's Farms

82. Rita Reif, 'Auctions: Old Masters From Duke of Devonshire, Works by Wright', in *New York Times*, 5 July 1987, p. 26Y.

83. Rita Reif, 'Illinois Gets a Bargain at a New York Auction', in *New York Times*, 13 December 1987, p. 21Y.

84. Leaflet on 'National Center for the Study of Frank Lloyd Wright at Domino's Farms', issued by Domino's Farms Corp., 1987.

85. Daralice D. Boles, 'The Selling of Frank Lloyd Wright', in *Progressive Architecture*, November 1987, p. 118.

Usonian House Living Room at Solomon R. Guggenheim Museum, New York City
Frank Lloyd Wright Exhibition, 1953
Credit: Ezra Stoller © ESTO All Rights Reserved

formalized as the National Center for the Study of Frank Lloyd Wright. The Wright artifacts are its most obvious possessions. In addition to a wide selection of art glass windows, unusual works on display include a side table from Fallingwater and a print stand designed to exhibit Japanese prints from Wright's collection at the Art Institute of Chicago in 1908. The collection is diversified to include parallel works of designers like Sullivan and Stickley that influenced the context of design in Wright's time. The Smithsonian Institution plans to draw exclusively from this collection to mount a future traveling exhibit of Wright's work.

Two of the largest Wright objects in the collection will remain in storage until a permanent exhibition building exists. One of these is the bedroom wing from 'Northome', the second Wright home for the family of Francis Little, built in 1913 at Wayzata, Minnesota, and dismantled fifteen years ago. (The large living room from Northome stands restored in New York City's Metropolitan Museum.) The other is an entire Usonian house originally exhibited in 1953 on the site of Wright's Guggenheim Museum in New York. When the exhibit was dismantled, its fragments were stored for thirty years by David Henken, a former Taliesin apprentice; he offered

them for a public television auction in which Monaghan acquired the pieces. Reassembling them will be a puzzle, however, for they are very incomplete and dilapidated. If one or both shells are resurrected with furnishings found or recreated, their context will be even more demonstrative than the best of artifacts deprived of their setting.

The archives form the third of the Center's programs, along with the furnishings and the preservation activities. The archives constitute a growing collection of drawings, documents, and books (for example, a second edition copy of Wright's *Autobiography* in the collection was annotated by him for further revisions). The Annual Frank Lloyd Wright Symposium and Festival brings this archival and scholarly activity to life. Domino's Pizza sponsors this conference in cooperation with the University of Michigan College of Architecture and Urban Planning, meeting at Domino's Farms and the university campus. For the second conference in 1987 the archive staff edited a *Prairie House Journal* of essays.[86] Altogether, the Center's activities fulfill a longtime dream of Tom Monaghan.

Of all the prolific ideas and activities conceived by Tom Monaghan, the most far reaching one could become an organization known as Legatus.

86. *The Prairie House Journal* (Ann Arbor, MI: Domino's Pizza, Inc., April 1987), 52 pp.

This is an alliance of corporate chief executives belonging to the Roman Catholic faith. Its primary goal is to promote and reinforce Christian ethics in a business community that stands increasingly discredited for greed and a want of ethics. Of interest to our topic is a collateral purpose of encouraging executives to contribute leadership and resources to their communities—individually, rather than as a joint endeavor of the organization.[87] In this sectarian way, at least, Legatus could help to broaden the sort of corporate activity that Domino's Pizza has brought to its community and to contribute to cultural enrichment of exurban and suburban communities around the country.

Tom Monaghan's founding of Legatus is a product of his Catholic upbringing, including his living in an orphanage and his one-time candidacy for the priesthood. Monaghan has given generously to Catholic charities; he tries to preserve anonymity for these gifts, but one acknowledged gift was funding toward a Vatican computer installation.[88]

Within the Prairie House at Domino's Farms is a chapel to foster the spiritual side of his employees, just as the exercise suite attends to their physical wellbeing. Present plans propose another chapel to occupy the summit of the tower he intends to build opposite the Prairie House. High in the building, it could not accommodate more than a very small party for want of adequate fire exits for a crowd. With this limited practicality, it becomes a votive offering and another facet of the idealism that holds Tom Monaghan to the cause of his tower.

87. George White, 'Pizza King Delivering Ethics Lesson,' in *Detroit Free Press,* 24 June 1987, p. 1A, 15A.

88. White, 'Ethics Lesson,' p. 15A.

The Tower

9

Skyscrapers are only the latest manifestation of a family of towers that poetic aspirations have raised a little taller than some mundane purpose would require. Towers were unusual in the serene landscape of antiquity, yet the majority of the Greeks' chosen Seven Wonders of the World were towerlike. In a later pious age, a single elevated platform was enough for a sexton or muezzin to work in, but the spirit craved more to excess. Istanbul's Blue Mosque was given six minarets, while nine spired belfries were projected at Chartres.

Ethereal visions of imaginary towers stimulated the Romantic poets, whether the sublime, venerable 'ivy-mantled tow'r' of Gray's country churchyard or the exotic imagery of Death's 'proud tower' presiding over Poe's ephemeral city in the sea. The Romanticists were reacting to smokestacks and mine shaft housings and other towers of the new industrial landscape. In time, the best of the skyscrapers redeemed the cause of poetry, but pragmatism could sanction them only amidst others of their kind in a dynamic city.

Johnson Wax Office, 1936-1939, with Research Tower, 1947, Racine, Wisconsin
Credit: Courtesy S.C. Johnson and Son

The thought of an attainable Golden Beacon brought on Tom Monaghan's obsession with a tower. He had had eyes only for Prairie horizontality before the limitations of his Green Road office property raised the question of a vertical alternative. Larry Brink's suggestion of the Golden Beacon was the catalyst of his conversion. Frank Lloyd Wright displayed a similar obsession in raising his postwar tower at Racine to house research laboratories that were not really suited to such space. The client accepted a research tower as a symbol of a progressive company. Today, the research department has moved elsewhere, and Johnson Wax is pondering some future use for a magnificent tower standing empty.[89]

Building the Golden Beacon became the fundamental objective at Domino's Farms, although deferred, but as at Racine its utility had become ambiguous. It was already obvious that the Golden Beacon would be impractical as office space, which use, of course, Wright never intended; the Prairie House was built to house the offices instead. The idea of a conference center with hotel rooms in the tower arose sometime after the amended zoning had authorized the Golden Beacon. There were several

other such projects being promoted in the Ann Arbor area when the Golden Beacon version was announced in the spring of 1986. But gradually the Golden Beacon proposal was refined to become a 'corporate campus', the like of which was not to be found in the states between Chicago and the East Coast.

A corporate campus would exist to train executives and future executives. Its programs could help to expedite the upward mobility of Domino's Pizza people into positions of greater responsibility and let them enjoy the process. Other Fortune 500 companies could send groups of their own employees to Domino's Farms for similar training programs to account for excess capacity in the facility. The rural setting promised for Domino's Farms would be conducive to the contemplative activity in such a campus, rather like a university college; recreational facilities would be on hand for satisfying the whole person. Freeways would make the corporate campus accessible to a major metropolitan area and its airport. On weekends when the student clients departed, tourists could take their place to enjoy Domino's Farms.

The special nature of a corporate campus was outlined by Stephen Harrison, who brought most

89. Paul Goldberger, 'Wright's Vision of the Civilized Workplace', in *New York Times,* 1 November 1987, p. 44H.

of these facilities into existence. Harrison suggested that the guest arriving in the lobby should quickly comprehend that this was no mere convention hotel; why not seat a registrar behind a desk with a computer terminal in place of the usual front desk counter? The lobby should help to get the newcomer involved by showcasing some adjacent features like a media resource center and indoor tennis courts. Classrooms should be close to breakout areas for informal gatherings between sessions, and they should be equipped for teleconferencing and other up-to-date technology. An intimate gourmet restaurant should complement the dining room. On special occasions, the indoor tennis courts could double as a banquet hall or host corporate annual meetings, saving the need for such a permanent facility to keep occupied. Racquetball courts, a swimming pool, and a game room were among the essential leisure facilities, together with a golf course nearby.[90]

Domino's Farms Development Corporation promulgated a program for an eighty-million-dollar campus in November, 1986. A full-height Golden Beacon of fifty-seven stories was now proposed, rather than a stunted one of thirty. Taliesin Associated Architects did not participate this time. Gunnar Birkerts declined to draw up a Golden Beacon, and he was invited to submit an alternative tower of his own design. Giffels Associates took up the task of fleshing out the Golden Beacon, in the hands of Bruce Johnson of their staff, who had been a Taliesin apprentice. A third design was solicited from the Boston firm of Shepley, Bulfinch, Richardson and Abbott, which had designed other corporate campuses. Meanwhile, a thirty-foot mockup of the Golden Beacon stood on high ground in the fields near the tower's intended location; it was merely an ever-present reminder of one of the most compulsive of goals Tom Monaghan habitually set before himself for business objectives to fulfill.

Sometime before Christmas Gunnar Birkerts met with Tom Monaghan just before they departed on their own holiday vacations. The architect found himself regaling his client on what made architecture 'so exciting that people will come a million miles to look at it—the pyramids, the Eiffel Tower, the Leaning Tower of Pisa...'. At that instant of intuitive leap, Birkerts knew that his design must be a leaning tower, something that nobody in the world had purposely designed. 'Give me through New Year's and I will give you something to think about', Birkerts added as he left. 'I didn't sleep for a week', he recalled afterward. 'I went to New York, and then I did the sketches.'[91]

90. 'Architectural Program: Domino's/Whitney Corporate Campus', prepared by Whitney Learning Centers Inc., March 1987.

91. Author's interview with Gunnar Birkerts, 7 July 1987.

Cathedral Campanile, Begun 1174, Pisa, Italy
Credit: Balthazar Korab

92. Frampton, *Modern Architecture,* p. 170; Nikolaus Pevsner, *Pioneers of Modern Design from William Morris to Walter Gropius* (New York: Museum of Modern Art, 1949), p. 145.

93. Gunnar Birkerts, 'Notes on the Tower' (typewritten memorandum dated August 12, 1987), 1p.

94. Correspondence dated 5 June 1987 from M. Rohde (Domino's Pizza, Inc.) to Edward R. Heaps (Federal Aviation Administration).

95. Memorandum No. 3 dated June 16, 1987, Gunnar Birkerts & Associates, item 4.

Of course, even a purposely-leaning tower is not really new, and Birkerts was aware of modern precedents. The slant of the Tower of Pisa was an accident, of course, slightly corrected in the topmost story. But there was Vladimir Tatlin's unbuilt Monument to the Third International. This was a Constructivist design of 1919 with an open framework spiraling upward supposedly to half again the height of the Eiffel Tower; within its cagework rotated enclosures in geometrical shapes. There were the four openwork legs of the Eiffel Tower itself, leaning inward toward one another while ascending to the first and second platforms. There were the Futurist apartment houses and other city buildings as imagined by Antonio Sant'Elia in his *Citta Nuova* designs of 1914; some of these tilted back as slabs of corbelled stories, but stabilizing props were drawn in behind them.[92]

None of these modern towers cantilevered out noticeably beyond the perimeter of its own foundations. Birkerts' tower would do so while leaning at an angle of fifteen degrees from the vertical (three times the cant of the tower at Pisa, the Sunday guides at Domino's Farms will tell you). According to Birkerts, this was 'a modest one by comparison to Frank Lloyd Wright's Fallingwater, which is a ninety degree cantilever off the vertical.'[93]

The fate of the Golden Beacon design was probably settled by early spring of 1987, whatever the economics of building it might be. The Federal Aviation Authority advised Domino's Pizza that the 550-foot tower proposed would obstruct the flight approaches to nearby airports. The height of the tower must not exceed 435 feet above ground level.[94] Once again, a Golden Beacon of less than full height was mandated. Tom Monaghan swallowed his disappointment in a meeting at Domino's Farms on June 15, 1987; he accepted Birkerts' design for the cantilever tower.[95]

Gunnar Birkerts describes his cantilever tower as 'rural sculpture'. The slanting form is too dynamic to share a city skyline with other buildings. Neighboring buildings and future neighbors create accidental, unpredictable relationships with the unorthodox mass and conceal vital aspects of its form. Another owner's building in close proximity may send unintended symbolic messages about its relationship to Domino's Pizza. Birkerts points out that zoning setbacks and other codes make such a building unlikely on an urban site in any case. Wright's towers, too, were criticized as being too lively to coexist with a typical urban fabric, and we remember that he wanted a rural opportunity for them.

If the cantilever tower is not urban, then what will make it rural? The answer lies in the limits of a controlled composition. At Domino's Farms there will be only the Prairie House and the tower's own low conference center pedestal to encounter. Encircling all will be a green landscape in which zones of parked cars will be the most intrusive element. Without the owner's acquiescence (and that of the township planners) no other building will be within range to interrupt this visual dialogue.

Tatlin Model of Monument to the Third International, 1920
Credit: Statens Konstmuseer, Moderna Museet, Stockholm, Sweden

Eiffel Tower, Paris, France, 'Looking Up'
Credit: Gordon Bugbee

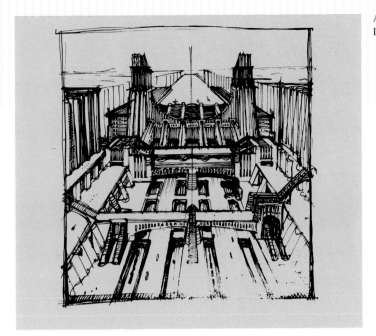

Antonio Sant'Elia, Central Station
Project for Milan, Italy, 1914
Credit: Museo Civico
Como, Italy

Across a ponded gap of about twice the width of the Prairie House itself, the cantilever tower will point toward its long consort, acknowledging a relationship actively. At its full length, the Prairie House will be equal to the presence of this dynamic partner. A conventional tower—the Golden Beacon included—would be more self-centered, expressing mostly its own challenge to gravity.

There is an illusion of motion in both buildings, but that of the cantilever tower is most obvious. The tower is in the tradition of Futurism and Expressionism from early in the century. Sant'Elia's city, with its canting structures, demanded to be wholly new and well coordinated, lest fragments of its forms be at odds with existing urbanism, just as Birkerts' tower would be. The cryptic expressionistic sketches that Erich Mendelsohn jotted down as a soldier in the trenches of World War I raised similar challenges. Sant'Elia and Mendelsohn belonged to an age experiencing mechanized travel at high speeds for the first time. At this distance in time, we can reasonably wonder why Mendelsohn's railroad station should want to empathize with its rolling stock. Four decades later the heir to Mendelsohn's sketches in Expressionism was the suspended catenary roof of the Dulles Airport Terminal outside Washington. This was Eero Saarinen at his best, at the dawn of jet airplane travel attended by his terminal.

The nagging question lingers why buildings should want to appear in motion, except in normal opposition to gravity. Eliel Saarinen's Tribune Tower design was a logical prototype of the soaring skyscraper, an illusion of motion that is easier to accept.

People also quickly became accustomed to the metaphor of hovering flight in his son's air terminal.

The two buildings at Domino's Farms will offer differing visual sensations of motion. At its ultimate length the long Prairie House will seem to vibrate longitudinally, rather like the wave action of a taut violin string between fixed ends. (Only from the tower will the restraining berms of the terminal ends be visible in one scanning glance.) The illusion of motion in each building will be heightened by the presence of its partner.

The tower's own illusion of motion will be more complex. A slanting mass suggests imbalance or great effort to remain in place. Birkerts describes this as 'a dynamic interaction, almost kinetic, with the gravity force visibly searching for the ground.' He adds that 'it is intended to evoke emotional response to it.'[96]

But the excitement of a building straining to avoid collapse is distressing to a visitor arriving with a room reservation, no matter how reassuring engineering and elapsed time may be. Birkerts is not merely indulging in applied engineering, however; he is manipulating form. The crest of the tower is curved to give the whole mass a sense of upward surge or of attenuation from some unseen hand pulling on its comb as a handle (the parallax of upward perspective as seen from the ground will enhance this sensation). Birkerts has put his tower in apparent jeopardy and then begins to rescue it. The contest between what seems to be opposing forces is a more sporting one, constituting the drama of the design.

In this tower Birkerts has reined in the vigorous structural features of earlier buildings like the

96. Gunnar Birkerts, 'Notes on the Tower', 1p.

105

Federal Reserve Bank in Minneapolis. The shape of the mass is responsible for the dynamic tension. The role of structure expressed in the form of the tower tends to be supportive where it can be reassuring and to be minimized where it would send a disconcerting message.

The boldest structural forms are the stair towers projecting as thick ridges from both sloping surfaces. They appear to stiffen the mass (as they do in fact, their side walls being continuations of the parallel corridor walls containing both vertical columns and diagonal bracing in an opposing direction). The elevator shafts emerge as a vertical prop at the lower face of the cantilevered facade. It became necessary when the elevator manufacturer declined to engineer elevators for a sloping shaft. To the purist it will be a vexing intrusion, but to others it will offer reassurance.

Against the side walls, preliminary studies show a smooth skin which is intended to be of bronze anodized aluminum panels with joint lines expressed. Windows of the guest rooms will become a punched texture in an allover pattern within the slanting lines of column cover panels. On these sides the early studies show a subtle expression of the columns on the faces, leaving the wall as an apparent diaphragm resisting wracking. Letting these side columns project more boldly would suggest that the unbraced supports can't resist sliding sideways in collapse. (Of course, at this writing when early studies are still being developed, any closer examination of building features may be premature.)

The motorist approaching on the freeway will see the tower from afar, for this will be the tallest habitable building in Michigan outside of Detroit and its suburbs. The motorist may welcome the opportunity for orientation that a directional tower offers. The student client of the corporate campus will find the way to the tower through the freeway cloverleaf and exit ramp to connecting roads and drives, guided by such orientation. If a motorist seeking the Domino's Pizza headquarters reaches the tower by mistake, there remains the best possible approach to the Prairie House on the bridge crossing the pond from the base of the tower.

The value of a unique corporate symbol is the justification for the cantilever tower. 'I wanted a building that is memorable, that can be described', Birkerts has said. 'Maybe you come back to it, or you tell others about it. It is a landmark, and at the same time it promotes who built it. "What building is it? Blue, red, or green?" "No, it is leaning."' [97]

The role of a corporate symbol is the primary thrust of the program. Equally essential, the cantilever tower recognizes the owner, just as the Prairie House respected his wishes for Wrightian forms. The Chairman of Domino's Pizza is known to enjoy things that are the biggest, the best, or unique in some definite way, like his Bugatti Royale, or the champion Tigers, or the longest copper roof in the world. It will inevitably be called the 'Leaning Tower of Pizza', but it will measure up.

To Birkerts, 'The architecture of this building has expanded its traditional role of functional accommodation, visual complacency, and the general structural and technological attitude of generic highrise structures. It is destined to excite, compel, and to deliver a new facet in modern architecture.' [98]

Against the giant scale of the tall cantilever tower and a headquarters building whose length is seven times the height of the tower, a natural landscape will be essential. Only the prairie grass originally intended can live up to the mammoth buildings. Arnold Palmer and his associate, Ed Seay, have been commissioned to design an eighteen-hole golf course, of which only eleven holes can be accommodated on the perimeter fringe of the 300-acre site (the rest may be situated across Highway M-14). It, too, will benefit from the prairie grass in contrast to its own clipped fairway lawns. Paul Raeder compares the reflexive compulsion to trim all grass with the embarrassment a corporate executive would feel if his front lawn went uncut for the summer. The context of Domino's Farms is entirely different from a suburban ranch house.

The Domino's Pizza executive may be evangelized in favor of a Wrightian house for which such formalities are unneccessary, however. A 400-acre tract north of Highway M-14 is intended as an executive subdivision with its own golf course. Tom Monaghan plans to have Fay Jones design a house for his family there.

The future of this greater Domino's Farms remains to be unveiled. Sites remain to be announced for the Mime Center and the permanent museum quarters, among other buildings. This is an opportunity for a harmonious array of farms, residences, and other buildings. It is an opportunity for buildings compatible with one another and with the design philosophy of the existing work, each according to its purpose, instead of a set of art objects scattered capriciously. And this opportunity may offer a real model of an ideal community for the present day instead of more of suburbia and exurbia 'in the haphazard making'.

97. Author's interview with Gunnar Birkerts, 7 July 1987.

98. Gunnar Birkerts, 'Notes on the Tower', 1p.

BOOK THREE

Epilogue

Conclusions

1

1. As cited in Antoinette Martin, 'Down on the Farms', in *Detroit* magazine, *Detroit Free Press*, 11 October 1987, p. 21; and in Lowell Cauffiel, 'Eye of the Needle', in *Detroit Monthly*, January 1988, p. 84.

2. Merrill Folsom, *Great American Mansions and their Stories* (New York: Hastings House, 1963), pp. 122, 125, 129; Stewart H. Holbrook, *The Age of the Moguls* (Garden City, NY: Doubleday & Company, 1953), pp. 309-10, 358-59.

People who are not accustomed to praising buildings seem to enjoy Domino's Farms instinctively. The Sunday tourists and the Christmas Lighting spectators come seeking little more critical understanding than perhaps some notion of what Frank Lloyd Wright has to do with what they see.

Those who find fault with Domino's Farms tend to settle on one of two issues. Some dismiss the whole spread as Tom Monaghan's ego trip, along with the costly purchases of classic cars and Wrightian chairs. Others, as critics of aesthetics, question the nature of the link to Wright.

The first critics often compare Domino's Farms to San Simeon, the baronial enclave of William Randolph Hearst.[1] In his younger years as an incipient press lord backed by a fortune in gold mining, Hearst conceived yellow journalism and, some say, the Spanish American War to win newspaper subscriptions. By the twenties he owned a nationwide newspaper empire. On a California estate one-fifth the size of Delaware, Julia Morgan designed for him a truly eclectic melange much grander than any palace. It had cathedral ceilings in real life and chambers and components pried loose from venerable castles of Europe. Life at San Simeon was a hedonistic movie-set existence staged for Hearst and his actress companion, Marion Davies, and whatever close friends could live up to their supporting roles with a straight face.[2]

William Randolph Hearst's Castle, La Cuesta Encantada, 1919-1925, San Simeon, California
Credit: © Hearst San Simeon State Historical Monument, All Rights Reserved. Photo by John Blades.

Stewart Holbrook considered Hearst to be the last of a line of moguls he traced back to Commodore Vanderbilt. The Edwardian moguls showed off their trophies to their peers in privacy as part of a spectacle the public beheld only distantly through closed gates. The public shared the treasures only later, if at all, as a commemorative museum bequest. The state-owned San Simeon is now one of California's chief tourist attractions.

The analogy is unfair to Tom Monaghan. Office workers and tourists set Domino's Farms apart from San Simeon and its Edwardian predecessors. The pizza magnate is entertaining the public and his Dominoids *now*. The cars in the new exhibition building will indulge public nostalgia in the favorite topic of the nearby Motor City. The Wrightian exhibits upstairs will be more pedagogical for a cause their patron believes in much more positively than with mere dilettantish affectation. Finally, it is not really cynical to recognize that the whole campus brings exposure to Domino's Pizza in places where paid advertising doesn't penetrate.

The question of architectural pedigree is more complex. Some critics feel that Domino's Farms does not go far enough in imagery and detailing to deserve comparison with Wright's work. An opposing view expresses surprise that a work of a perceived Minimalist like Birkerts goes as far as it does in donning Prairie house mannerisms. A third view challenges Domino's Farms philosophically as organic architecture.

The first two objections tend to neutralize each other. The headquarters building cannot satisfy both positions, and it doesn't go very far to satisfy either. It hardly suggests what Wright might have designed for Domino's Pizza if he had been given thirty more years to live. Nor does the building resemble any particular building of Wright's, the Banff summer hotel notwithstanding. At best, like Birkerts' proposal for the cantilever tower, it is the sort of bold gesture Wright achieved with projects like the Mile High tower or the Marin County civic buildings in California. There is latent historicism in the owner's original prescription of hipped roofs, horizontal ribbon windows and the like, in the correlations with window and wall patterns of Prairie houses, and in the raked horizontal joints of Robie house brickwork (which was also a common Usonian detail). This is all rather general as executed, however. A better comparison might be made with current interest in context.

It is easy to forget that the headquarters building was designed to be a good neighbor to an unfulfilled Golden Beacon tower, which presumably

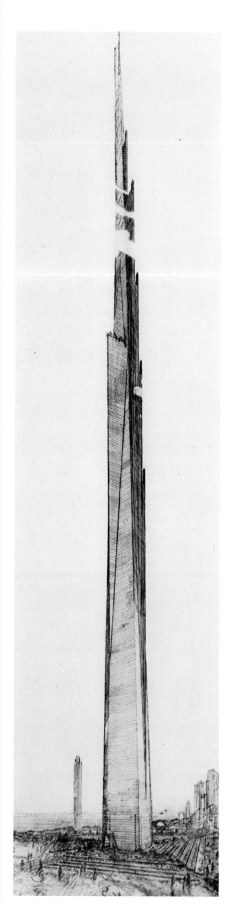

Mile High Skyscraper 'The Illinois', 1959 Chicago, Illinois

would have had more impeccable Wrightian credentials. Respect for context, more commonly in urban settings, is one of the more attractive themes of Postmodernism. It sees merit in the human record of a locale as deserving as much consideration as a rock outcropping to be built upon in the most natural wilderness. Design extracts an essence of the best of accumulated forms and improves upon them, reconciled with modern experience in space and materials. Frank Lloyd Wright could not have accepted this argument at face value, having spent a lifetime creating an architecture more innately American than comes from such imagery. But for architects whose buildings must coexist with others at close range, contextualism offers one way to begin.

Second generation Art Deco towers like those of Philip Johnson and Helmut Jahn are a current example. They reinforce a sense of place in the Chicago Loop or the New York Battery skyline, already rich in the stalagmite skyscrapers of the twenties.

When fashion scatters the new towers across the country indiscriminately, however, cities begin to look as much alike as they did with glass boxes of the International Style. A new tower breaks the spell in Philadelphia where previous buildings could rise no taller than the City Hall tower. Seattle and Indianapolis are receiving their first tall examples. The glass boxes were at least claiming to represent a universal architecture, however little we care for the notion today.

The question remains how contextualism can be reconciled with principles of organic synthesis. Tom Monaghan's instinctive choice of a Wrightian Prairie idiom for a Michigan meadow might have been as good a start as any. As Birkerts suggests, such directives become part of the data to be synthesized. At some point, however, a developing contextual approach will sacrifice the organic design process for a preconceived envelope, as would have been true of an enlarged McCormick house with a change of program.

Marin County Civic Building, 1959, California
Credit: Joshua Freiwald

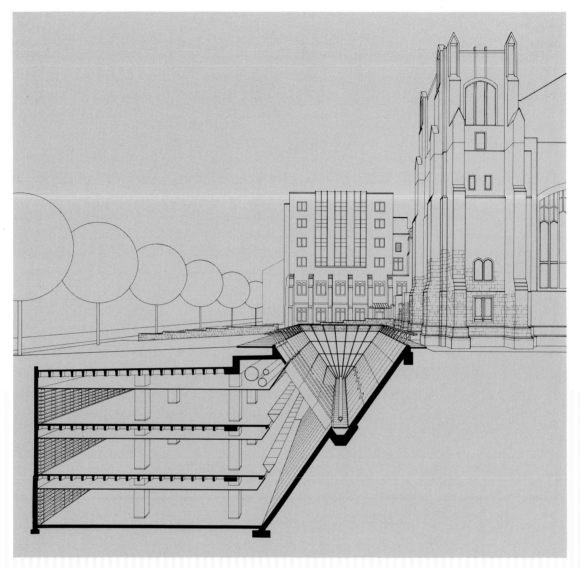

University of Michigan, Law School Addition, 1974-1981, Ann Arbor, Michigan
Credit: Courtesy of Gunnar Birkerts and Associates, Inc. Architects

Gunnar Birkerts rarely seems so accommodating to the current spirit of contextualism as here. His closest previous encounter would have been the unbuilt embassy in Finland or the Lincoln School in Columbus, but both belong to his vocabulary. The underground building has become his customary response to a setting charged with specific character. His addition to the Law School Library at the University of Michigan is buried under a lawn. Daylight reaches it through a 'moat' of sloping glass set in metal mullions. The contemporary components hardly intrude upon the 'Oxford college quadrangle' aura of the Law School buildings beyond, and preserved open space is a dividend. For similar reasons he placed a library ad-

dition within a berm at Cornell University. Birkerts recently proposed comparable underground extensions to the century-old Michigan State Capitol building in Lansing.

In this question of imagery, the architectural critic Robert Benson prescribed a suitable role for Domino's Farms in previewing the newly-occupied first phase building for *Inland Architect*. When he wrote, only contractors' earthwork suggested the magnitude of the present southerly extensions. Professor Benson concluded:

'If, when it is finished, Domino's World Headquarters is successful as pure architecture, it will be because Birkerts has in fact managed to project his own personality through the Wrightian matrix imposed on him. He will have produced a synthesis that indeed transcends and overreaches the initial personal demands of the patron in the commission. That will probably bring Birkerts closer to the spirit of Frank Lloyd Wright than any approximation of the Prairie School could. And it will also inaugurate a new period in Birkerts' career: One which is endowed with a richer and more pluralistic imagery than is possible in the exclusive world of totally abstract form.[3]

The extreme ends of the ultimate headquarters building suggest such an example of Birkerts' personality in design. Buried in terminal berms, they expose little more than a giant triangle of the hipped roof floating on eaves over a ribbon of tinted glass as a shadow line. The broad glass sheets separated by slender metal mullions retain only a memory of Prairie house art glass in a ribbon of wooden casements. Except in its eave detailing, the sixty-foot-wide expanse of hipped roof is relieved only by a texture of parallel seams.

This triangle abides by the abstract geometry Birkerts prefers in his other work. Even the first master plans of John Howe and of Birkerts himself could not resist breaking up the broad expanse of the blunt ends with triangular bay projections, which their client considered annoying excrescences. Wright brought the end of his Marin County building close to the ground too, but embellished the curved roof with decorative circular forms. Birkerts' simplification lives up to the magnitude of the executed building, which steps down in scale primarily at the main entrancing, which steps down in scale primarily at the main entrance trellis, where visitors will be more comfortable. In its simplicity the building will be an equal partner with the can setting for the rich, delicate jewel of the supplanted Golden Beacon. (This is not to denigrate background buildings; they are part of the real meaning of contextualism.)

To appraise Domino's Farms as organic architecture is separate from the issue of Wrightian resemblances. Bruno Zevi[4] and Birkerts[5] between them have suggested some two dozen names of architects (happening to be mostly European in this instance) known to have subscribed to organic design principles. Organic architecture concerns a process, we remind ourselves. We must not be surprised that hardly any Wrightian look-alikes turn up in pictures of their best-known work. To examine Domino's Farms as organic architecture summons some basic principles. Its example may suggest what an architect may learn today from Wright, although a more comprehensive discussion of Wright's value today is beyond the scope of this writing.

Organic architecture invokes a process 'growing out of the inner functioning, the inner meaning, the inner necessity', to repeat Birkerts' interpretation.[6] The result should be an integrated architecture of a harmony between small and large elements, from within to the outdoors and the interfacing world. It must respond indiscriminately and satisfactorily to such criteria as space conception, construction, materials, structure, visual ordering, environment, site, and, where appropriate, metaphor.

This is no mechanistic process, and a logical diagram does not constitute a building. The architect's creativity must intervene to invoke specific architecture. Birkerts ascribes this extra step to intuition. The product of intuition may seem correct in retrospect, perhaps in the way Wright felt that only a specific building would result from given circumstances. But the achievement of intuition is hardly automatic, and only experience can guide the architect's choices. Most important, the product of intuition cannot arbitrarily set aside the synthesis that should have led toward it.

The prerogatives of intuition also invite the diverse imagery possible in contemporary architecture. Organic principles must remain as an axiomatic foundation of design, however. Postmodernism may suffer in the degree to which an architect may set these principles aside in favor of merely manipulating pictorial conceptions. Organic principles are more than a historical residue of Wright. Even without his polemical voice to support them, they remain as a conscience for good practice as a starting point in design. With Wright's example in their past, architects cannot be innocent enough to revive the eclectic Battle of the Styles: To reconstitute the Art Deco supplanted by Modernism just as, nearly a century ago, Ralph Adams Cram tried to retrieve the cause of English Medieval architecture overwhelmed long before by a 'pagan' Renaissance. If intuition is a path to diversity, however, its unpredictable results cause insecure architects and critics to hedge it about with *a priori* theoretical controls as a substitute for the organic synthesis. Except as *a posteriori* discipline for analyzing a design, theory in this role can be as academically blighting as were the inhibitions of mainstream postwar Modernism.

Space is the initial reality of the architect's conception, even before form begins to materialize. The flow and modulation of space should respond

3. Robert A. Benson, 'Gunnar Birkerts and The Domino Theory', in *Inland Architect,* January-February 1986, p. 27.

4. Bruno Zevi, 'Frank Lloyd Wright and Contemporary Architecture', address to symposium, 'The Wright Hand', at University of Michigan, 13 April 1985 (reprinted in unpaginated proceedings).

5. Refer to page 71 above.

6. Refer to page 71 above.

to human movement and being at rest and to visibility which is vicarious movement. The modulation of space, large and small, high and low, should communicate order, however rich the experience may be.

Birkerts' 'track' master plan constitutes his most basic claim to be implementing organic design principles at Domino's Farms, with options anticipating the orderly extension of interior space. Organic architecture provides for the needs of a building which may never be considered finished. A building starting with a symmetrical plan is almost always suspect in this way, except with the most basic program. The ultimate appearance of Domino's Farms should not really match the model the Sunday visitors examine in the main lobby, but there should be an affinity between the two. In an extreme scenario of corporate growth, Birkerts would add more tracks to the present seven.[7]

As we have observed, the principal weakness of Domino's Farms as organic architecture also concerns interior space. There seems to be a gap in the process that allows critics to see mere caprice in the resulting building envelope of cascading roofs. The work spaces, where the observer is at rest, are compatible with the building shape in cross section. The ambiguity lies in the intervening spaces for movement. Meaningful modulation of space, rather than great spaces in themselves, constitutes the remedy. Exasperated visitors get lost in and around the great atrium spaces of many buildings of the recent past, made needlessly complex in order to be interesting.

The cantilever tower offers a limited prospect of redemption, and this is primarily in manipulating the public areas within the base from which the tower springs. At this writing it would be premature to judge the result of evolving preliminary designs. The tower itself is cellular in small guest rooms and is reached by elevator travel. It can hardly achieve even the play of interior space in the two-story apartments of Wright's Price Tower.

A building designed by organic principles must respect constructional needs. We have seen that Wright favored large buildings in reinforced concrete offering integrity of structure and surfaces. Yet it would seem needlessly rigid to equate concrete construction with organic architecture. Critics seeing brickwork carried on steel framing at construction sites of Domino's Farms may consider that a throwback to similar construction in the Robie house and the Larkin Building, built before Wright fully embraced concrete. But such criteria as speed of erection and flexibility in accommodating future changes in con-

cealed electronic utilities are valid objections to casting concrete floors and walls.

Tom Monaghan speaks of 'organic materials,' and we easily understand that these include the traditional brick, stone, wood, and copper. Wright was the first American architect to use concrete creatively, however, and he was not averse to new materials like the tubular glazing at Racine. Materials are not foreordained to be new or traditional; circumstances prescribe their choice. Stone obtained on site tied Taliesin to its setting, and in that locale it was the only affordable building material in the Depression era.[8] Birkerts takes pride in investigating innovative materials, but he attains one of the most pleasing subtleties of the Prairie House in traditional materials. The lower edges of roofs growing greenish in weathered copper are bordered in grayish lead-coated copper. The effect distinguishes the roof slopes from one another.

The roofscapes contribute a metaphor of 'home,' taming the magnitude of Domino's Farms. The Sunday visitors recognize this instinctively, and this is a test of an effective symbol. Symbolism is useful in communicating order, whether instructively as in Wright's 'tree' towers or poetically as in Wrightian names of houses like 'Snowflake.' Symbolism need not be blatantly apparent, for this sacrifices something of a joy of discovery. When it is needlessly obscure or lacks empirical ties to public awareness, however, symbolism risks becoming artificial imagery shared only by an informed elite.

The same becomes true of the search for archetypes in history to mold and explain the corporate headquarters building as a building type. The architect who originally conceived his Codex Headquarters design as a classical villa now compares it to a New England village common.[9] Both analogies are meaningless to office workers who know neither Hadrian's Villa nor Deerfield. Even as skyscrapers, the modern office building arrived with no archetypes except the farfetched classical column, and the sort of synthesis of fundamentals that produced the Larkin Building occurred rarely. In the site plan of Domino's Farms one could posit the Baroque palace as an archetype, with a paved entrance court of honor on the opposite side of the building from a formal garden. The parade ground pavement where the Sun King received awestruck ambassadors at Versailles explains little about the modern problem of parking lots, nor would its literary conceit make parking lots any more palatable. In any case, the archetype vanishes in the third dimension, as it should.

7. Author's interview with Gunnar Birkerts, 23 June 1987.

8. Edgar Tafel, *Years With Frank Lloyd Wright: Apprentice to Genius* (New York: Dover Publications, Inc., 1979), p. 137.

9. Julie V. Iovine, 'The Elusive Model,' in *Metropolis,* December 1987, p. 50.

The goal of organic architecture is a richer way of life. The client has furnished this beyond the customary scope of a workplace at Domino's Farms. No master plan could really have anticipated the organism that evolved as the Domino's Farms community. One of the benefits of the ongoing construction work there is that the architect and the client can continually reappraise the work remaining to be built through experience with the occupied building and the way people use it. Without turning to such empiricism, architects are often poor sociologists. One of the failings of Modernism was the architects' imposing a seemingly logical routine on people unwilling to behave so mechanically. Today's architects are more often criticized for letting aesthetic preoccupations make them oblivious to improving a way of life.

The organism is habitually called the 'Domino's Pizza family' by company officials. The word 'family' is felicitous. Americans tend to equate capitalism with individualism, but the two are not necessarily equivalent. One is a type of economy, and the other is a personal philosophy. The Japanese have become successful in combining aggressive capitalism with a familial corporate style that meets human needs of workers for input and recognition. The corporate family supports the individual.

The American alternative is too often a macho 'bottom line' regimen drawn from analogies to sports or the military. This can be divisive as egos struggle to assert themselves. In sports there is ultimately only one winner, while everybody wins in a properly functioning family.

An architect cannot plant this ingredient in his building, but his preconceptions and neglect can frustrate it. Suppressing barriers can encourage a familial organism. The lowrise Domino's Pizza World Headquarters brings all departments under the same copper roof, from executive offices to warehouses. In the open office areas, departments flow together without boundaries apparent to a visitor passing through, and they can borrow space from one another as needs change. This is not true of tall buildings where each floor is limited arbitrarily and work processing travels between floors.

Loss of boundaries need not suppress departmental and personal identity. At Domino's Farms the entrance courtyards offer 'front door' identity that should extend upstairs in an internal node to a single department or several sharing departments. Staff members come to work each morning through the same path departmental visitors will use during the day. Within a department, personal

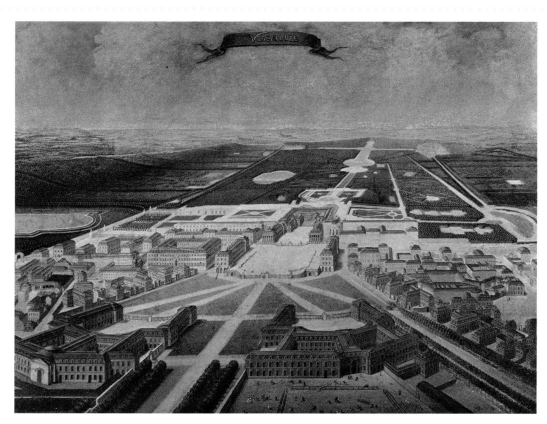

Versailles France—Late 17th Century
Credit: Haeseler/Art Resource, New York

identity can survive without degenerating into a scramble for status symbols like a larger office. One possible answer would be to offer choices in available furnishings and arrangements in combinations too variable to confer status. Space should exist for family pictures and personal effects in a place where staff members spend a majority of their waking hours. Above all, private office cubicles should not monopolize all the windows overlooking the green outdoors justifying the suburban office building.

Too often, the view is of parked cars and pavement, of course. For Domino's Farms, parking spots for staff and visitors can be close to the dispersed departmental entrances. Islands of plantings mitigate the extent of pavement, together with the more distant view of the site's peripheral greenbelt. An exposed parking lot is indispensible for most suburban office buildings. For all but a single story building, it must measure several times the footprint of the building.

Parking garages on several levels are usually the only option for a suburban office tower. Their customary utilitarian appearance is improved primarily with earthwork and plantings. Hiding them beneath a lowrise office building deprives it of contact with the surrounding landscape, elevated on a monumental pedestal. Public transportation is rarely an effective alternative in metropolitan suburbs, although some companies keep or hire their own bus fleets for their employees.

The greenbelt is pleasant, but at the noon hour it signifies isolation from town. Thirty years ago, planners for the prototypical Connecticut General headquarters outside Hartford recognized that 'because there would be no noontime opportunity for downtown errands and shopping, services such as barber and hairdressing and a well-stocked club store' would have to be provided inside the building.[10] Remote suburban headquarters buildings have furnished such amenities ever since. A progressive company breaks down other barriers by minimizing use of an executive dining room in favor of upgrading the employee cafeteria into something comfortable for all. Sometimes this will be a completely detached building to help office workers get away from their working environment during the precious lunch hour. At Domino's Farms, of course, a pizza store is an alternative to the regular E. B. A. ('Everything But Anchovies') Club, soon to be supplemented by other snack shops for additional options. The physical fitness suite and the chapel there provide

for other personal needs, and a downstairs tenant for sports medicine constitutes a medical presence in the building. There are plans for a day care center to ease the burden of the two-income family.

The weekend events and extracurricular activities at Domino's Farms bring real families together on strictly social occasions. Involving the public as well helps to make these activities viable without implying obligations for office workers who have their own weekend preferences. These activities enrich and reach out to the surrounding community. Retirees keep in touch with former colleagues there, a reminder that life has continuity beyond the working years.

An ample peripheral greenbelt and relatively direct access to highway connections help Domino's Farms to coexist with the community beyond it. Roofscapes do their part to make a large building feel at home. The decision to make the tower a conference center instead of office space mitigates the ultimate traffic load, especially at rush hour. Office work and training programs keep different hours, and the latter tend to ensnare their charges on the premises for days at a time. The golf course serving the conference center will also assure a meadow uncluttered with additional buildings and their parking lots.

Some observers feel that people must move closer to their workplaces to make the metropolitan suburbs viable and unclog their expressways and streets.[11] Too often this is unrealistic. The same land speculation Wright disliked in cities now raises suburban land values to price homes beyond the reach of younger families. Dispersion and traffic result. In an extreme case like Los Angeles, large houses or duplexes are replacing smaller homes on the same lot, leading to a compact way of life that is the antithesis of the easygoing openness that drew people to California in the past.[12] It becomes easy to accept this as an era of diminished expectations.

There were probably never more diminished expectations than in the Depression era when Frank Lloyd Wright conceived the Usonian house and formulated Broadacre City as promises for a better future. To conserve a way of life and fulfill a suburban dream of long standing, a balance must be kept between buildings and nature. An office building in the countryside may stay within reach of appropriate homes its workers can afford to own. The future plans of Tom Monaghan at Domino's Farms may demonstrate how this compact with nature and the countryside can be kept.

10. 'Background of the Connecticut General Building', undated pamphlet Z1719 of Connecticut General Life Insurance Company (available for building tours in 1958), pp. 22-23.

11. Charles Lockwood and Christopher B. Leinberger, 'Los Angeles Comes of Age', in The Atlantic Monthly, January 1988, p. 54.

12. Philip Langdon, 'Where Sprawl Comes to Squeeze: Solving New Problems of Density in Los Angeles', in The Atlantic Monthly, January 1988, p. 85.

BOOK FOUR

Prairie House Portfolio

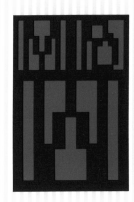

Special Note:
All illustrations in
Prairie House Portfolio, unless
otherwise credited, are
provided by Gunnar Birkerts
and Associates, Inc.,
Architects.

Corporations and the suburban developers who build for them are among the most conspicuous patrons of architecture in the eighties. Pushing beyond the nodes of the suburban shopping centers, the new corporate home offices and regional headquarters buildings line the expressways beyond green lawns in the same way those equally inaccessible corporate emblems, the Edwardian mansions, once lined the Lake Shore Drive. The new products are slick and competent, becoming fragmented boxes surfaced in colored reflective glass or in horizontal stripes of windows and spandrels, perhaps with a glazed atrium exposed. They seem interchangeable, and personnel transferred between regions or between corporations would quickly feel at home again. The common facade vocabulary shows only slight competitive inroads of the Postmodernism that distinguishes most of the new towers downtown. In the suburbs, the publicly held corporation is fastidious, but not adventurous, in its taste.

Domino's Farms is a major exception in this highway panorama. The tyranny of the flat roof is suppressed. The great mass housing Southeastern Michigan's largest privately held corporation is subdued in scale by its roofs reaching down toward the ground. The untamed landscape in the foreground suggests the previously existing rural setting into which the Prairie House blends so well. The prospect is far different from the previous development proposals of 1,100 houses filling up the site. Domino's Farms has readily responded to the individual taste of one corporate leader, something few publicly held corporations can accomplish. On behalf of his company, Tom Monaghan has become one of the most colorful patrons of architecture in our era. A pizza maker as a recognized critic of good building seems incongruous to some, but the example helps to break the elitist pretensions of architecture, and the results at Domino's Farms speak for themselves. It is certainly more edifying than the spectacle of a New York casino king as tastemaker to our cultural capital.

One may envy Tom Monaghan for being able to make things happen with a wave of the hand. In reality, building the Prairie House by stages has required teamwork drawing from many disciplines in design and construction, responding to the corporation's own staff under its monitor, John McDevitt. The continuity in participating organizations since the initial groundbreaking in 1984 suggests that a successful working relationship has prevailed. A chart accompanying this writing identifies these organizations and their key personnel. A separate time chart arrays significant events in the ongoing design and construction of the Prairie House, with an informative special focus on the intensive sixteen months between groundbreaking and moving day in the first construction phase. The prolific ideas of Tom Monaghan take time to germinate, but authorized projects proceed quickly. The cost of borrowed money and the needs of a growing organization intrude on any dream world.

For all the necessary teamwork, the process functions best when it funnels through a single design architect to achieve a coherent conception, like sand passing through an hourglass. Tom Monaghan's unorthodox preferences assured a project of character, but the specifics belong to the designer's pencil. A selection of conceptual sketches of Gunnar Birkerts is included in this portfolio to reveal several exploratory intervals in the design process.

Do these sketches signify an organic approach to design? It would be unfair to expect a small number of drawings to represent the full range of harmonizing even the smallest components with the overall conception. It is of course disconcerting to know that much of the internal appearance was considered to be outside of Birkerts' scope, and one would like to know of any compensating strategy for resolving these gaps in the future. The clearest manifestation of an organic design approach lies in the early appearance of the track format in the conceptual sketches leading to the accepted master plan. Equally significant are the ground level penetrations of the building, acting as dispersed departmental front doors and suggesting the possibility of order within. By contrast, imposing the McCormick House format of courtyards and wings on the aborted master plans inhibited any organic approach. What is an attractive residential setting for a garden party provokes anxiety instead when transposed to an office context at larger scale, whether for a stranger trying to keep an appointment or a new employee delivering a report. Unlike the differentiated rooms of a mansion, the homogeneity of office space encompassing a maze of courtyards accentuates this ambiguity.

Can the tower be considered to embody organic design principles, or is it merely a sculptural corporate symbol? The several conceptual studies presented are concerned with refining form arrived at intuitively, and do not yet show the 'filling in the gaps' between intuition and synthesis to produce the structural and spatial integrity under the skin. The answer would concern possible benefits that the cantilever form contributes to guest rooms, something more positive than a lack of inconveniences. For example, some rooms would enjoy a dramatic view through a slanting window sash directing attention to the Prairie House roof below, as seen from a room seemingly floating in space. One photograph in the accompanying portfolio shows such a view from the position of the proposed penthouse, as taken from a helicopter.

The photographs and drawings in this portfolio illustrate the story of the Prairie House as told in Book Two of this writing. It is an interrupted story, for the design and construction will continue at Domino's Farms. The most recent design changes place a glazed atrium beside a future main entrance. Photographs of a modified model show this atrium sheltered under stepped planes of a glazed trellis resembling the sloping open trellis work at secondary entrances. This promises one of the great spaces now wanting in the Prairie House, but of course the model is only a prediction of the moment. The vitality of the Prairie House lies in its favorable resilience to growth and change. Perhaps this lesson is as important as any other that Domino's Farms offers us.

The home offices of Domino's Pizza, Inc., came to occupy a 300-acre site that included the Zeeb farm, seen here in 1984 before the first of many groundbreakings. The barns still serve a children's petting farm, and tractors cultivate the fields beyond the offices. Even when the new buildings at Domino's Farms are complete, the site will still preserve a rural aspect that would have been obliterated by the building of more than a thousand homes originally proposed here.

From the beginning Domino's Farms promised to be much more than a corporate office complex in the view of Thomas Monaghan. The many activities he anticipated for the site are shown in this early site study prepared in 1984 by the design architect, Gunnar Birkerts.

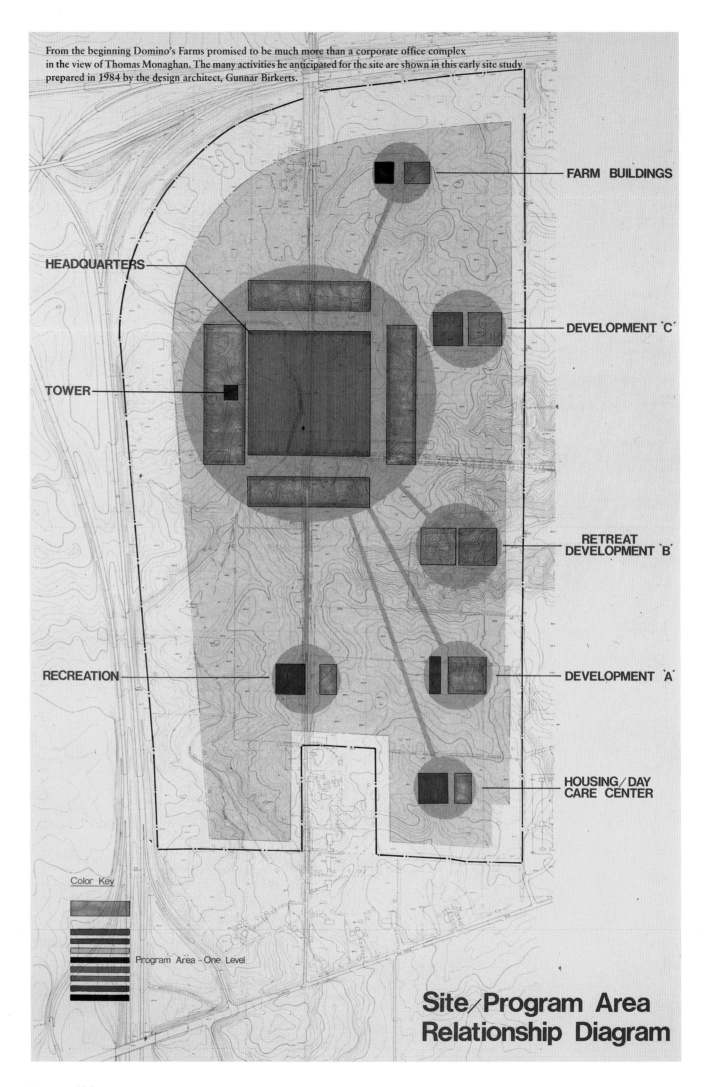

FARM BUILDINGS

HEADQUARTERS

DEVELOPMENT 'C'

TOWER

RETREAT
DEVELOPMENT 'B'

RECREATION

DEVELOPMENT 'A'

HOUSING/DAY
CARE CENTER

Color Key

Program Area - One Level

Site/Program Area
Relationship Diagram

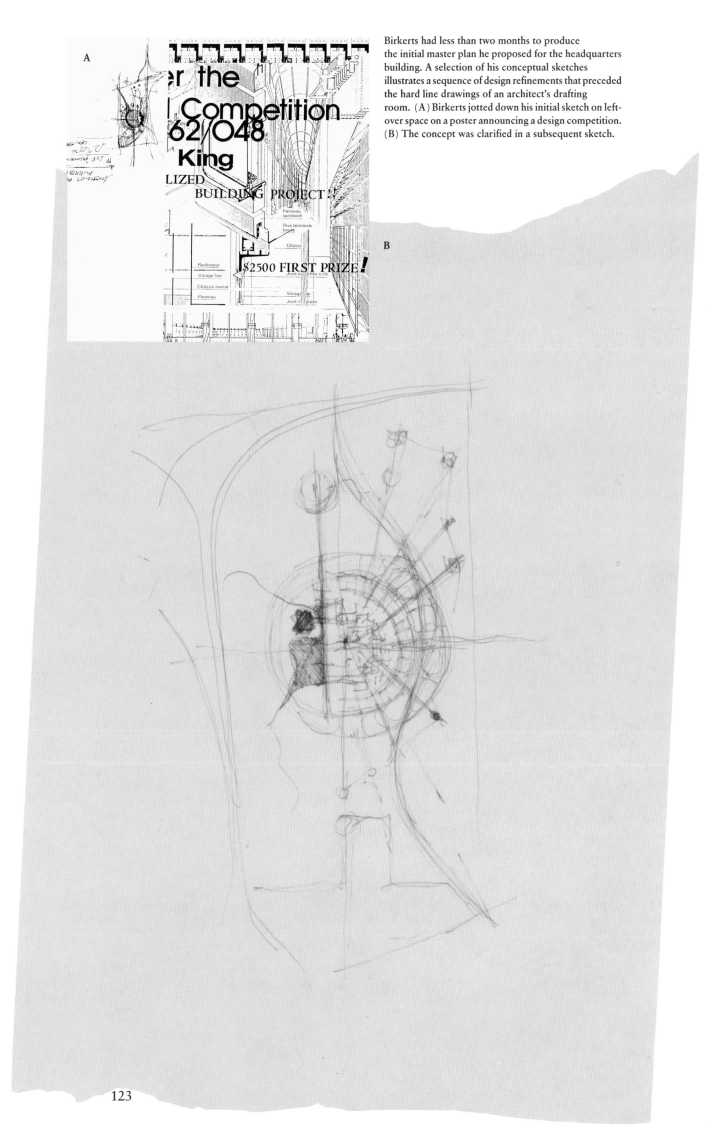

A

Birkerts had less than two months to produce the initial master plan he proposed for the headquarters building. A selection of his conceptual sketches illustrates a sequence of design refinements that preceded the hard line drawings of an architect's drafting room. (A) Birkerts jotted down his initial sketch on left-over space on a poster announcing a design competition. (B) The concept was clarified in a subsequent sketch.

B

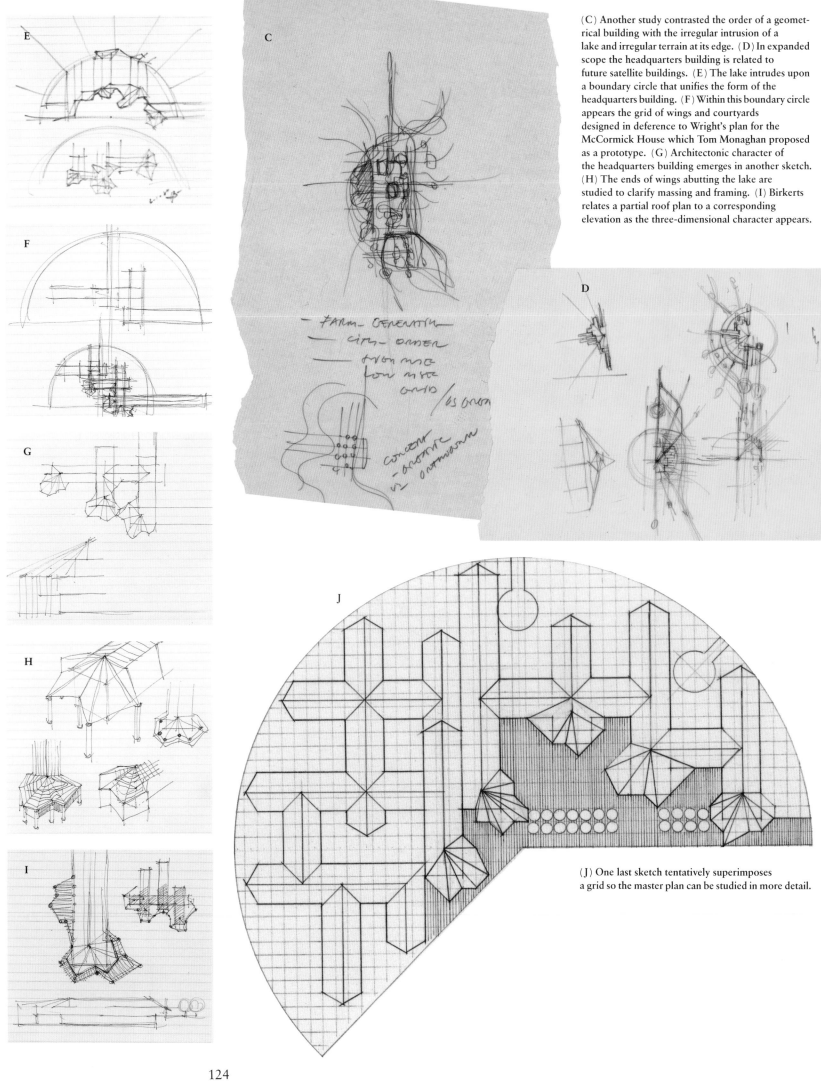

(C) Another study contrasted the order of a geometrical building with the irregular intrusion of a lake and irregular terrain at its edge. (D) In expanded scope the headquarters building is related to future satellite buildings. (E) The lake intrudes upon a boundary circle that unifies the form of the headquarters building. (F) Within this boundary circle appears the grid of wings and courtyards designed in deference to Wright's plan for the McCormick House which Tom Monaghan proposed as a prototype. (G) Architectonic character of the headquarters building emerges in another sketch. (H) The ends of wings abutting the lake are studied to clarify massing and framing. (I) Birkerts relates a partial roof plan to a corresponding elevation as the three-dimensional character appears.

(J) One last sketch tentatively superimposes a grid so the master plan can be studied in more detail.

124

Birkerts' initial proposal did not satisfy the imagery Tom Monaghan expected
of an enlarged McCormick House. Mr. Monaghan turned down this initial master plan,
presented to him on February 21, 1984, in the form of a model.

Birkerts' preference for circles may have seemed foreign to the Wrightian Prairie house vocabulary that Monaghan wanted for his corporate headquarters. In retrospect, Birkerts sensed that the real limitation of the unifying circle was in being 'too finite'.

Two weeks after his initial proposal was turned down, Birkerts returned with new recommendations.
On March 10, 1984, he presented a pair of rendered models to suggest alternative proposals for the headquarters building.
One was an elongated recollection of the original master plan, with the circle becoming a gentle arc.
After some deliberation, Mr. Monaghan chose the other alternative, a longitudinal building that could be six-tenths of a mile long.

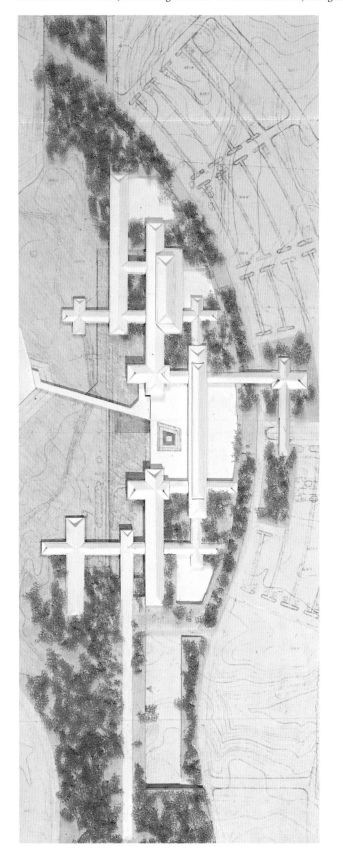
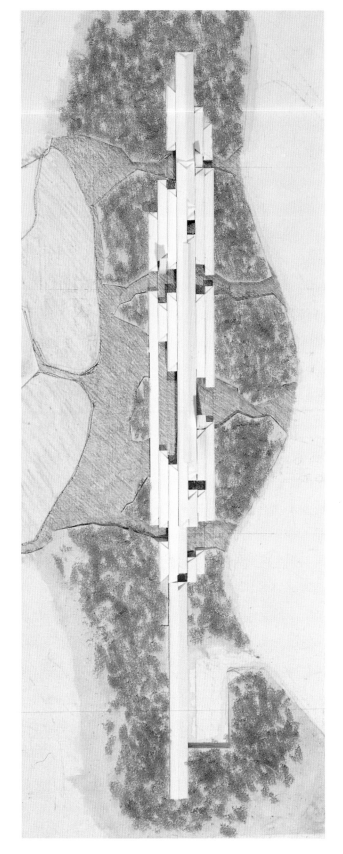

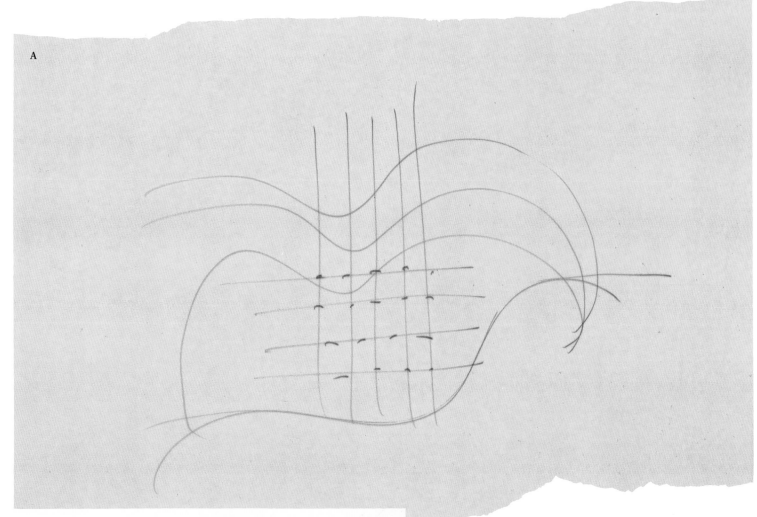

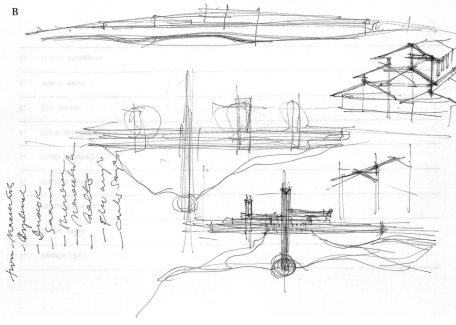

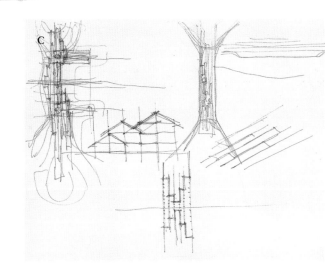

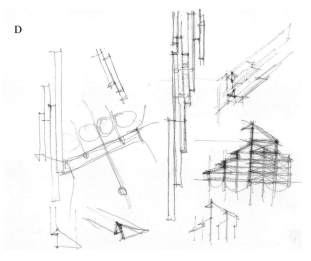

The essence of the chosen master plan crystallized quickly as seen in this selection of Birkerts'
conceptual sketches. (A) Once again an early gesture was to set a geometrical building in contrast with
a free landscape. (B) The most fundamental feature appeared quickly, the track format as a
strategy for controlled growth and the resulting building profile of cascading roofs. (C) Intermediate
courtyards at ground level began to penetrate the mass at intervals as links to the surrounding
landscape. (D) Another sketch studied the ends of the tracks in their staggered array.

The first straight lines of the T-square suggested a concept ready for refinement.

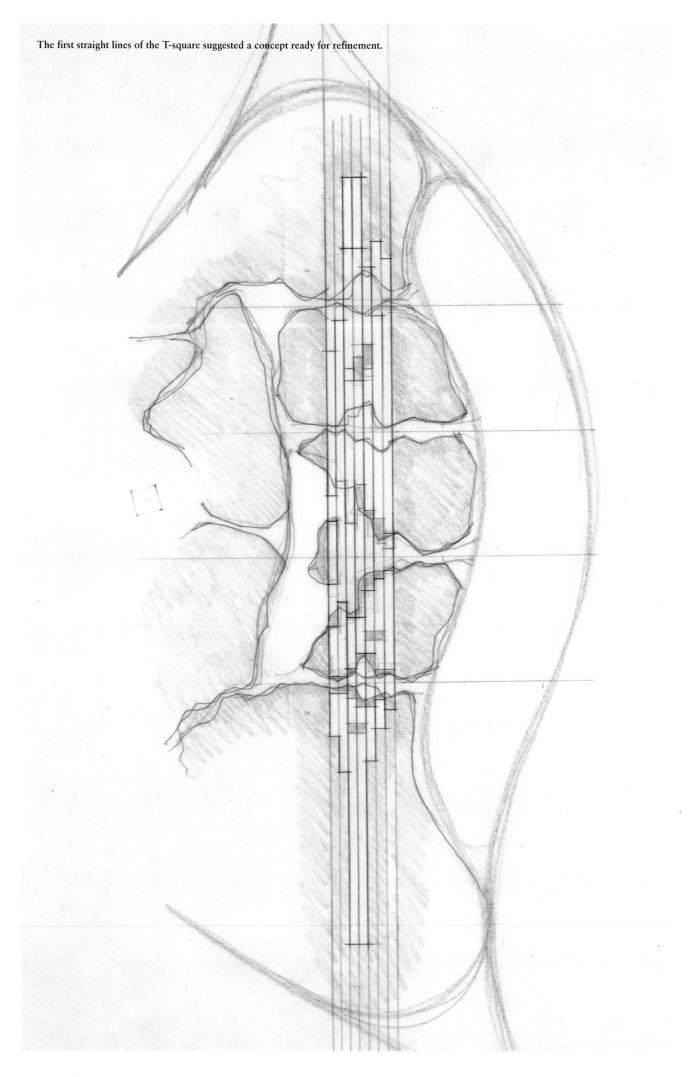

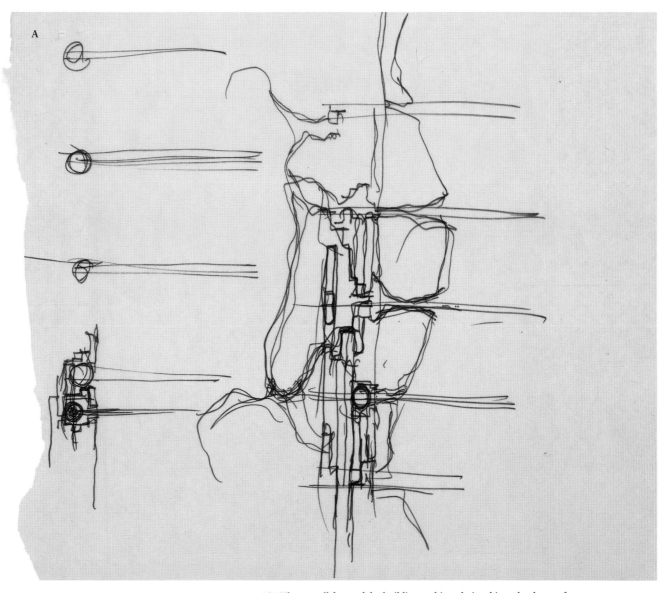

A

(A) The overall form of the building and its relationship to landscape features began to take shape. (B) A typical intermediate penetration of the building was studied.

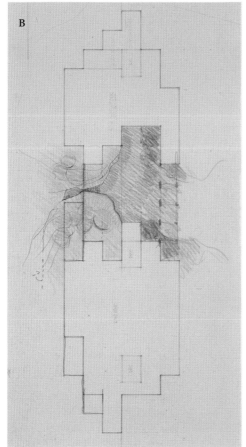

B

(A) The modular grid was imposed to reconcile the concept with measure. (B) Another sketch explored an alternative form of the intermediate courtyards.

A perspective sketch developed the architectonic
character of the long headquarters building,
which would become known as the Prairie House.
Taking its position across the lake was the
Golden Beacon, adapted from Wright's 1956 design
by Taliesin Associated Architects as an office
tower for Domino's Pizza, Inc.

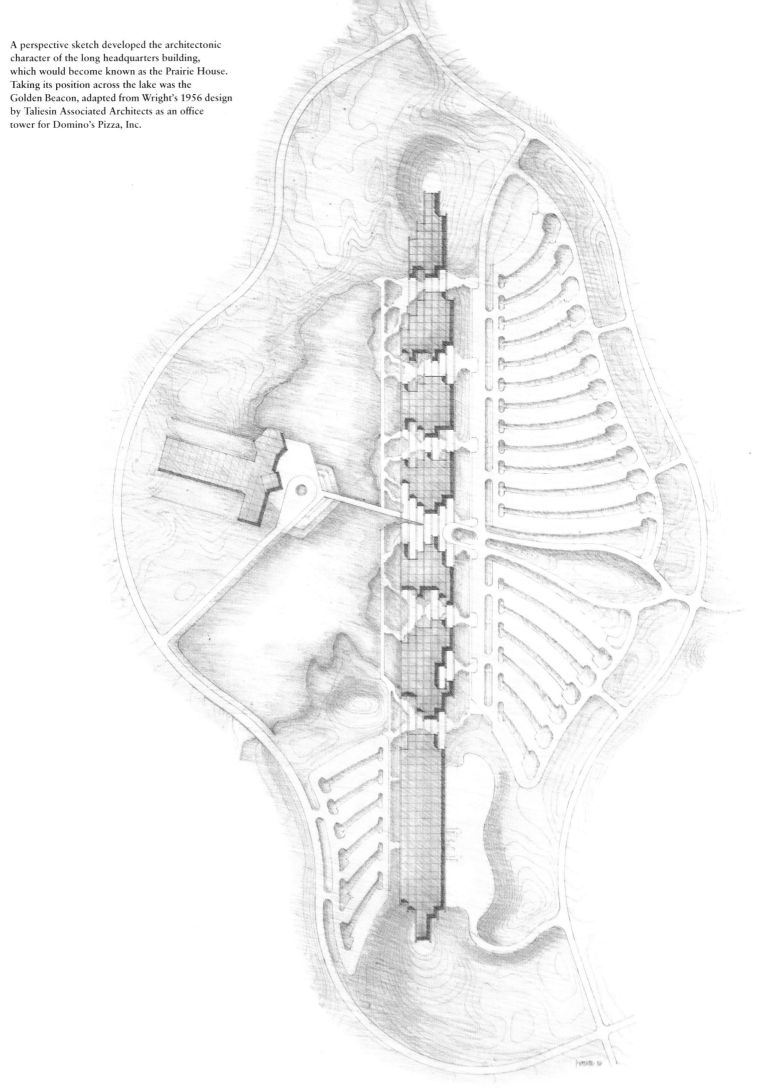

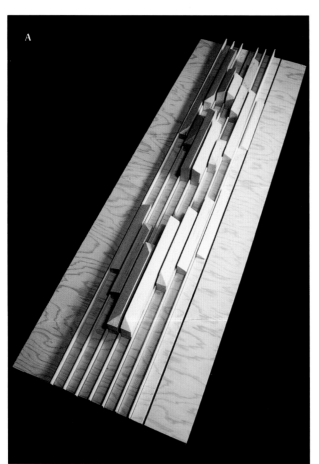

A

(A) Shaped wooden blocks could be manipulated
in their tracks to study the building configuration in this working model
of the Prairie House.
(B) An isometric section drawing presents one of the intermediate courtyard penetrations as seen downhill on the west side which
rises a story taller than the opposite facade.

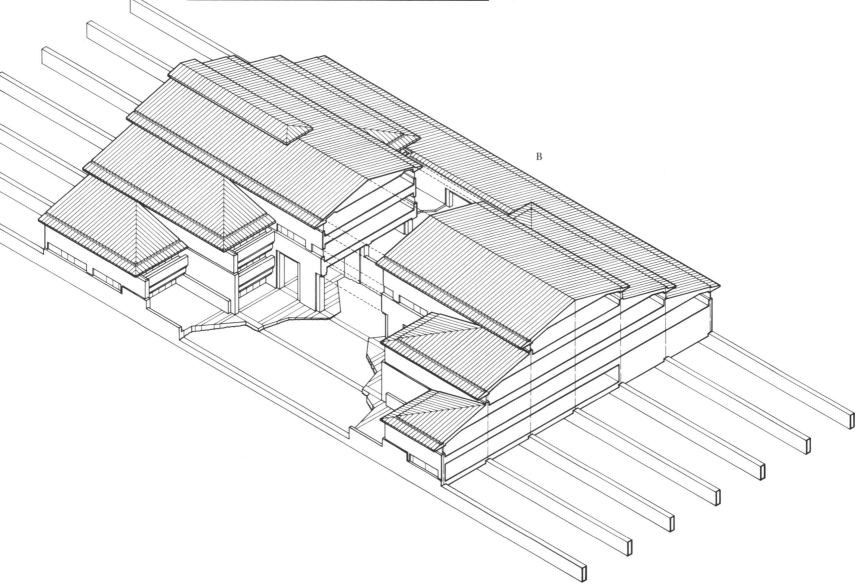

B

134

Particular features have been changed or refined, but the master site plan prepared in 1984 has governed the growth strategy for the Prairie House through its various construction stages.

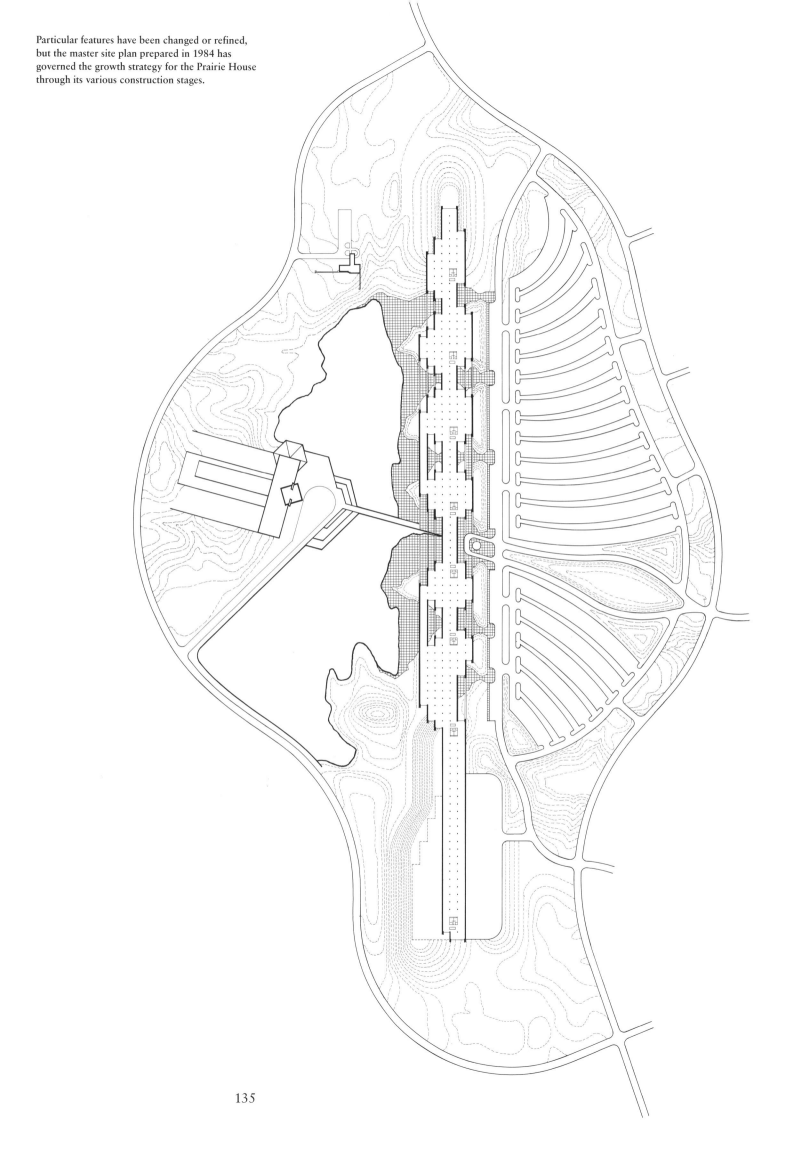

135

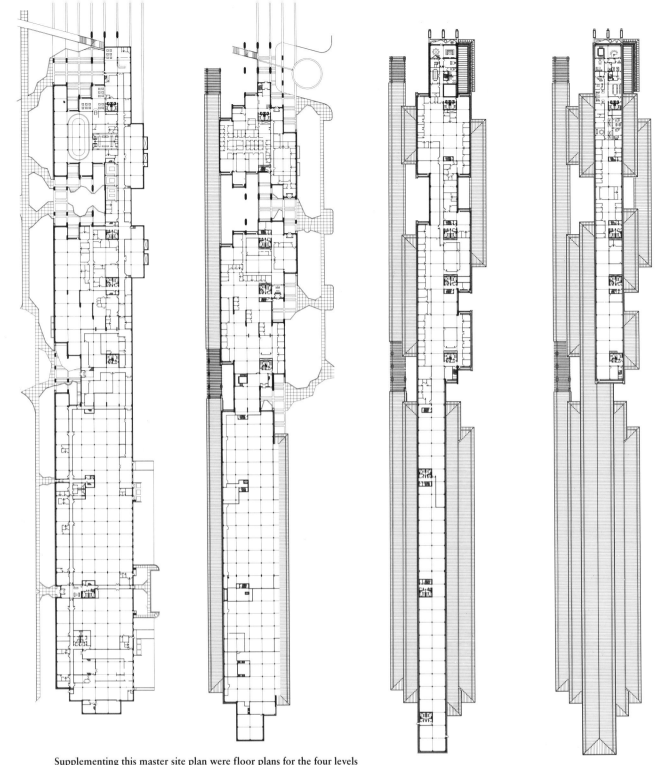

Supplementing this master site plan were floor plans for the four levels
of the Prairie House and a typical transverse section drawing explaining their relationship.

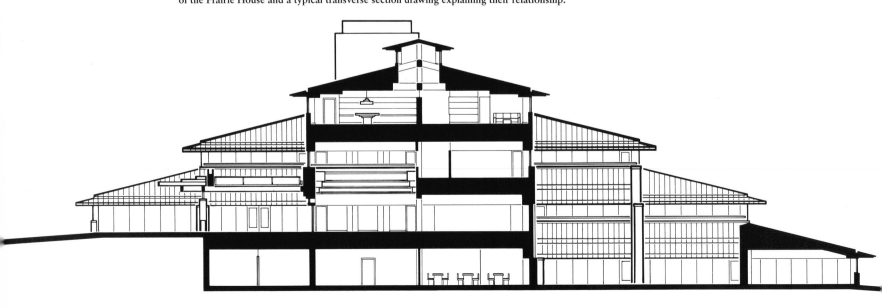

A rendered aerial photograph places the roof of the Prairie House, as proposed in 1984, upon terrain bordering the northeastern corner of the city of Ann Arbor. The strategic location of Domino's Farms is apparent, with U.S. Highway 23 parallel to the Prairie House and joining Michigan Highway 14 to the north.

Aerial photographs taken in the spring of 1988 show how much of the master plan for the Prairie House, including its two bermed extremities, has been fulfilled in four years. (A) The Prairie House is seen to the south of M-14, its closest portion being the detached exhibition building completed in the spring of 1988; it will be the northern end when intermediate portions are completed. In the foreground lies the sites for the Shire Horse farm (to the right).
(B) Another view southwestward shows the city of Ann Arbor on the distant horizon. (C) The northeastern fringe of Ann Arbor's residential suburbs cluster beside U.S. Highway 23; Domino's Farms lies beyond the highway in Ann Arbor Township. (D) An earth berm swallows all but the topmost story of the Prairie House at its southern end, housing the Michigan regional commissary. Beyond parking at left, a forty-two-foot mock-up marks the site of the cantilever tower Birkerts proposes for guest rooms of an executive training and conference center. (E) A northward view traces the visitor's approach to Domino's Farms along the winding path of Earhart Road, coming from the Plymouth Road interchange with U.S. 23.
    Credit: Keiichi Miyashita

The profile of the Prairie House has been compared to the roofs of the Norwegian stave churches, the oldest wooden buildings in the western world. The analogy is apparent in this view of the first wing of the Prairie House in frame in early 1985.

Domino's Farms assumes a pastoral setting, with white fences along the winding Earhart Road approach from the south, echoing the character of cross country roads.
Credit: Keiichi Miyashita

The executive offices of Domino's Pizza, Inc., including the two-story Chairman's Suite, occupy the upper floors of the northern end of the main building, seen here on its east facade.
Credit: Keiichi Miyashita

The entrance to the executive offices lies beyond this drive with flagstaffs bearing flags of the various countries where Domino's Pizza is active.
Credit: Keiichi Miyashita

A porch trellis in redwood and steel tames the scale of the Prairie House for the main entrance to the executive offices.
Credit: Keiichi Miyashita
Details of the porch trellis are shown in plan and section.

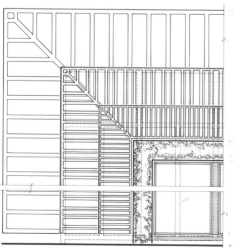

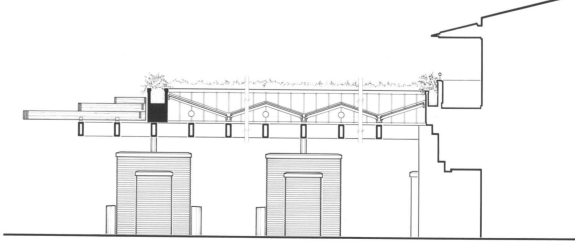

Lobbies at other entrances to the Prairie House
include one entered from the west side of the commissary wing
and a multistory lobby leading upstairs toward
the main offices of Domino's Pizza Distribution Corporation.
Credit: Keiichi Miyashita

The EBA Club is an upgraded cafeteria where all Domino's Pizza
people may feel at home. Once a month as seen here, all Domino's Pizza
staff don the uniforms of pizza throwers as a gesture of solidarity
with the franchises.
Credit: Balthazar Korab

All Domino's Pizza people are welcome to use the Physical Fitness Center.
Credit: Keiichi Miyashita

Banners give life to a passageway through a typical workspace in the newest office wing in the Prairie House.
Credit: Keiichi Miyashita

For open office space, the choicest workspace belongs to the top story where opposite walls of windows run parallel less than sixty feet apart.
Credit: Domino's Pizza Archives

Clerestory windows from a rooftop monitor shed deflected sunlight on the central reception area for the executive offices of Domino's Pizza, Inc., on the top floor.
Credit: Balthazar Korab

With the enthusiasm of a former architectural student, Tom Monaghan chose to work closely with Gunnar Birkerts on the design of his own Chairman's Suite. The several conceptual sketches for interior finishing shown here are from Birkerts' hand, however, dating from 1984. (A) One sketch features the entrance door to the suite. (B) Birkerts redesigned the fireplace wall at the lower level when Monaghan objected to a previous symmetrical design as being too 'Art Deco'. (C) Library shelving wrapped around the landing was a special feature of the staircase within the suite.

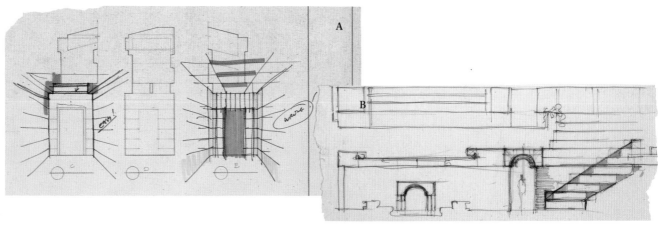

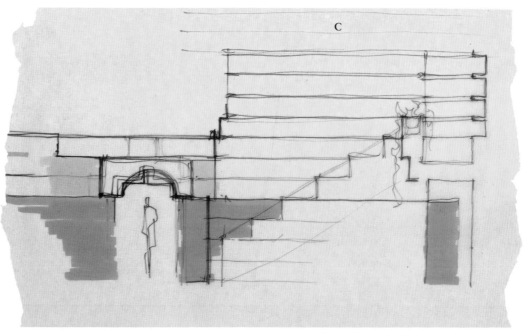

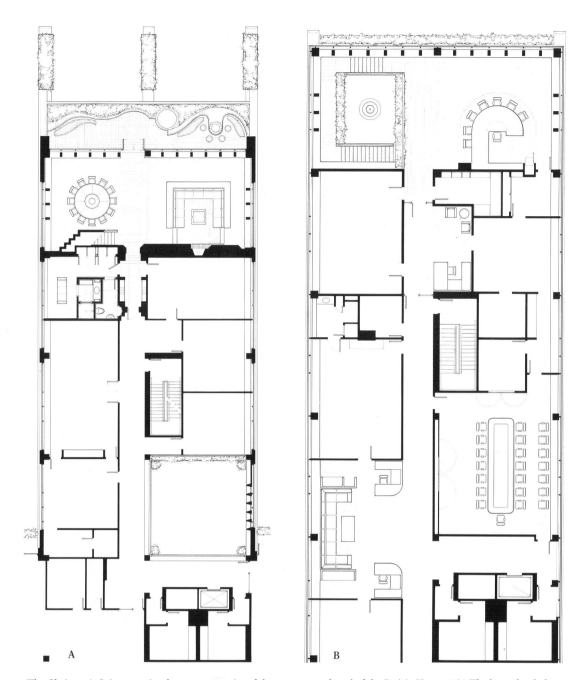

A

B

The Chairman's Suite occupies the two top stories of the present north end of the Prairie House. (A) The lower level plan (at third story level) features lounge seating beside the fireplace, with a conference table beyond, as a congenial setting for meetings and interviews. (B) The upper level is a mezzanine preserving visual privacy for the Chairman's desk when conferences take place downstairs. (C) A transverse section of the suite looks southward toward the fireplace wall. (D) The relationship of both areas is shown by a longitudinal section of the suite, looking eastward.

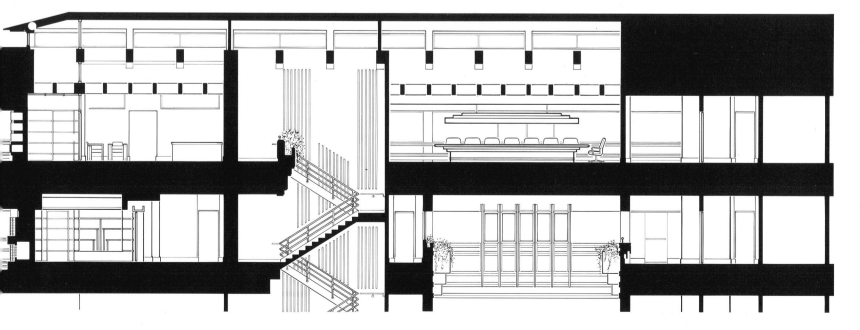

145

Leather lounge seats by the fireplace are gathered around a glass coffee table encasing a model of Tiger Stadium; the conference table stands beyond, near the stairs. Care in detailing of the Chairman's Suite appears in this close view of brickwork in the fireplace wall near the third level entrance.
Credit: Balthazar Korab

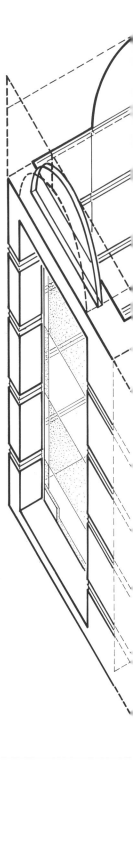

The private washroom is the enigma of the Chairman's Suite.
Despite the horizontal wall splines thematically shared with other walls
of the suite, the washroom seems to belong to a different world.
(A) The splined walls of the entrance to the lavatory compartment
show the greatest harmony with the conference space beyond,
but the golden groin vault of the ceiling seems Mediterranean.
(B) The groin vault modules of the ceiling distinguish the various
compartments of the washroom. (C) Greenish Italian marble replaces
the mahogany panels between the brass splines in the
wet compartments of the washroom.

Credit: Balthazar Korab

An isometric drawing of the washroom clearly shows
how the ceiling shape relates to the various lavatory, toilet and
shower compartments.

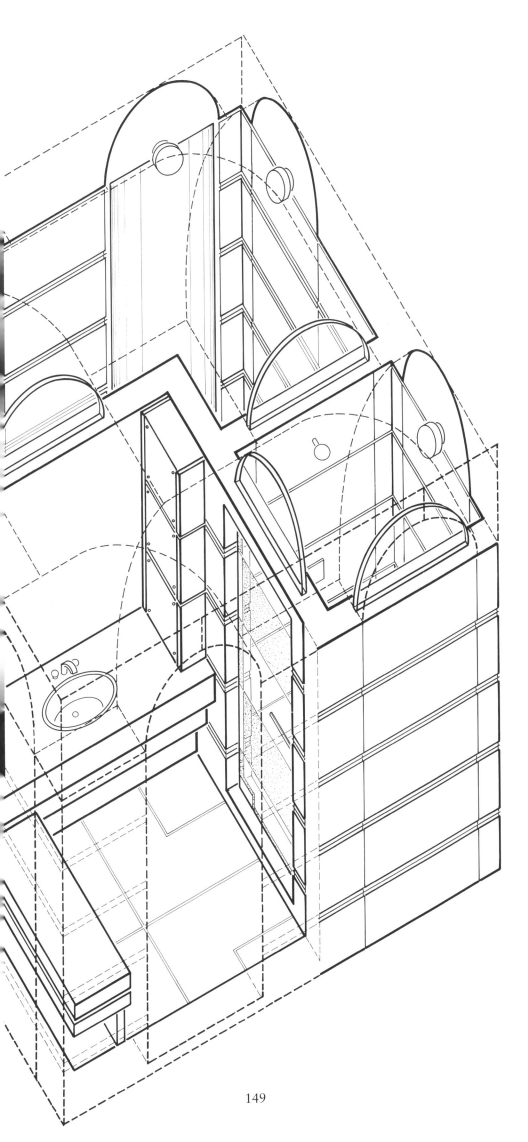

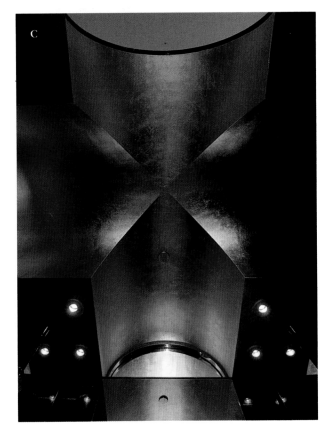

149

Tom Monaghan wanted the Chairman's Suite to have the warm feeling of a lodge, using brick and wood borrowed from the vocabulary of Wright's Usonian houses. The wood panels became African mahogany, however, and polished brass splines replaced the horizontal wood battens Wright would have used, giving a more pristine appearance.

In this view the conference table stands near the staircase to the mezzanine.

Credit: Balthazar Korab

The horizontal brass splines became a dominant theme of the Chairman's Suite, influencing other components.

On the stairway, for example, their interval sets the spacing for book shelving at the landing. Detail photographs show elements of the staircase. (A) A corner of the stair shows its brass railing and the brass spline set in mahogany paneling. (B) Another view becomes an elevation of the brass rail and its support. (C) A third view shows comparable elements at the landing level.

Credit: Balthazar Korab

On the upper level of the Chairman's Suite, the cage-like vestibule of the main entrance has brass framing recalling the wall splines. The colored and clear glass panels have a loose kinship with the Wrightian art glass casements hung decoratively nearby in the executive office reception area.
(A) A similar framed panel of clear and colored glass hovers over the vestibule.
(B) A display niche sets off the side plane of the vestibule.
     Credit: Balthazar Korab

Plan and elevation drawings illustrate the framing pattern of the vestibule.

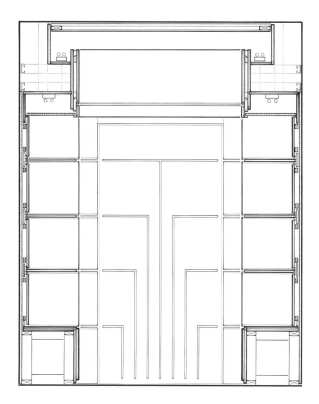

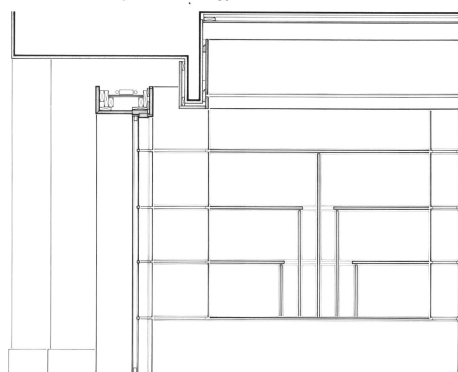

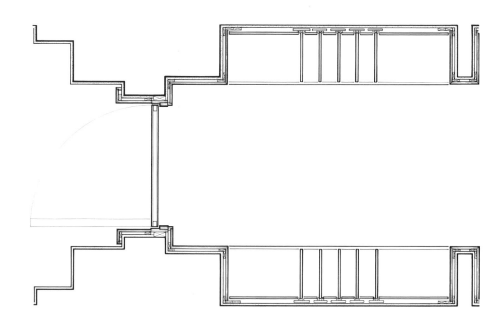

Leather is a significant material, whether used for lounge seating, floor tiles, or around the Chairman's desk top.
Credit: Balthazar Korab

The end wall of the Chairman's Suite, which now faces
northward toward the Zeeb barns and the exhibition building
beyond them, will someday look into a central atrium
of the completed Prairie House.
Credit: Balthazar Korab

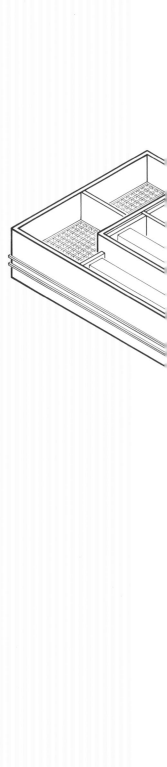

Adjoining the Chairman's Suite is the Board Room, especially distinguished by its rectangular chandelier designed by Birkerts. Harmony between accessories and their setting often results from repeating themes found elsewhere in the Prairie House, sometimes on a very different scale. The Board Boom chandelier has a stepped profile recalling the track cross section of the building, itself.
Credit: Balthazar Korab

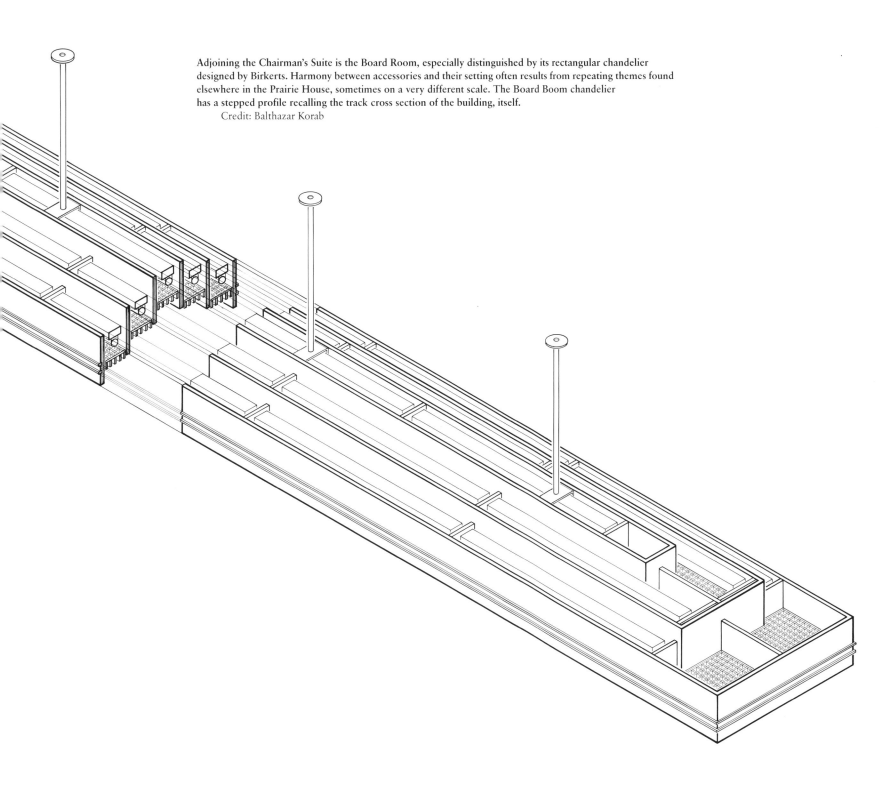

157

In the Chairman's Suite, a brass candelabra for the fireplace mantel, seen here in Birkerts' conceptual sketch and in a photograph, has parallel bars terminating in random order, again like the tracks of the building. A companion to the candelabra is the firewood carrier for the hearth, also seen in Birkerts' sketch and in a photograph.
  Credit: Keiichi Miyashita

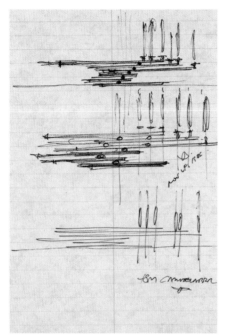

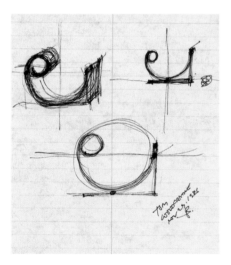

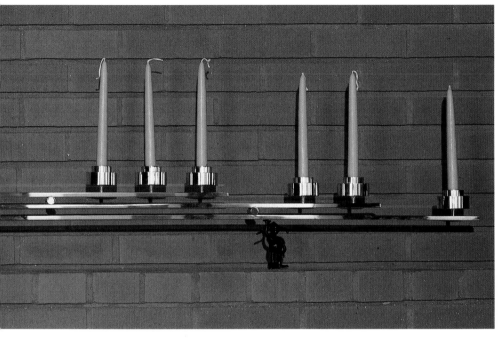

(A) Cigarette/trash containers stand at the building entrances.
(B) The grille on top of the floor standing torchiere offers a pattern
to be used elsewhere. (C) The torchiere grille pattern
is echoed in the debossed table placemats.

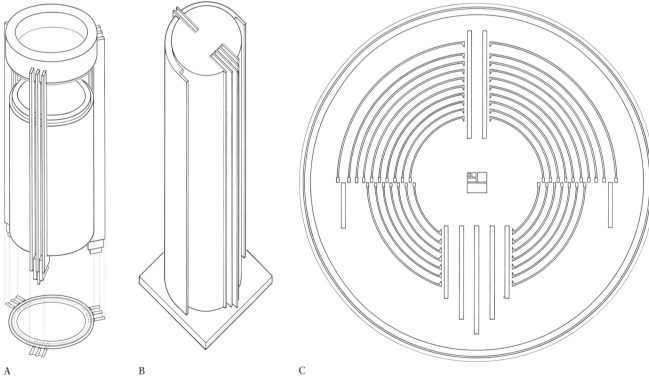

A   B   C

Newly opened in the spring of 1988 is a two-story building which will one day be linked to the Prairie House as its northern end. For the present it serves as an exhibition building for several significant collections belonging to Tom Monaghan and Domino's Pizza, Inc.

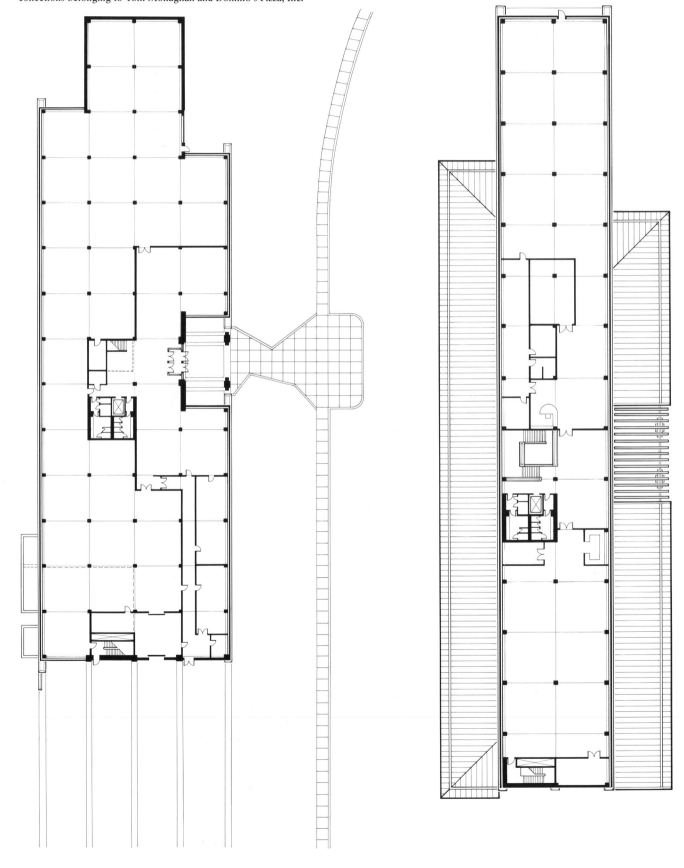

160

The ground floor houses Domino's Classic Cars, a collection of more than two hundred
distinctive automobiles owned by Tom Monaghan and by the curator, George Crocker. On the upper floor
is the National Center for the Study of Frank Lloyd Wright at Domino's Farms, the world's largest
collection of Wrightiana that is not 'in situ' at a Wright-designed building.
    Credit: Balthazar Korab

For a substitute to a tower adapted from Wright's Golden Beacon, Gunnar Birkerts devised his cantilever
tower design as a uniquely memorable corporate symbol. Birkerts developed these sketches early in 1987 for the
design accepted that June by Tom Monaghan for a Conference Center opposite the Prairie House.

A

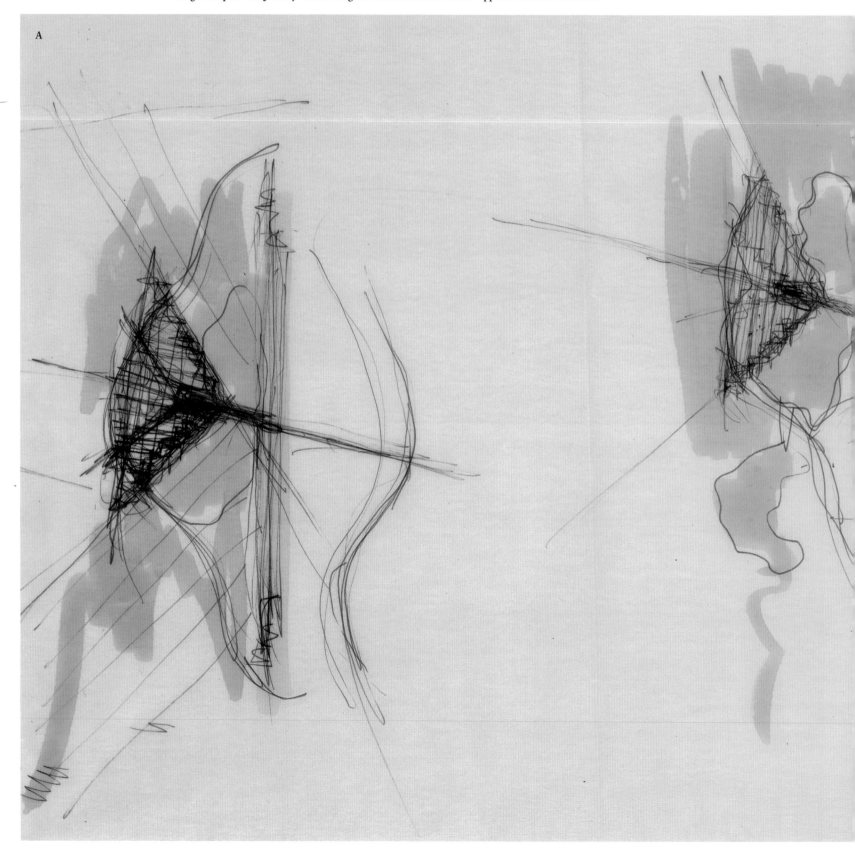

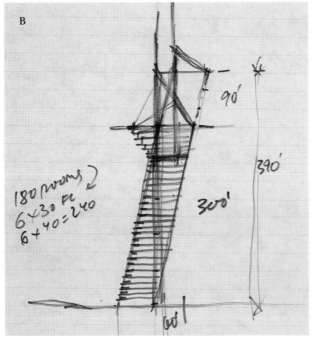

B

180 rooms
6×30 Fc
6×40=240

90'

390'

300'

60'

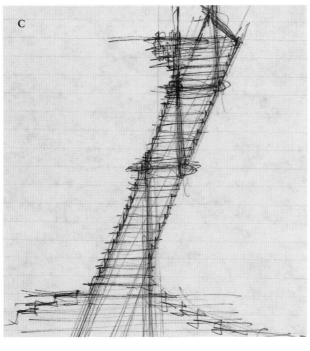

C

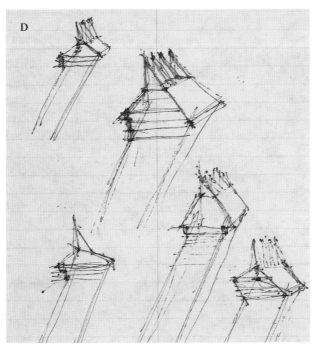

D

(A) Two initial sketches study the low base structure of the Conference Center, itself, and its relationship to a bridge crossing a lake to the Prairie House. (B) Annotated program requirements accompany an early sketch of the leaning tower, to contain guest rooms for executive training programs. (C) An additional sketch relates the tower to the Conference Center at its base, seen in section view. (D) Other studies explore alternatives for the top of the tower.

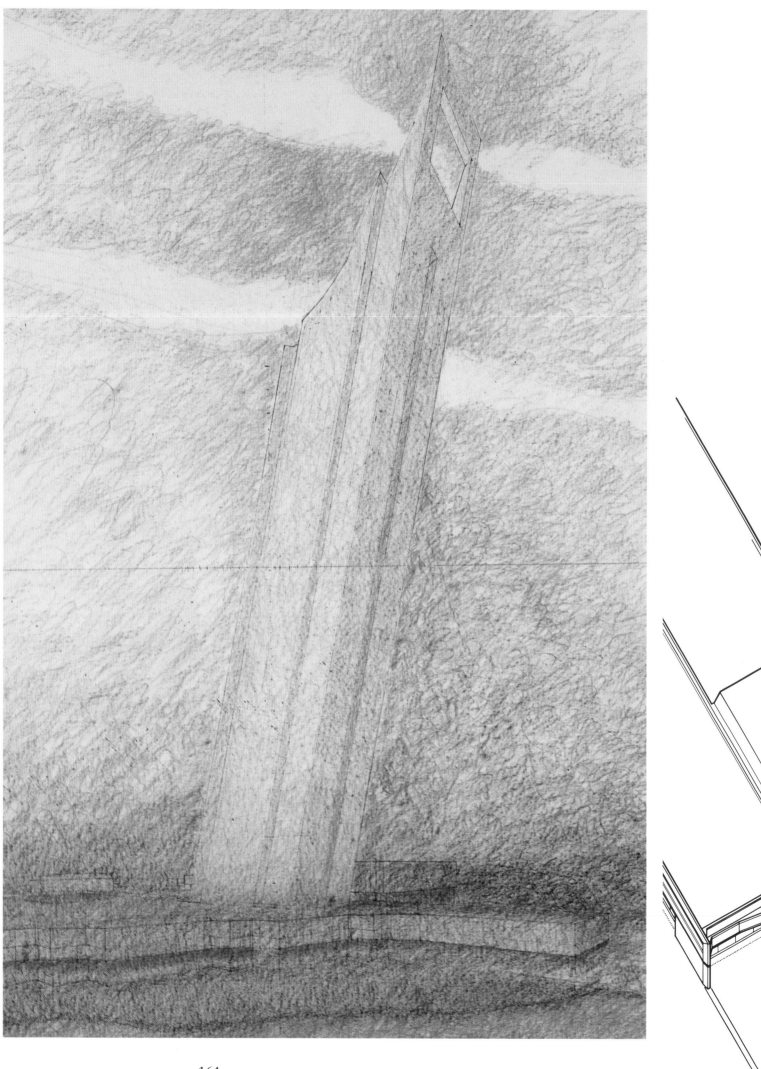

164

The chosen form of the tower, with its upswept top visually
countering the jeopardy of the tilting form, appears in a drawing
in colored pencil. Gunnar Birkerts conceived the cantilever
tower as 'rural sculpture' that is effective in counterpoint with the
Prairie House in a controlled setting; it is too dynamic
to appear amidst the random forms of an urban setting. An isometric
drawing shows the appearance of the tower and Conference
Center making up this corporate campus.

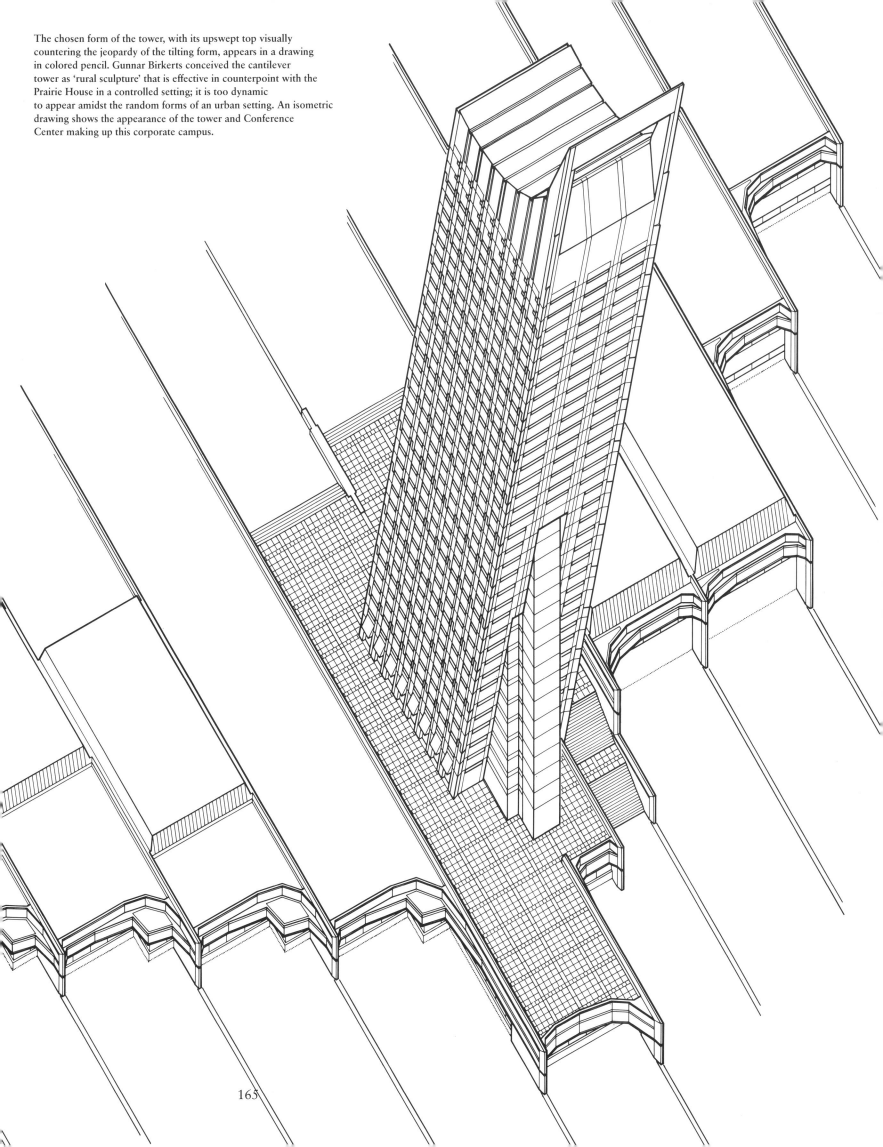

The cantilever tower is braced to resist its tilt within
the walls of the stairwells that continue as corridor walls,
as shown in these plan drawings of typical floors.

A section drawing of the tower shows the special care
taken to integrate the vertical shafts of elevators with the
sloped profile of the tower. The design requires
repeating combinations of special guest rooms interfacing
with the elevator shafts.

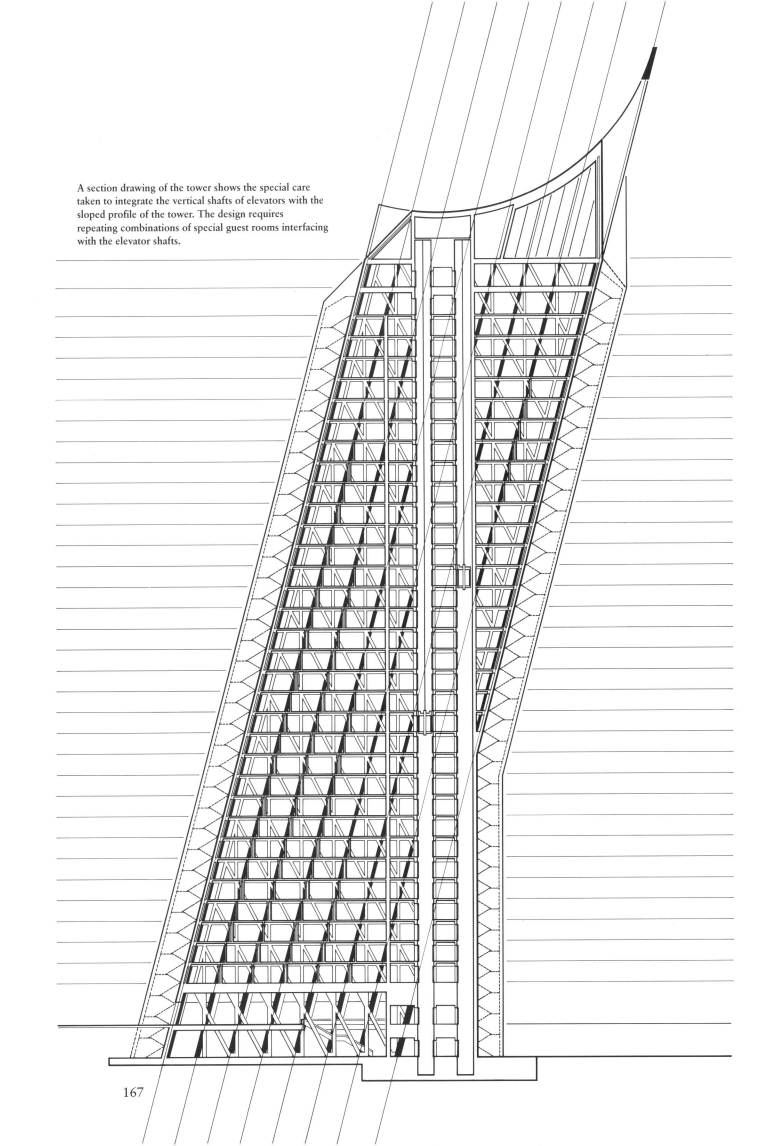

Gunnar Birkerts stands beside a one-tenth-sized steel
mock-up occupying the site of the 435-foot cantilever tower. The mock-up
replaced a wooden one for the Golden Beacon adaptation,
now placed like a stele at the entrance to the new exhibition building.
   Credit: Keiichi Miyashita

A view from the Domino's Pizza helicopter simulates
the vista from future penthouse windows of the cantilever tower,
looking down upon the Prairie House.
   Credit: Paul Chu Lin

The model of the Prairie House and its companion tower continues to change in its ongoing refinement, and a book illustration can only freeze the status for the moment. This view shows the design at the time the cantilever tower proposal was made public in September, 1987.

The next construction campaign may provide a new and enlarged main entrance to the Prairie House, shown here in the foreground with the cantilever tower beyond.

A model shows the current proposal for a glazed atrium at the future main entrance
to the Prairie House, using a cascade of framed glass roof planes resembling the open sloping trellis
now found at several secondary building entrances.

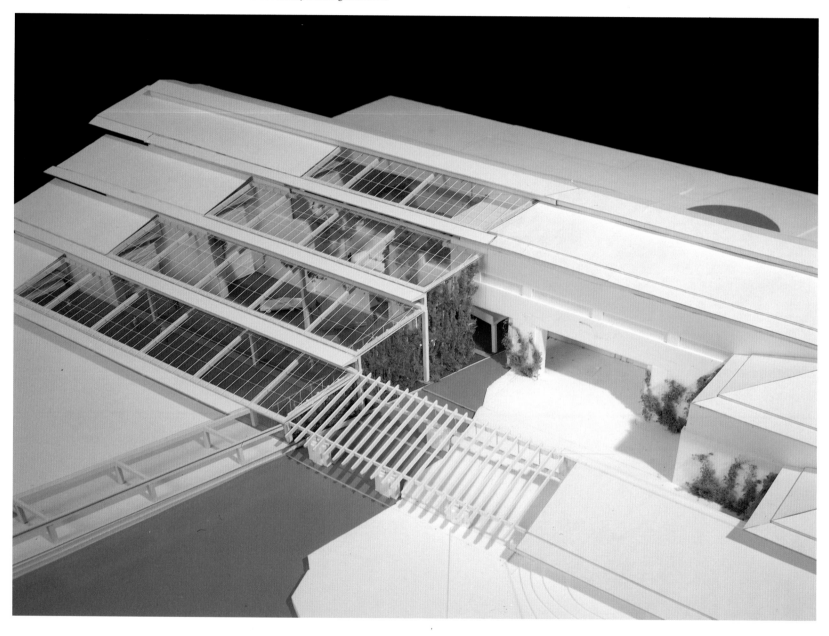

Swimming facilities and tennis courts are to be built to the south of the Prairie House, and they will need care to integrate inherently rectilinear forms into the landscape.

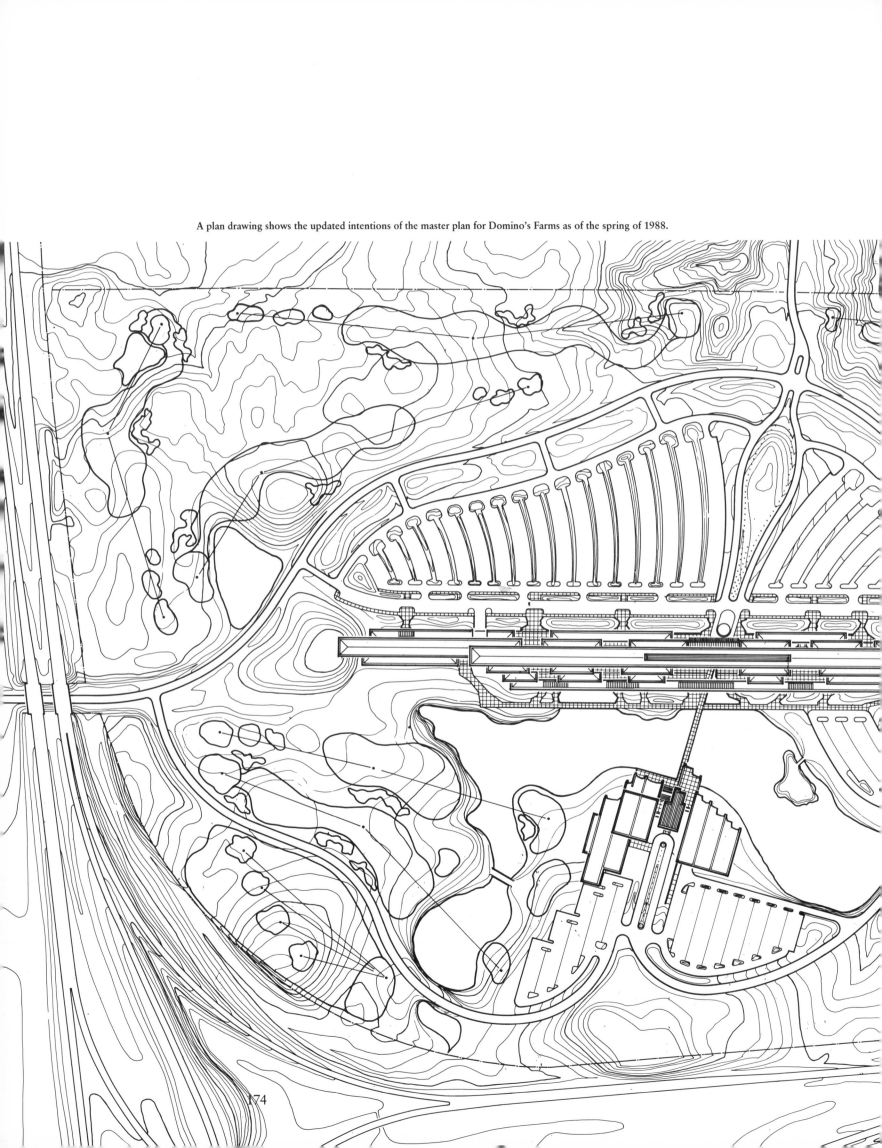

A plan drawing shows the updated intentions of the master plan for Domino's Farms as of the spring of 1988.

175

The lights of the Chairman's Suite are illuminated as dusk settles upon Domino's Farms.
Credit: Balthazar Korab

Domino's Pizza, Inc.
Project Participants, Headquarters Profile

Initial Design Architects
John H. Howe, Architect
Burnsville, Minnesota
William Wesley Peters
Taliesin Associates Architects
Taliesin West
Scottsdale, Arizona

Firm Responsible for Design
Gunnar Birkerts
and Associates, Inc. Architects
Birmingham, Michigan
Design Architect:
Gunnar Birkerts
Principal-In-Charge:
Anthony Gholz
Designer: Kevin Shultis
Design Development:
Anthony Duce
Interior Designer:
Mary Jane Williamson

**Firm Responsible
for Construction Documents**
Giffels Associates, Incorporated
Southfield, Michigan
Project Directors:
Donald Cuatt, Al Chartrand

Planning/Landscape Architects
Beckett Raeder, Incorporated
Ann Arbor, Michigan
Paul Raeder, Allison Arscott

**Consulting Mechanical
Engineers (Phase Two)**
James Partridge Associates, Inc.
Birmingham, Michigan
James Partridge

Construction Manager
Barton Malow Company
Southfield, Michigan
Kamal Sharma

Headquarters Profile
Total Land Area: 291.49 acres
Lot Area: 275.82 acres

Phase I   218,300 SF 760 Cars
Phase II   165,269 SF 296 Cars
Phase III   83,202 SF 328 Cars
Phase IV   67,100 SF 241 Cars
Phase V   292,000 SF 837 Cars

Building Module: 4 Foot

Structure: Steel frame

Hipped Roof: Standing seam
copper and lead coated copper,
redwood soffits

Exterior Wall: Continuous
ribbon windows, brick with
horizontally raked joints,
copper covered planters

Interior:
Height: 9'-0"
Ceiling: 2x4 acoustical panels
Floor: Carpet, rubber, brick
or ceramic tile
Walls: Metal studs and drywall

Mechanical: Fin tube
and air conditioned

Domino's Pizza, Inc.
Timetable Of Events

Giffels Associates, Inc.
Programming Phase
(problem definition)
Mid-August 1983 thru
Late October 1983

John H. Howe, Architect
Beckett Raeder, Incorporated
Master Plan Phase
Mid-August 1983 thru
Mid-January 1984

John H. Howe, Architect
Preliminary Design
Early September 1983 thru
Mid-January 1984

John H. Howe, Architect
Project Design Services end
January 11, 1984

Gunnar Birkerts
First Scheme for Master Plan
January 11, 1984 thru
February 21, 1984

Thomas Monaghan
rejects First Scheme
February 24, 1984

Gunnar Birkerts
presents two new
alternative Master Plans
to Thomas Monaghan
February 24, 1984 thru
March 10, 1984

Taliesin Associates Architects
Presentation to
Thomas Monaghan of
adapted 'Beacon' Tower
March 2, 1984

Thomas S. Monaghan
approves Prairie House scheme
as built
March 12, 1984

Gunnar Birkerts
and Associates, Inc. Architects
Beckett Raeder, Incorporated
Barton Malow Company

Land re-zoned for
commercial and tower use and
preliminary design work
continued. Parking and Phase I
building massing, road
relocation, site grading, landscaping and cost resolved.
Phase I defined.
March 12, 1984 thru
May 8, 1984

Gunnar Birkerts
and Associates, Inc. Architects
Phase I Schematic Design Phase
May 9, 1984 thru June 29, 1984

Gunnar Birkerts
and Associates, Inc. Architects
Design Development Phase
June 29, 1984 thru
August 31, 1984

Giffels Associates, Inc.
Working Drawings begin
June 29, 1984

Presentation to Ann Arbor
Township Planning Commission
of Headquarters Building,
Tower Master Plan and
Phase I Massing
July 23, 1984

Approval by Ann Arbor
Township Planning Commission
of Preliminary Site Plan
August 8, 1984

Approval by Ann Arbor
Township Planning Commission
of Phase I Preliminary Site Plan
August 27, 1984

Phase I Ground Breaking
August 30, 1984

Guaranteed Maximum Price by
Barton Malow Company
August 31, 1984

Phase I Construction Packages:
Site Preparation
Issued: August 1, 1984
Completed: September 30, 1984

Primary Steel and Decking
Issued: August 27, 1984
Completed: April 25, 1985

Foundations
Issued: September 7, 1984
Completed: April 1985

Building Enclosure
Issued: October 15, 1984
Completed: September 1985

Elevators
Issued: November 15, 1984
Completed: November 18, 1985

Mechanical, Electrical
and Controls
Issued: November 15, 1984
Completed: December 9, 1985

Building Interiors
Issued: January 16, 1985
Completed: December 9, 1985

Food Service Equipment
Issued: January 28, 1985
Completed: December 9, 1985

Interior Woodwork
Issued: February 4, 1985
Completed: December 9, 1985

Thomas Monaghan's Office
Completed: January 1986

Phase I Occupancy
December 9, 1985

Phase II Distribution Center/
Office Space
Ground Breaking:
November 14, 1985
Topping of Steel: May 28, 1986
Occupancy: October 7, 1986

Phase III Additional
Office Development between
Distribution Center
and First Phase Offices
Ground Breaking:
December 9, 1986
Topping of Steel: June 10, 1987
Occupancy: August 28, 1987

Phase IV Museum
Ground Breaking: July 15, 1987
Topping of Steel:
September 30, 1987
Occupancy: March 1, 1988

Gunnar Birkerts
works on new Tower Design
Late December 1986

Gunnar Birkerts
presents new Tower Design
to Thomas Monaghan
January 6, 1987

Tower Presentation
to Domino's Pizza, Inc.
Management
January 9, 1987

Tower Presentation
to Ann Arbor Township
Planning Commission
July 6, 1987

Press Conference
Tower Presentation
October 6, 1987

Index For Domino's Mansion

Index For Domino's Mansion (continued)

Index For Domino's Mansion (continued)